THE COURAGE OF FAITH

THE COURAGE OF FAITH

MARTIN LUTHER AND THE THEONOMOUS SELF

MARY GAEBLER

Fortress Press
Minneapolis

THE COURAGE OF FAITH

Martin Luther and the Theonomous Self

Copyright © 2013 Fortress Press. All rights reserved. Except for brief quotations in critical articles or reviews, no part of this book may be reproduced in any manner without prior written permission from the publisher. Visit http://www.augsburgfortress.org/copyrights/ or write to Permissions, Augsburg Fortress, Box 1209, Minneapolis, MN 55440.

Cover image: © Can Stock Photo Inc. / Boris15

Cover design: Laurie Ingram

Library of Congress Cataloging-in-Publication Data

Print ISBN: 978-0-8006-9752-5

eBook ISBN: 978-1-4514-3862-8

The paper used in this publication meets the minimum requirements of American National Standard for Information Sciences — Permanence of Paper for Printed Library Materials, ANSI Z329.48-1984.

Manufactured in the U.S.A.

This book was produced using PressBooks.com, and PDF rendering was done by PrinceXML.

This book is dedicated to Pastor William H. Lazareth.

CONTENTS

Acknowledgments	ix
Abbreviations	xi
Introduction	1
1. God's Prophet	23
2. Freed to Serve	83
3. Luther and Self-Love	117
4. Life in the Spirit	155
Conclusion	191
Index	203

Acknowledgments

When a project takes as long as this one has, there are many people to thank—too many to do justice to here. Still, I wish to acknowledge a few people who have been central to the development of this work. It was while I was living and working in New York City that William Lazareth's preaching initially grasped me and set my life on a very different course. It was he who first put Martin Luther into my hands and into my head. Then there were the extraordinary teachers whose own love for Luther continues to expand my understanding: George Forell, Scott Hendrix, Timothy Lull, and George Lindbeck. These scholars in particular stand out among the many whose work has influenced my thinking.

Special thanks must go also to Gene Outka and Margaret Farley, who invited me into a conversation that opened up a wider view of the Church, the place Luther occupies within it, and the possibilities that Luther's theology continues to provide today. Margaret Farley's careful and faithful work on human agency has served to focus my own questions, and her intellectual influence is discernible throughout the pages that follow. More than teachers, these scholars have been friends and mentors, encouraging, prodding, and urging me forward with a kind of vocational devotion that would have delighted Luther.

My colleagues here at Gustavus Adolphus College have likewise gifted me with their confidence and support; those within the Religion Department especially have helped me carve out the time necessary to complete this project. They have also challenged and informed my thinking with the generosity and care that exemplifies the best sort of scholarly solidarity.

In addition to these, I give special thanks to Linda Backman, my longtime friend and theological conversation partner, who first invited me to come hear Pastor Lazareth preach. Without Linda's hospitality and steady confidence I could not have stayed the course.

Finally I thank my family, and in particular my father, whose life in the ministry and in pursuit of meaning paved the way by teaching us the power of historical perspective and the importance of honoring curiosity for its own sake.

Abbreviations

Br   Martin Luther. *Briefwechsel*. 18 vols. in WA.

LW   Luther's Works. Edited by Jaroslav Pelikan and Helmut T. Lehmann. Saint Louis: Concordia; Philadelphia: Fortress, 1958–1986.

Tr   Martin Luther. *Tischreden* (Table Talk). 6 vols. in WA.

WA   D. Martin Luthers Werke (Weimarer Ausgabe). *Weimar: Böhlau, 1883–1993.*

Introduction

When Philip Watson produced a study of Luther's theology titled *Let God Be God*, many applauded this succinct rendering of Luther's prophetic theological vision.[1] In the post–World War II context of an overconfident culture driven by the desire for conquest and personal achievement, Luther's attack on human arrogance appeared to have found its mark. But this assault on pride has been reassessed in recent years, with growing skepticism. Focusing on the reluctance among women to assume their God-given responsibilities, feminist theologians have challenged the traditional view of human nature and original sin that underscores Reformation thought, arguing that for many women sin takes a different form. Daphne Hampson, for example, tracing the Reformation doctrines of sin and grace back to Luther, argues that the central convictions of feminism, including the cultivation of self-empowerment,[2] must be recognized as incommensurate with Luther's theocentric emphasis. Pointing to the need for "women to come into their own,"[3] Hampson argues that Luther's rejection of self-love only exacerbates the problems many women face. When the issue is not self-assertive pride but rather passive self-abnegation, she continues, "To advocate, as does the Lutheran tradition, that the self should be broken . . . [is a practice that] must be judged highly detrimental."[4] Thus, by recontextualizing the Reformation attack on pride and self-righteousness within a larger frame—one that includes the experience of both women and men—feminist theologians have added a new dimension to an old debate about Luther's anthropology. Hampson's challenge, along with the growing body of literature

---

1. Philip Saville Watson, *Let God Be God! An Interpretation of the Theology of Martin Luther* (Philadelphia: Muhlenberg, 1948).

2. The self is of central importance in this study. As Daphne Hampson points out, "Luther would not have used the term 'self' and lacked a post-Enlightenment conception of the self, but this is the best word to use when translating his insight into a modern idiom" ("Luther on the Self: A Feminist Critique," *Word and World* 8, no. 4 [1988]: 334–42 [334]). Judith Plaskow provides us with a pertinent quotation from Paul Tillich: "It is time to end the bad theological usage of jumping with moral indignation on every word in which the syllable 'self' appears. Even moral indignation would not exist without a centered self and ontological self-affirmation" (Judith Plaskow, *Sex, Sin and Grace: Women's Experience and the Theologies of Reinhold Niebuhr and Paul Tillich* [Lanham, MD: University Press of America, 1980], 112. Cited from Paul Tillich, *The Courage to Be* [London and Glasgow: Collins, 1952], 90).

3. Hampson, "Luther on the Self," 340.

4. Ibid., 339.

that expresses similar concerns, raises important questions about the status and role of human agency in Luther's theology.

Valerie Saiving is usually credited with the initial insight that the Christian (and especially Reformation) doctrines of sin and grace are gender-specific. In her article "The Human Situation: A Feminine View,"[5] Saiving correlates the traditional Reformation understanding of sin with underlying psycho-biological structures[6] peculiar to males, which culminate in the manifestation of pride and/or self-assertion. This form of sin, she explains, fails to take the experience of many women into account, and has been viewed as "the [universally present] imperialistic drive to close the gap between the individual separate self and others by reducing those others to the status of mere objects which can then be treated as appendages of the self and manipulated accordingly."[7] Saiving concedes that those who experience sin in this way are effectively judged under the influence of Reformation doctrine. Redemption, in this case, is expressed in a newly created vulnerability—a softening of those boundaries by which the survival of identity was previously maintained. And in this situation, she suggests, the goal of a self-annihilating Christlike love is not inappropriate.[8] But Saiving is interested in female development; and girls, she argues, have a potentially equal and opposite problem from their brothers. Rather than building up self-protective boundaries, separating themselves from their neighbors, women frequently suffer from inadequate personal boundaries, leaving them instead without a secure self-identity. Such an individual, according to Saiving, is therefore vulnerable to a loss of self in relationships with others—she is too easily absorbed into the neighbor, whom she serves and from whom she is apt to seek an identity that is never her own. Thus, Saiving writes,

---

5. Valerie C. Saiving, "The Human Situation: A Feminine View," in *Womanspirit Rising: A Feminist Reader in Religion*, ed. Carol Christ and Judith Plaskow (San Francisco: HarperSanFrancisco, 1992), 25–42.

6. "The process of self-differentiation," Saiving contends, "plays a stronger and more anxiety-provoking role in the boy's maturation than is normally the case for the girl." Unlike their brothers, girls have a psychologically easier task in accomplishing the work of sexual maturation, Saiving argues. Girls "passively" develop the sexual identity that they observe in their mothers, with whom they have already bonded as infants. The ease of this task, so the theory goes, frees females from the arduous task of sexual differentiation, thereby leaving them psychologically free to risk the vulnerability of other-identification (ibid., 38). This naturally grounded psychological freedom allows females to become the nurturing, self-giving mothers their infant children will require in order to survive and mature into healthy adults (ibid., 36–37).

7. Ibid., 33.

8. Ibid., 33.

the temptations of women as women are not the same as the temptations of man as man, and the specifically feminine forms of sin—"feminine" not because they are confined to women or because women are incapable of sinning in other ways but because they are outgrowths of the basic feminine character structures—have a quality which can never be encompassed by such terms as "pride" and "will-to-power." They are better suggested by such items as triviality, distractibility, and diffuseness; lack of an organizing center or focus; dependence on others for one's own self-definition; tolerance at the expense of standards of excellence; inability to respect the boundaries of privacy; sentimentality, gossipy sociability, and mistrust of reason—in short, underdevelopment or negation of the self.[9]

In this "underdevelopment," persons fall away from their God-given freedom and responsibility, becoming instead "chameleon-like"[10] creatures, dependent upon others for affirmation and identity.

Judith Plaskow, in a dissertation published in 1980,[11] enlarges on Saiving's initial insight. Given the wider range of human experience made visible by the inclusion of women's voices in the theological conversation, Plaskow agrees that the Reformation tradition in particular addresses matters of sin and grace too narrowly—a conviction that by 1980 was shared by many. Summing up twenty intervening years of theological work, Plaskow notes that "in all this material, the inadequacy of understanding sin solely as pride has become almost a commonplace."[12] Following her conviction that such differences are not inherent, but socially constructed, Plaskow takes up Saiving's insight and carries it forward with a careful analysis of women's experience.

The key issue for Plaskow is the social construction of the "feminine" and the effects this has on women's self-identity.[13] The locus of sin, she argues, is (for women) primarily outside of the self,[14] though Plaskow is also interested in what she sees as the subjective collusion of women in the distortion of identity, which is deeply influenced by social formation.[15] In attempting to

---

9. Ibid. "They become aware of the deep need of almost every woman, regardless of her personal history and achievements or her belief in her own individual value, to surrender her self-identity and be included in another's 'power of being'" (ibid., 43).

10. Ibid., 47.

11. Plaskow, *Sex, Sin and Grace*.

12. Ibid., 2.

13. Ibid., 14–15, 31–32.

14. Ibid., 9.

15. Ibid. 170.

address both aspects of the situation, Plaskow defines women's experience "as the interrelation between cultural expectations and their internalization."[16] Taking the work of Simone de Beauvoir's *The Second Sex*[17] as instructive, Plaskow tests the argument that "the central dilemma of women's lives . . . is that women do not shape their own experience, but allow their life choices to be made for them by others."[18] Plaskow finds confirmation of this theory, first, through an examination of empirical evidence, both psychological and anthropological, and again, by way of literary confirmation, in her presentation of Doris Lessing's fictional character Martha Quest.[19] "Martha's problem," Plaskow writes, "is that there is no one she can commit herself to be."[20] Martha is a character who "drifts into and out of relationships and obligations by way of other people's choices. Against her better judgment, Martha is swept along into marriage. She is caught [up] in current[s] which she cannot resist. There is no Martha Quest as a responsible, willing being."[21]

Martha's lack of agency—her refusal to accept the responsibility for autonomous personhood—is her besetting sin. "We might say," Plaskow suggests, "that women's traditional tasks and characteristics are not problematical *per se* but become so when they are not chosen."[22] Martha manifests what Plaskow takes to be the common feminine experience of passive acceptance—an inability to initiate choice and action out of one's own identity. "All the while [that Martha is married], she feels that someday something will change, must change, but she cannot plan to change things, cannot see herself as the agent of action."[23] With Saiving, Plaskow concludes that Reformation doctrines of sin and grace, which describe a self-assertive pride redeemed and re-created into self-sacrificial *agape*, do not address the feminine situation. "[Women's] sin cannot be seen as the product of over-glorification of the self, for the problem is precisely that she has no self; she has not yet become a self and will not take the responsibility for becoming one. Her form of sin must be comprehended on its own terms, and that means it must be seen to have its roots in human nature, independent of pride."[24]

16. Ibid., 167–68.
17. Ibid., 31.
18. Ibid., 32.
19. Ibid., 34.
20. Ibid., 37.
21. Ibid., 36.
22. Ibid., 41.
23. Ibid., 65.
24. Ibid., 66–67.

Both Saiving and Plaskow describe the "feminine sin"[25] in the context of the larger feminist argument—that is, they claim that women's experiences have been traditionally overlooked. As in the case of Saiving, Plaskow's central point is that Reformation teachings on sin and grace do not address those who find themselves in bondage to passivity rather than to self-assertive pride.[26] Plaskow's project builds on Saiving's insight by analyzing the theologies of Reinhold Niebuhr and Paul Tillich.[27] Plaskow concludes her examination of these two theologians with the following remarks: "The question remains . . . as to whether the Protestant doctrine of justification *per se* is a response to the sin of pride and therefore more relevant to men's than to women's experience. Where sin is perverse inaction rather than self-assertion does the message that the self is forgiven despite persistence in sin foster a passivity which is women's real problem?"[28] Perhaps, Plaskow suggests, "one could formulate a doctrine of justification which would judge the failure to become a self and open up into a process of self-actualization."[29] If self-assertion is a sin that invites judgment and transformation, she suggests, might not the failure to become a self be similarly displeasing to God, and likewise open to regeneration?

The question of what is pleasing and displeasing to God is an important one, particularly in light of the Kantian influences in Western culture that calls individuals to their duty as autonomous human beings. As we have seen so far, the experience of women, as it is manifested in a self-abnegating passivity, has itself been taken to justify the claim of divine condemnation. Plaskow's confidence in divine judgment, however, is problematic, resting as it does on the assumption that nonflourishing is epistemologically sufficient to warrant the claim. Is her argument from nonflourishing really grounded in our created human nature? Or is it, like the socially constructed view of the feminine that Plaskow deplores, the reflection of (possibly sinful) cultural expectations?[30]

Mary Stewart Van Leeuwen raises this epistemological problem directly.[31] "What does the [biblical] creation account tell us about gender relations?" she asks.[32] "The Bible," she suggests, "tells us not about natural or social history so much as about 'metahistory'; that is, it deals with universal truths about God, human beings, and their interaction throughout time. . . . So the distinction between natural and social accounts of gender on the one hand and the supernatural, biblical account on the other is the first thing we need to

---

25. Saiving, "Human Situation,"2.
26. Plaskow, *Sex, Sin and Grace*, 4.
27. Ibid., 3.
28. Ibid., 157.
29. Ibid.

recover."[33] She notes that among "evangelical biblical scholars, well-trained in Hebrew exegesis," there is wide agreement on the interpretation of the Genesis creation accounts, despite differing church affiliation.[34] All of them, she argues, "affirm that God called both sexes, without favor, to exercise accountable dominion over the creation. . . . Men and women were meant from the beginning to be 'joint heirs' of creation, just as they are joint heirs of salvation in the third act of the biblical drama."[35] Pointing to a study by Gilbert Bilezikian, Van Leeuwen interprets the text from Gen. 3:16 ("your desire shall be for your husband and he shall rule over you") as the source of that gendered distinction in sin identified by Hampson, Saiving, and Plaskow. The verse, explains Van Leeuwen, is really "talking about an unreciprocated longing for intimacy."[36]

> [The woman's] desire will be for her husband, so as to perpetuate the intimacy that had characterized their relationship in paradise lost. But her nostalgia for the relation of love and mutuality that existed between them before the fall, when they both desired each other, will not be reciprocated by her husband. Instead of meeting her desire . . . [h]e will rule over her. . . . [T]he woman wants a mate, and she gets a master; she wants a lover and she gets a lord; she wants a husband and she gets a hierarch.[37]

---

30. Ibid., 29–30. Plaskow asks, "From what standpoint can [the] illegitimacy [of traditional descriptions of theological anthropology] be demonstrated?" She goes on to examine empirical, anthropological, and literary data for confirmation that her description of women's experience is justified—providing evidence to support an argument from natural law. That is, if some cultural construction promotes nonflourishing across a broad spectrum of human experience, such a construction appears to work contrary to the goal of nature and is therefore (presumably) condemned by God, who calls for creation to flourish (as Adam and Eve are called to be "fruitful"). But this assumes human beings have the capacity to accurately assess what counts as flourishing. (Given the central role sin plays in distorting human reason in Luther's thinking, the point needs to be considered.) Plaskow reveals an underlying commitment to some form of essentialism (even if human nature can only be approximately known by way of particular experience) when, in her final reflections, she writes: "If it is inadequate to view pride as the human sin, then, in the light of women's experience, the sin of failing fully to realize one's freedom, failing fully to become a self, must be seen as equally firmly rooted in human nature" (Ibid., 175).

31. Mary Stewart Van Leeuwen, "The Christian Mind and the Challenge of Gender Relations," in *Reformed Journal* 37, no. 9: 17–23.

32. Ibid., 18.

33. Ibid.

34. Ibid.

35. Ibid.

36. Ibid., 20.

Van Leeuwen suggests that "as a result of the fall there will be a propensity in man to let dominion run wild—to impose it in cavalier and illegitimate ways not only upon the earth and upon other men, but also upon the person who is 'bone of [his] bones and flesh of [his] flesh.'" The corollary is "the particularly female sin," whereby women will seek to preserve relationships in their quest for intimacy "as an excuse not to exercise accountable dominion in the first place."[38] "If women insist on peace at any price—if they settle for an abnormal quietism as a way of avoiding the risk and potential isolation that may come from opposing evil—then they are not exhibiting the fruit of the Spirit; they are sinning just as surely as the man who rides roughshod over relationships in order to assert his individual freedom."[39] In support of Bilezikian's claim, Van Leeuwen compares the well-known story of King David's rape of Bathsheba on the one hand (an example of male sin) with the story of Queen Esther's courageous defense of her people on the other (an example of women's sin narrowly avoided). Queen Esther, Van Leeuwen explains, offers a parallel "paradigm of the female evasion of responsibility, which needs just as much to be renounced."[40] After Mordecai's prophetic rebuke, and Esther's turn from fearful passivity to faithful courage, "the Jews are again spared to continue as God's carriers of the Messianic promise, in part because a young queen overcame the negative legacy of Genesis 3:16."[41]

Thus Van Leeuwen turns to Scripture for epistemic confirmation that the nonflourishing so widely experienced by women reflects, not cultural presuppositions alone, but the failure to meet God's call to faithful and decisive action in the world. Queen Esther's courageous response to Mordecai's

---

37. Ibid. Van Leeuwen is quoting Gilbert Bilezikian, *Beyond Sex Roles* (Grand Rapids: Baker Book House, 1985), 55, 229.

38. Plaskow, *Sex, Sin and Grace*, 20–21.

39. Ibid., 21.

40. Ibid., 20, 21. By way of explanation Van Leeuwen offers the following: "Esther, after all, was the darling of King Ahasuerus's harem. She seemed quite happy to keep her Jewish identity a secret, and even when her uncle Mordecai asked her to intercede with Ahasuerus to rescue the Jews from Haman's genocidal plot, she answered, in effect, that she would rather not take the risk. But then comes Mordecai's rebuke, as telling as the prophet Nathan's judgment of David: 'Think not that in the king's palace you will escape any more than all the other Jews. For if you keep silence at such a time as this, relief and deliverance will rise for the Jews from another quarter, but you and your father's house will perish. And who knows whether you have not come to the kingdom for such a time as this? (Esther 4:13-14)' Esther, like David, is turned around by this prophetic rebuke, and after asking the Jews to fast and pray for her (thus manifesting the *right* sort of communal solidarity), she finally says, 'I will go to the king, although it is against the law; and if I perish, I perish'" (ibid.).

41. Ibid., 21.

prophetic judgment provides us with an example of human responsibility faithfully, and courageously, enacted—an example women (and men) are called to emulate.[42]

As with Plaskow, Van Leeuwen buttresses her argument with a story. A young woman named Kari Malcolm, raised by missionary parents in China, and a survivor of three years in a Japanese internment camp during World War II, wrote of her dismay "when one of her most vibrant friends decided against medical school and the mission field."[43] In an act, which seemed to Malcolm a faithless failure of nerve, her friend let "the dreams and aspirations of many years . . . die"[44] when she became engaged to marry. "I could not see why marriage and medical school had to be an either/or proposition,"[45] Malcolm writes. "For many women marriage was such a top priority that careers, as well as love for Jesus, had to be relegated to second place."[46] Reflecting on Malcolm's experience, Van Leeuwen writes, "Malcolm is well aware of the psychological and sociological forces that contribute to women's desire to evade risk and responsibility by attaching themselves to other people.[47] But as a biblically literate Christian, she realizes this is not the whole story. Underneath these mechanisms lies the fear of losing security, family, and even one's femininity—a fear that can be cast out only by the redemptive love of Jesus Christ."[48] Van Leeuwen too notes the dual nature of sin so widely affirmed elsewhere. "One of the tragic things about our fallenness, as expressed in Genesis 3:16," she writes, "is that it seems to be so horribly complementary in its effects on the sexes: the male propensity to abuse dominion seems compulsively matched by the female propensity towards the securing of relationships, even unhealthy ones, no matter what the cost."[49] Reflecting the same insight, Daphne Hampson explains, "The reality of women's lives has been that they had to circle round other people. What plans they might have had gave way to what others determined should be, resulting in a sense of powerlessness, of lacking control even in their own lives. Meaning had to be found through the lives of others. Typically, the 'problems' that women have manifested have been those resulting from the lack of a sense of self-worth, leading to depression, anorexia, or suicidal

---

42. Ibid.
43. Ibid. See Kari T. Malcolm, *Women at the Crossroads: A Path Beyond Feminism and Traditionalism* (Downers Grove, IL: InterVarsity Press, 1982).
44. Ibid.
45. Ibid.
46. Ibid.
47. Ibid., 22.
48. Ibid.
49. Ibid.

tendencies. . . . Feminism has [therefore] stood for empowerment."[50] Arguing that there is simply no way to square one of the central aims of feminism—the empowerment of the self—with the theology central to Luther's understanding of the God-human relationship, Hampson concludes, "The whole dynamic of being a self is very different from what Lutheranism has proposed. Thus its prescription must appear irrelevant, indeed, counter-productive."[51]

Central to Hampson's objection is her reading of Luther's anthropology, which she believes presents insurmountable difficulties for the necessary incremental building up of the self. "Luther's achievement lay in his reconceptualization of the human relation to God," Hampson notes.[52] Yet, she continues, it is precisely this reconceptualization, with its emphasis on a relational ontology, that presents problems for the feminine quest toward self-transformation and empowerment. Unlike Roman Catholicism, where one may "speak of the person as existing through creation and then as having the capacity to choose to relate to God,"[53] Luther's God (in Hampson's view) "is conceived to be fundamental to the very constitution of the self in each moment. . . . Luther contends that each moment I must anew base myself on God and so be the creature I was intended to be. To think that I could in some sense first possess myself, then relate to God as to another, would be to have an idol—one with whom I think I can deal."[54]

"It is not natural," Hampson claims, "for humans so to base themselves on God."[55] Noting Luther's remark that "progress is nothing other than constantly beginning,"[56] Hampson concludes that "it follows from this that there is no history of the development of the self; no movement within ourselves from being a sinner to being righteous."[57] Not only, in Hampson's view, has Luther

---

50. Hampson, "Luther on the Self," 339.

51. Ibid.

52. Ibid., 334

53. Ibid., 336. Notably, this kind of fundamental unity of God and self is not, for Hampson, problematic. She writes, "I believe that Luther's understanding that, if one is to speak of God, one must say that the self cannot be itself except as God is fundamental to the constitution of that self, must be retained within theology, and indeed can appropriately be developed by feminists" ("Luther on the Self," 334). It is the otherness of God—that God stands outside the self (according to Hampson's reading of Luther)—that Hampson finds irreconcilable with feminist commitments. Notably, she adds, "It becomes all the more imperative to develop Luther's insight that God must be seen as one who is fundamental to our being ourselves, not as some exterior other with whom we inter-relate. In that respect his thought surely needs to be taken up" ("Luther on the Self," 341). This is one of the primary goals of my discussion of the thenomous self in ch. 4.

54. Ibid., 336–37.

55. Ibid., 335.

failed to provide an ontology that supports continuity of the self through time, but he has also sought to do so precisely because he has no interest in spiritual transformation. "He has," she suggests with some irony, "got away from any such self-preoccupation."[58]

Emphasizing Luther's doctrine of justification so much that it obscures his robust (if relatively unknown) teaching on regeneration in the Spirit, Hampson naturally sees it as unresponsive to the feminine form of sin. Unfortunately, this understanding of Luther's anthropology is widespread—the result of an influential group of theologians, frequently read and taught in the United States, who have energetically imitated Luther's early prophetic denunciation of human agency. Luther scholars such as Helmut Thielicke, Gustav Wingren, and Anders Nygren have assiduously worked to undermine the self-righteous pietism that both Luther and Paul viewed as dangerous to faith. Given their historical context, this emphasis is not surprising. Following World War II, they gained a new recognition of sin that had been largely absent earlier in the century. So that, just as Luther had to struggle against the semi-Pelagianism of his own age, Lutheran theologians felt likewise compelled to undermine the overweening confidence that had been blind to the demonic tendencies within. But Luther moved on after 1521 to develop an anthropology that opened toward an active, cooperating agency with the indwelling Spirit—a move these theologians have refused to make. Reluctant to engage in any discussion of the volitional work of the faithful in the incremental growth of righteousness and faith (which Luther takes to be a key feature of the Christian life), they instead take every opportunity to present precisely the sort of Lutheran anthropology Hampson dismisses as "incommensurate" with feminism. We find Thielicke, for example, focusing on Luther's early description of those good works that spring forth "spontaneously" from faith.[59] "We lay particular emphasis on the term *sponte*," Thielicke writes, "because it describes most felicitously the directness of the relationship between justification and works. . . . The new obedience is 'automatic' in the sense that it cannot be otherwise."[60] Gustav Wingren, echoing this denial of human efficacy, locates agency in the external vocational

---

56. Ibid. Hampson quotes from Gerhard Ebeling, *Luther: An Introduction to His Thought*, trans. R. A. Wilson (Philadelphia: Fortress Press, 1972), 162. Notably, these references are from Luther's early lectures on the Psalms (1513–1515) and Romans (1515–1516). These represent the teachings of the early Luther, prior to the full development of his doctrine of God's twofold reign—a development that had important consequences for his anthropology.

57. Hampson, Luther on the Self," 335.

58. Ibid.

59. One of many examples from "The Freedom of a Christian" (1520): "He does the works out of spontaneous love in obedience to God." *LW* 31:359.

call as it applies to relationships within the family. "At work in marriage," he writes, "is a power which *compels* self-giving to spouse and children. So it is the 'station' itself which is the ethical agent, for it is God who is active through the law on earth."[61] And again, he argues, "That which the office does is not part of man's account, but of God's."[62] Indeed, Wingren is so eager to discourage any exploration of the process by and through which human agency engages the Spirit volitionally that he soundly rejects two earlier attempts to explore this process. Responding to works by Karl Eger (1900) and Paul Heinz Schifferdecker (1932),[63] both of whom tried to establish a systematic relationship between faith and action, Wingren writes, "If Luther had shown by logical principles how faith must express itself in love, as Eger and Schifferdecker desire, he would not have developed his view more systematically. Rather, he would have replaced the reality of God with an intellectual construction and denied the miraculous character of something which is a miracle. Luther knew very well what he was doing when he merely asserted the relationship between faith and love without proving it." "Why is it," Wingren asks, "that faith does not stop [with the believer], but becomes love which is concerned about a neighbor? *Faith is God, and God is like that.*"[64] One cannot help noticing that by the time Wingren reaches his conclusion here, the *person* of faith has dropped out of the picture altogether.

What women need," writes Hampson, is to "come to themselves . . . to come to have an adequate sense of self,"[65] so that salvation is "a healing,"[66] or "a coming into their own,"[67] rather than an ontology that makes self-existence, or selfhood, dependent on a God who is other.[68] Recalling Plaskow's

---

60. Helmut Thielicke, *Theological Ethics*, ed. William Henry Lazareth (Grand Rapids: Eerdmans, 1979), 63.

61. Gustaf Wingren, *Luther on Vocation* (Philadelphia: Muhlenberg Press, 1957), 6.

62. Ibid., 8.

63. Each sought to make sense of volition under the impact of faith; each determined in the end that Luther had failed to provide a coherent motivational explanation. Eger, in his 1900 *Die Anschauungen Luthers vom Beruf*, concludes that "serious consequences followed from [Luther's] theoretical lack of a systematic relationship between justifying faith and the fulfillment of vocation in the service of love" (Wingren, *Luther on Vocation*, 40). Schifferdecker, in his 1932 *Der Berufsgedanke bei Luther*, argues that "the necessary inner unity between faith and the power proceeding therefrom for action in vocation Luther has not been able to establish" (Wingren, *Luther on Vocation*, 41).

64. Wingren, *Luther on Vocation*, 41 (emphasis added).

65. Daphne Hampson, "On Power and Gender," *Modern Theology* 4, no. 3 (April 1988): 234–50 (241).

66. Ibid., 242; see also 248.

67. Ibid., 248.

68. Hampson, "Luther on the Self," 336–37. See also Hampson, "On Power and Gender," 248.

argument that "salvation" or "redemption" comes not from "dying and rising" daily in Christ, but rather from communities of women who listen and speak one another into being, Hampson notes that "the feminist response of recent years has been 'consciousness-raising' groups, in which women were enabled to find voice, therapy that allowed a feminist analysis of the situation in which a woman was placed, and assertiveness training in which women learnt to hold their own."[69] But, according to Wingren, Thielicke, and Hampson, "there is no self [in Luther's anthropology] which is indeed a self."[70]

This rendering of Luther's anthropology, however, leaves too much out. In time, Luther modified his early focus on justification, which initially colored all other aspects of his thought, by expanding his interest in the temporal realm and developing an anthropology associated with it. There is much in Luther's writing, especially after 1522, that reveals quite a different view of human agency than is visible in the accounts offered by Thielicke, Wingren, and Hampson. In fact, there is a good deal of evidence to suggest that Luther shared the conventional assumptions about the ontic structures and capacities that support life and personhood; and there is no doubt that he expected the same zealous disciplining of "worldly lusts" under the guidance of the Spirit as did his scholastic colleagues.

While Luther's anthropology has been problematic in light of feminist commitments to self-development, Hampson, Saiving, and Plaskow raise another distinct but related issue. This is Luther's focus on self-sacrificial love, or *agape*, understood as the shape that Christian love must take. Whether any theology that teaches the faithful to assume the cross of Christ in self-sacrificial love could be commensurate with the kinds of concerns raised by these women appears doubtful. "A sacrifice of self, leading to the nurture of others," writes Hampson, is a paradigm that "feminist women seemingly reject . . . with unanimity."[71] Saiving agrees that for women who too easily "surrender [their] individual concerns in order to serve the immediate needs of others,"[72] a theology of self-sacrificial neighbor-love appears to be highly problematic. This "religion of self-sacrifice," Hampson suggests, is dangerous because it may so easily become "the opium of women, reinforcing the position to which a woman has already assigned herself, compounding her belief that 'one should not put oneself forward.'"[73] Such a view of agape, says Saiving,

---

69. Hampson, "On Power and Gender," 242.
70. Hampson, "Luther on the Self," 336.
71. Hampson, "On Power and Gender," 239.
72. Saiving, "Human Situation," 44.
73. Hampson, "On Power and Gender," 239.

encourages a woman to abandon becoming "an individual in her own right."[74] Given the opportunity, she will believe, for example, "That having chosen marriage and children and thus being face to face with the needs of her family for love, refreshment, and forgiveness, she has no right to ask anything for herself but must submit without qualification to the strictly feminine role."[75] "The Gospel of [a self-sacrificial] powerlessness," concludes Hampson, "has been appropriated by those to whom it should never have been directed."[76] Given Luther's remark that "self-love is something wicked by which I love myself in opposition to God,"[77] and Nygren's claim that, for Luther, self-love is "wholly under the dominion of sin"[78] (a view of self-love Gene Outka calls "wholly nefarious"),[79] it is hardly surprising that those who already attribute a problematic deficit of self-regard to women would spurn Luther's analysis.

Without doubt, a good deal of Luther's early work, as well as his ongoing rejection of "free will,"[80] could be said to justify Hampson's concerns. The theocentric vision undergirding Luther's thought informed both his theology and his use of language as he battered away at what seemed to him a naive and dangerous confidence in human beings. Not surprisingly, Luther's theology offended many in his own day, including those who had little interest in gender-related issues. Erasmus of Rotterdam, for example, the most celebrated humanist of Luther's time, challenged Luther publicly over Luther's surprising and dangerous repudiation of free will. "Was it necessary," Erasmus argues in his response to Luther's teaching, that "in avoiding the Scylla of arrogance, you should be wrecked on the Charybdis of despair or indolence?"[81] Luther's prophetic denunciation of human efficacy before the grandeur of God is indisputably a key element of Luther's early theology. But the crux of the

---

74. Saiving, "Human Situation," 45.

75. Ibid.

76. Hampson, "On Power and Gender," 239.

77. *LW* 26:297.

78. Anders Nygren, *Agape and Eros* (Chicago: University of Chicago Press, 1982), 23.

79. Gene H. Outka, *Agape: An Ethical Analysis* (New Haven: Yale University Press, 1972), 56–63. Notably, Outka adds, "Certain strains in Luther himself resist assimilation into Nygren's program.... One finds in some of Luther's writings a view close to [one in which] ... the agent's own interests serve as the paradigm of all others, and may be taken as the standard for treating others in the sense of the golden rule" (ibid., 62).

80. While Luther rejects this terminology, it is by no means clear that he rejects the content, when understood according to the Catholic tradition as a freedom of choice within the bounds of God's providence. See ch. 4.

81. E. Gordon Rupp and Philip S. Watson, eds., *Luther and Erasmus: Free Will and Salvation*, Library of Christian Classics (Philadelphia: Westminster Press, 1969).

argument here is derived from Luther's work during the years that followed. The Luther we will observe in the pages ahead reveals important theological developments that began to emerge after 1522, when he returned to Wittenberg and assumed new vocational responsibilities as a civic leader. His refocusing on the social and political situation resulted in a correlative opening up of his theology to include the temporal realm. As a thinker who constantly theologized at the intersection of experience and Scripture (with the important additional influence of the church fathers), it is no surprise that Luther's marriage in 1525 also spawned important theological developments. In chapter 3, for example, I track Luther's growing confidence in God's reliable creational gifts, his discovery of joy in this world, and his deepening embrace of a friendlier God.

But in all of this, it is important to view Luther against the backdrop of his early work. In order to tell the later story, we need to understand his earlier thinking, including the situation out of which Luther's prophetic rejection of the world in general, and scholastic optimism in particular, sprang; for Luther's prophetic calling continued to shape his thinking in the years that followed. If no longer exclusively, it nonetheless remained an important component of his thinking, though in time it became but one element among others, embedded in a considerably larger theological vision.

Chapter 1, then, opens with the story of Luther's early years and continues through his theological discovery up to his excommunication from the Roman Church in early 1521. This first chapter illuminates some of the causes behind Luther's early and vehement rejection of human efficacy and self-love. We begin with Luther's passion for security in an insecure world. Exacerbated by lifelong bouts of intense anxiety, Luther's tenacity in maintaining the theological presuppositions entailed by his solution should not surprise us, given the real existential repercussions for him personally. A second element at work derives from his theological training. The semi-Pelagian scholasticism Luther was taught encumbered the young monk with an untenable approach to salvation—one that nearly drove him to despair and the devil; it was, therefore, a theology he considered extremely dangerous to the salvation of others, who like himself might flounder under the uncertainty of God's predestining will. But we must also take into account Luther's discovery of the German mystics, with their fusion of opposites, such that death implies life and suffering promises hope. Luther embraced these oppositions in his "theology of the cross,"[82] allowing him to reinterpret his bouts of anxiety as signs of God's love rather than God's wrath. While this fusion of opposites made sense of his own experience, it also resulted in the absolute condemnation of self and world—a dimension of Luther's early theology we find difficult to grasp today. Another factor responsible for Luther's most radical denunciations was his conviction that God's saving Word comes to condemned sinners through the words of Scripture. Given his vocational responsibility as a teacher of the Bible and his conviction that God had delegated to him the protection and deliverance of this liberating Word of salvation, Luther's pugnacious response to Rome can be better understood in light of papal claims to exclusive interpretive control of the text. Luther's devotion to his pastoral calling also played a significant role, since (he believed) nothing less than eternal salvation was at stake for all those souls that had been given into his keeping, souls for whom he was responsible before God. Thus Luther was prepared to say and do whatever was necessary to cultivate a saving faith, thereby fulfilling the duty God had thrust upon him. Finally, and probably most important of all, was Luther's unusual sensitivity to the power and presence of the living God. This prophetic sensibility provided the frame for everything else, causing Luther to view temporal reality as the stage upon which God and Satan played out their roles in a cosmic drama. And it was into this same drama that Luther understood himself to be drawn—prepared by God to lead the multitude of souls into battle against the devil. Only when we appreciate the enormity of Luther's vision can we grasp the correlative radicalism of his theology. In chapter 1, then, we observe the Luther who turned away from everything temporal in service to that which is infinite, understanding this as an either/or proposition.

If chapter 1 explores Luther's monastic departure from this world and the controversy that thrust him back out and onto the world's stage, then chapter 2 tracks that development. In meeting the new social and political demands of the day, Luther's theology underwent important changes. It was in addressing these changes that his still-developing two-kingdom thinking, which had previously focused almost exclusively on spiritual concerns, expanded to meet the political exigencies requiring Luther's attention and leadership.

Luther expanded his two-kingdom thinking by adapting his earlier dualistic view of the self into a considerably more complex configuration that was correlated with God's two metaphorical "hands." Through these, God is always busily at work in the world, on the "left hand" in the civil or temporal realm, and on the "right" through a spiritual realm in which Christ brings people to faith. Luther's adaptation of Paul's eschatological framework, based

---

82. See Heidelberg Disputation, thesis 20: "He deserves to be called a theologian . . . who comprehends the visible and manifest things of God seen through suffering and the cross" (*LW* 31:40). See also thesis 21: "A theologian of glory calls evil good and good evil. A theologian of the cross calls the thing what it actually is" (Ibid.).

on Paul's notion of an "old" and a "new" Adam, provided this wider frame that could now accommodate both an inner and outer self. In its final form, Luther's mature model of the two realms became his primary vehicle for working out responses to various social challenges as these arose. Most interesting to us, however, is the revised anthropology that Luther's new model generated. His early, dualistic view of the self, understood as wholly sinful or righteous before God (*coram Deo*), remains, but in this new configuration is designated as the inner self. Given Paul's understanding of persisting sin (and Luther's experience of it), Luther posits an outer self, which continues in this present age to fight in the Spirit against the residual "substance of sin." Thus there is one person, wholly sinful or righteous before God while at the same time partly righteous and partly sinful before the world. This is the self in transition under the cooperating agency of the Holy Spirit. Though persisting sin is not counted as sin on account of Christ, it is nevertheless still very real.

In light of this remaining need for reform, we take up Hampson's concerns about Luther's anthropology, paying particular attention to his presuppositions regarding the reliability of persisting ontic structures that undergird the potential for incremental growth. Luther's expectation of an outworking of faith through works of love directed toward the neighbor is thus coupled in midcareer with a sanctifying discipline that focuses on the self.

Parallel to this new model, we find in Luther's work a revised eucharistic understanding of Christ's body and blood fully present in the bread and wine, which nevertheless remains wholly bread and wine. Reflecting the "totally human, totally divine" description of Christ in the church's historic creeds, Luther's understanding of the Eucharist does not allow for the transubstantiation of the temporal bread and wine into the similarly fully present body and blood of Christ. Not only does this affirm the full value of the created order (and the outer self), but it also works to sacramentalize the entire created order. God is ubiquitous in Luther's theology, everywhere at once, not only in, with, and under the bread and wine, but also in, with, and under the whole creation.

This understanding of God's near presence is also worked out in Luther's new understanding of vocation, which emerges alongside his developing two-kingdoms model. Under Luther's novel use of the word *vocation*, every ordinary task of this world becomes a holy calling for those who can discern God's work in and under their own. The priesthood of all believers is expected to "preach" in word and deed, so that worldly occupations become an important delivery system by way of which Christ's presence and work breaks into this world, creating a new sacramental secularity. This work on vocation develops in the context of Luther's attack on monasticism, as he relocates God's activity in Christ throughout the whole created order rather than under the sacramental control of Rome alone.

Chapter 3 addresses Luther's infamous rejection of self-love. While in chapters 1 and 2 we observe his prophetic renunciation of the self, this chapter addresses his growing acknowledgment of a legitimate and godly concern for one's own well-being. Beginning with Luther's return to Wittenberg in 1522, and influenced by the great joy he discovered in his marriage to Katie in 1525, Luther largely reversed his earlier condemnation of self-care. In time, and especially in the context of plague-ridden Wittenberg, Luther found self-love both reasonable and prudent—indeed, an obligation. Not only is the mandatory care for oneself derived from an obligation to protect others from contagion, but Luther also very clearly affirmed a desire to protect oneself as a natural good, woven into the fabric of creation, and an attitude pleasing to God. Surprisingly, he supported the relocation of the university to Jena while the plague ravaged Wittenberg; the lives of his students and colleagues were of such value that their worth overrode an imprudent self-sacrificial stance that Luther now described as "tempting God." Here we see quite a different appreciation and valuation of the self from that of the young Luther, who "tempted God" with excessive fasting and other self-destructive activities—the very behavior he now publicly repudiated. Luther's marriage, which he entered into in order to "spite the devil,"[83] provides further evidence of his growing affirmation of worldly joys, as he discovered the unexpected pleasure of fatherhood and the deepening friendship and love he shared with Katie.[84] When his teenaged daughter died, Luther's grief reveals to us the depth of his natural love,[85] making it clear that his theology no longer envisioned earthly life and eternal life as opposites. Rather, God's gifts are present in both realms. No longer hidden under the form of its opposite, joy is both natural and God-pleasing. As Luther's confidence in God's redemptive love grew ever stronger, his earlier terror of God's judgment was reconfigured within the larger frame of God's mercy.

Chapter 4 addresses the question of agency in light of the free-will debate. Beginning with the difficult issues raised by Luther's infrequent, but nonetheless unsettling, rants against free will (given the necessitarian logic these display),[86] this chapter argues that Luther's pastoral concerns and theological

---

83. *LW* 49:111. See also Heiko Augustinus Oberman, *Luther: Man between God and the Devil* (New Haven: Yale University Press, 1989), 280.

84. William Lazareth, *Luther on the Christian Home: An Application of the Social Ethics of the Reformation* (Philadelphia: Muhlenberg Press, 1960) 31–32.

85. Ibid., 32.

battles allow us to interpret these texts in light of his far more usual Augustinian approach to human freedom. If his remarks fail to honor the careful scholastic distinctions normally employed, Luther is not engaging in sloppy thinking so much as intentionally refusing to collude with an impious use of language. Luther's extraordinary understanding of the power of language to construct reality becomes clear as we see him manipulating conventional theological constructs in new, and purposefully unsettling, ways.[87]

Despite Luther's apparent disregard for human freedom, he did not fail to hold human beings responsible for their failure to honor God. Not only does he explicitly affirm this, but it is also visible in his frequent and passionate exhortation, as he attempted to move people to choose for rather than against God. In both his pastoral letters of consolation to those on the brink of despair and his frequent exhortations to the baptized via sermons and lectures, Luther consistently called upon the baptized to cooperate with the indwelling Spirit, both in their service toward the neighbor as well as in their discipline of "worldly lusts." Luther's theology of vocation conflates these two aims in the notion of vocation as a "school for character." Of note (particularly in light of Hampson's critique) are Luther's warnings that to fail in this—to passively ignore the Spirit's calling into the work of reforming old habits and assuming new challenges—is to turn one's back on God faithlessly, thereby relinquishing all the promises of the gospel. Though his constant urging of this warning upon those who would ignore it, this presupposition presents a curious tension. On the one hand, persons are told that they can do nothing at all in relation to faith, which clearly includes for Luther the active outworking of faith in love. On the other hand, Luther frequently suggests that persons do in fact have the capacity to choose to work with the Spirit; further, that these decisions have eternal consequences suggests that, whatever Luther preaches about free will, his presuppositions on the ground suggest a considerably more optimistic view than his theology of passive righteousness suggests.

Luther's oddly illogical juxtaposition of an attack on free will with a simultaneous call to battle against the flesh might be interpreted as Luther's enactment *in time* of the scholastic *consequentiae/consequentis* distinction that he

---

86. Rupp and Watson, *Luther and Erasmus*, 140, 180. See ch. 4.

87. See *LW* 32:94: "I would wish that the words, 'free will' had never been invented." And also *LW* 25:372: "What else does the expression 'to be contingent' mean than to be a creature and not God?" Luther is taking the word *contingent* (used to describe human free will) and reapplying it to the radical dependency of human beings on God's free will. Human beings *are* contingent (dependent), but are not able to make choices contingently (freely) in light of God's predestining will (see ch. 4). Note also Luther's reapplication of the concept of holy *vocation* to ordinary work.

so energetically rejected.[88] That is to say, from within the temporal context, one's choice for or against God is always open (or free) and the possibility of salvation is thus always available. Yet, simultaneously, from the perspective of eternity, and *without the opening that time provides*, God's providential predestining foreknowledge is absolute. The mystery of human responsibility in the face of God's predestination is thereby maintained by way of created temporality. Luther intentionally left the logical disjunction unexplained, but nonetheless present, in his description of God rendered as both *Deus absconditus* and *Deus revelatus*. Luther appears to be preserving the mystery of God's providence and human responsibility beyond our ability to logically package it. Thus Luther never stopped exhorting people to cling to the *Deus revalatus* in the face of the *Deus absconditus*—at least as long as they are capable of conscious choice;[89] and he normally paired this exhortation with teaching about the integral part each choice plays in the cosmic battle between God and the devil. Thus the work of choosing (to opt, for example, for passive neglect rather than dangerous engagement) in the presence of the indwelling Spirit is more than a personal choice. Every opportunity to choose (as possibilities are presented by the Spirit) becomes an opportunity to grasp the promise or to ignore it, to struggle on behalf of God against Satan, or to succumb. The work of resisting temporal temptation thus becomes part of something larger—something infinitely important in ways that exceed individual gain. Christian life consists in this ongoing struggle to choose well in cooperation with the in-forming and empowering Spirit. Christian life, in other words, involves a clear call to active engagement rather than passivity.

Chapter 4 closes with a modest phenomenological exploration of how such a struggle in the Spirit might be experienced and actively engaged.

The conclusion expands on this program. After a brief summary of key points in the overall argument of the book—that is, for an interpretation of Luther's theology which is more conducive to addressing feminist concerns—we turn, once again, to address the inner movement that allows

---

88. See n87. Luther rejects a scholastic distinction between *necessitas consequentis* (the necessity of occurrences based on God's choice and foreknowledge) and *necessitas consequentiae* (the free choice by human beings according to their given capacities). The distinction protects human responsibility on one side and God's overarching providence on the other. It remains a mystery as to how both God and human beings can be genuinely free to choose different ends while at the same time affirming that God's will is absolute. Hence Luther rejects calling free a choice that cannot, ultimately, change God's predestining will with regard to salvation.

89. During the plague, Luther refused to make pastoral calls to those already so close to death that they were no longer consciously able to hear and receive the gospel's promise. See ch. 3.

one to break free. As a model reflecting the feminine situation, we return to the story of Queen Esther, who was quite happy to passively keep her Jewish identity a secret when to reveal it would put her life in danger. "Even when her uncle Mordecai asked her to intercede with Ahasuerus to rescue the Jews from Haman's genocidal plot," writes Van Leeuwen, "she answered, in effect, that she would rather not take the risk."[90]

> But then comes Mordecai's rebuke, as telling as the prophet Nathan's judgment of David: "Think not that in the king's palace you will escape any more than all the other Jews. For if you keep silence at such a time as this, relief and deliverance will rise for the Jews from another quarter, but you and your father's house will perish. And who knows whether you have not come to the kingdom for such a time as this?" (Esther 4:13-14).[91]

Van Leeuwen's description of faithful action seems to be precisely that ongoing engagement with the Spirit that Luther sees as central to the life of faith. "Esther, like David, is turned around by this prophetic rebuke," writes Van Leeuwen, "and after asking the Jews to fast and pray for her (thus manifesting the right sort of communal solidarity), she finally says, 'I will go to the king, although it is against the law; and if I perish, I perish.'"[92]

In the opening paragraph of his book *Freedom of a Christian*, Luther describes the experience of faith as something that cannot be understood until one has "tasted the great strength" faith offers in dangerous situations. "It is impossible to write well about it or to understand what has been written about it unless one has at one time or another experienced the courage which faith gives a man [or woman!] when trials oppress him. But he who has had even a faint taste of it can never write, speak, meditate, or hear enough concerning it."[93]

This is the courage of faith—a critical contribution of Luther's theology to the plight of those in bondage to passivity; persons, that is, like Queen Esther, who preferred to hide out from the responsible, and dangerous, engagement with the world into which she was called. The courageous agency that faith inspires is demonstrated both in the way Luther lived his life and in the theology of sanctification that he developed midcareer. Faith is subjectively active in the

---

90. Van Leeuwen, "Christian Mind," 21.
91. Ibid.
92. Ibid.
93. Luther, *Career of the Reformer I*, 343.

process of choosing freely from within the limited options of choosing with, or in defiance of, God through a multitude of everyday decisions that matter infinitely.

When Luther convinced the laity that their ordinary jobs were holy vocations, no less significant than the work of the priest who stands at the alter consecrating the bread and wine, he ignited a powerful response from those whose lives had seemed to themselves insignificant. In the same way, Luther's view of the Christian life, understood as an ongoing series of decisions, drawing one into a cosmic drama of infinite importance, moves persons, not toward an "oh, so what—" shrug-of-the-shoulders passivity, but toward a new understanding of the self *and the choices one makes* as valuable in an ultimate sense. For those whose temptation is to see themselves as beings of no real significance, this is an invitation to accept what Luther takes to be already true. There is no neutral ground; and so each choice is another skirmish between God and Satan—a battle subjectively engaged from below through the consciences and the choices of individual human beings. Heiko Oberman names and describes this drama in his book *Luther: Man between God and the Devil*. But Luther did not consider this his private story; it is rather the story of every person. And such an understanding of the Christian life, viewed from the subjective perspective of the actors, has the power to ignite action and to transform lives. The new doctrine of justification that Plaskow longs for, "which would judge the failure to become a self and open up into a process of self-actualization,"[94] *is* Luther's doctrine of justification, embedded in a later and larger theology that includes human choice and action. As always, the gold in Luther's theology is God's gospel promise, which remains an opening—an authentic freedom to embrace new possibilities—offered to all, even as it is also the ground of that courage one needs in order to take the risk. Hampson's objections to *Lutheranism* are not misplaced, given the systematic refusal of Luther scholars to protect against the dangers of self-righteous striving by presenting Luther's theology as one devoted to the obliteration of the self. It is my hope, on the brink of the five hundredth anniversary of the Reformation—a Reformation ignited by Luther's theology and his personal courage—that this book may help to fan the dying embers, unleashing some hint of the warmth that Luther's fire generated half a millennium ago.

---

94. Plaskow, *Sex, Sin and Grace*, 157.

1

God's Prophet

LIFE IN THE MIDST OF DEATH

Born in 1483, Luther lived in a world that knew death intimately.[1] And while the terrors of finitude and human limitation were hardly unique to his time, it is nevertheless difficult for us today, with our scientific grasp of reality, to understand Luther's world. For the people of his day, one thing was clear—once born, there was no escape. This temporal life was but the tip of an eternity that promised either perfect rest or the fury of God's wrath—forever! Life in this world was hard and short, at least by our modern Western standards. For most ordinary people, this meant years of grueling hard work in the fields, eking out a living by bare subsistence. It meant a life ordered by the cycle of the seasons, and disordered by the disaster of unexplained disease and drought. It meant scrambling to keep a roof over one's head and food on the table. The death of children was a familiar occurrence. Medicine as we know it today was still a long way off; and in a world not yet knowledgeable about germs and viruses, reason could only construe illness as an evil wind blowing unpredictably through the village, mysteriously spreading plague to some homes but not to others. Viewed as an unwelcome visit by otherworldly forces, the suffering that accompanied disease and starvation was often

---

1. See Bernhard Lohse, *Martin Luther's Theology: Its Historical and Systematic Development*, trans. Roy A Harrisville (Minneapolis: Fortress Press, 1999), 325: "The Reformation understanding of the righteousness of God and the justification of the sinner is unintelligible apart from its eschatological context.... Certainly, Luther's view owed much to the waning medieval period, when the universal power and presence of death was experienced and reflected on with great intensity." Lohse notes two authors behind this generalization: Hans-Jurgen Prien, *Luthers Wirtschaftsethik* (Gottingen: Vandenhoeck & Ruprecht, 1992), and Hans Pruss, *Die Vorstellungen vom Antichrist im spatern Mittelalter, bei Luther und in der Konfesionellen Polemik: Ein Beitrag zur Theologie Luthers und qur Geschichte der Frommigkeit* (Leipzig: J. Hinrichs, 1906).

explained as divine punishment for some unacknowledged sin, or the devil's army capriciously thwarting God's creative ends.

It was by way of the institutional church, with its narrative of judgment and salvation, that people were able to make sense of their lives. Without scientific explanations, their desire to understand why and how things happened was satisfied by a deeply held belief in devils, magic, and divine providence. In that world, as in our own, the experience of death was devastating and often incomprehensible. But set within the context of the Christian story, their personal lives (and deaths) were taken up into a larger frame of meaning. This life became the opportunity for achieving something better in the next. With the vision of heaven so prominently displayed in the religious art around them, people lived their lives toward the achievement of this end,[2] a goal that promised perfect peace beyond the daily bumps and bruises of this world.[3] But it was a heaven not easily won. A person had to live rightly in obedience, and to die rightly, formed in the virtues of faith, hope, and love.[4]

Life's purpose was derived not only from the vision of heaven that drew one forward but also from the fear of hell, which provided an equally powerful motivator.[5] Men and women, from their birth surrounded by the formal authority of the church and the informal influence of biblical (and extrabiblical) stories, had only to observe the pictures of judgment, carved above the great cathedral doorways, to grasp the trial that awaited each human being.[6] It was

---

2. From Thomas à Kempis, *The Imitation of Christ*, in *A Reformation Reader: Primary Texts with Introductions*, ed. Denis Janz, 2nd ed. (Minneapolis: Fortress Press, 2008), 4. According to Janz's introduction, "Thomas à Kempis (1380–1427) joined the Order of Hermits of St. Augustine in 1406 and was ordained to the priesthood in 1413.. . . . He wrote his *Imitation of Christ* between 1420 and 1427. Written in all probability for novice monks, it soon became one of the most famous devotional books of the age, for laity and religious alike" (Janz, *Reformation Reader*, 4). The piece gives us an excellent picture of the kind of piety in which Luther was formed. Themes important to Luther included the fragility and uncertainty of life, flight from the world, divine judgment, the dualist conviction that the appetites of the body are evil and that reason is to be informed by grace in order to help discipline the will and impose virtue, life as a project focused on the incremental acquisition of virtue under the threat of purgatory and hell for those who failed. "If you remain faithful in all your doings, be sure that God will be faithful and generous in rewarding you" (Thomas à Kempis, *Imitation of Christ*, 11). "Always keep in mind your last end, and how you will stand before the just Judge from whom nothing is hid. . . . Why do you not prepare yourself against the Day of Judgment" (ibid., 10). "The more you spare yourself now, and indulge the desires of the body, the more severe will be your punishment hereafter, and the more fuel you gather for the flames" (ibid.).

3. Ibid., 10: "Keep your heart free and lifted up to God. . . . Daily direct your prayers and longings to heaven, that at your death your soul may merit to pass joyfully into the presence of God."

4. Ibid., 12: "Always remember your end, and that lost time never returns. Without care and diligence, you will never acquire virtue."

in preparation for this inevitable ordeal that Christendom taught people to order their lives.[7] Thus life in Luther's day had meaning because it had a goal—heaven, if you lived and died righteously in the Lord, or hell, if you gave up the good fight and succumbed to the devil, who was always there, eager to confuse and corrupt.[8] And for those who wanted to make the most of the opportunity life offered, there was also the fast track to salvation provided by the church—the monastic life, which provided spiritual training for those who were specially gifted.

It was this route that young Luther chose. In the year 1505, as he was returning to the University at Erfert to work on a law degree, Martin was caught out in the open in a great thunderstorm. Terrified by what he took to be his imminent death, and with lightning and thunder crashing all about him, Luther experienced that divine judgment he so feared. Eternity yawned before him as he stood there in the very face of God's wrath. "Saint Anne, Saint Anne," he cried. "Save me. I'll become a monk."[9]

---

5. Heiko A. Oberman, *Luther: Man between God and the Devil* (New Haven: Yale University Press, 1989), 6. Oberman includes a woodcut from Ulm featuring a skeleton with the serpent wrapped around it is disappearing into the mouth of a monster, with flames coming from its mouth. The feet of the skeleton have already disappeared into the mouth. The woodcut is titled: *Whether master or servant, rich or poor, all the living are alike: a framework of bones, threatened by Hell, Death, and the Devil.*

6. Ibid., 89. A woodcut from *Der Antichrist* portrays a picture of Jesus as a judge, sitting on the rainbow with a lily coming out of his right ear, the faithful beneath walking toward heaven with penitent, downcast eyes. The virgin Mary hovers over them in prayer. From the left ear of the Judge protrudes a sword. Beneath this there are the powerful people in Luther's world—nobility of church and world, with their crowns and miters; they are chained together and are being herded into the mouth of the monster that awaits them. The appended text reads: "Christ, Judge of the World, the Virgin Mary and St. John intercede for the imperiled faithful, To the just, the Judge is saying, 'Come,' and to the evil, 'Go'—to Hell." Also from à Kempis: "Many die suddenly and unexpectedly; for at an hour that we do not know, the Son of man will come. When your last hour strikes, you will begin to think very differently of your past life and grieve deeply that you have been so careless and remiss" (*Imitation of Christ*, 9).

7. Dietriech Kolde, *Mirror for Christians* (1470), in Janz, *Reformation Reader*, 62–63: " . . . When bitter death is coming, then you should say the following repeatedly: . . . 'O holy God! O powerful God! O compassionate God! O strict and righteous judge, have mercy on me, a poor sinner, when I must answer to your terrifyingly strict court. . . . O dear Lord Jesus, then may your holy bitter death, your precious blood and your unspeakable manifold suffering stand between you and all my sins." See also in Janz, *Reformation Reader*, 61, a "Deathbed Struggle," from *The Art of Good Lywyng and Good deying* (1503). Books on the art of dying were some of the first products that appeared after Johannes Gutenberg invented the printing press in 1440. The first thing he printed was the *Poem of the Last Judgment* (1446).

8. Thomas à Kempis, *Imitation of Christ*, 11: "If the love of God does not restrain you from sin, the fear of hell at least should restrain you." "What will the flames feed upon, but your sins? The more you spare yourself now, and indulge the desires of the body, the more sever will be your punishment hereafter, and the more fuel you gather for the flames" (ibid., 10).

It's an interesting fact that Luther, in this moment of desperation, called on Saint Anne rather than on Jesus. For Luther, as for so many others, Jesus was not the loving intercessor he would in time become for the church. Instead, Jesus was the judge portrayed in chapter 25 of Matthew's Gospel, separating out the good sheep from the evil goats that were bound for hell. Jesus was known by way of the familiar Apostles' Creed as that one who "will come to judge the living and the dead."[10] This was a Jesus familiar to Luther and to all the people, as he was often portrayed, sitting upon a rainbow with a sword in one hand and a lily in the other.[11] In the face of eternity, the saints, or the Blessed Virgin Mary, offered a safer berth.

Luther was raised in modestly comfortable surroundings. His father, Hans, who came from a family of peasants, had hoped to attain greater family distinction through the education of his talented son Martin. But he was forced to relinquish this dream when Luther unexpectedly entered the Augustinian monastery at Erfert on July 17, 1505.[12] To become a monk meant that Martin would leave the world and his family behind.[13] Hans could expect no grandchildren from a son who took vows of celibacy. Nor could he hope any longer for the prestige that Martin's successful career as a lawyer might have brought to the family. The distinction that Martin in fact eventually did achieve as a great reformer of the church would have been unimaginable to old Hans. Years later, Luther spoke of his father's anger at his sudden and decisive change

---

9. Martin Brecht, *Martin Luther: His Road to Reformation: 1483–1521*, trans. James L. Schaaf (Philadelphia: Fortress Press, 1985), 49.

10. *Lutheran Book of Worship* (Minneapolis: Augsburg, 1978), 65. The Apostles' Creed arose in the early Western church as a normative statement of faith and teaching. It remains an important part of the regular worship in Christian churches that retain the Western liturgical tradition, and would have been an important part of Luther's understanding of basic Christian doctrine. Trinitarian in form, the second article of the creed, which reflects the church's understanding of Jesus as the Christ, reads as follows: "I believe in Jesus Christ, his only Son, our Lord. He was conceived by the power of the Holy Spirit and born of the virgin Mary. He suffered under Pontius Pilate, was crucified, died, and was buried. He descended into hell. On the third day he rose again. He ascended into heaven, and is seated at the right hand of the Father. *He will come again to judge the living and the dead*" (emphasis added).

11. Oberman, *Luther*, 89. See also the woodcut mentioned in note 5 above. Oberman provides many pertinent illustrations throughout his book.

12. Brecht, *Martin Luther*, 50.

13. Oberman, *Luther*, 124. It was a "decision for the monastery and against the world." From à Kempis: "... The further she withdraws from all the tumult of the world, the nearer she draws to her maker" (*Imitation of Christ*, 6). "Many weak and foolish people say, 'See what a good life that man enjoys! He is so rich, so great, so powerful, so distinguished!' But raise your eyes to the riches of heaven, and you will see that all the riches of this world are as nothing" (ibid., 7). "For God with his holy angels will draw near to him who withdraws himself from his friends and acquaintances" (ibid., 6).

in direction. "I asked my father why he was angry at me," Luther recalls. "He answered, 'Don't you know the Fourth Commandment, Honor your father and your mother?' For he wanted to encourage me to study law, and in fact I already possessed a complete *Corpus iuris* [book of the law]."[14] But Luther was convinced that God had called him to the cloister; and in spite of his father's disappointment, he was determined to obey.[15]

Monastic life in those days was viewed as a radical break with the world—a kind of death;[16] and the Augustinian order that Martin chose to enter was especially strict. The Augustinians at Erfert were among a group of monastic communities that had rededicated themselves to the ancient rule of their order precisely to avoid the dangerous distractions of this world. Many monasteries had relaxed old, outdated traditions, adapting their vows to the practical necessities of the day. But the order Luther chose had responded to this loss of rigor by devoting themselves anew to the discipline of the old rule. Among the practices they chose to revive, the Erfert Augustinians adopted an enforced silence (excluding their daily recitation of prayers); they wore uniform clothing and left the monastery grounds only with the permission of their prior, who was the head of the community. They also agreed to banish all private property among themselves, including books.[17]

---

14. Martin Luther, *Luther's Works*, vol. 54, *Table Talk*, ed. Jaroslav Pelikan, Hilton C. Oswald, and Helmut T. Lehmann (Philadelphia: Fortress Press, 1999), 354.

15. Brecht, *Martin Luther*, 50.

16. Thomas à Kempis, *Imitation of Christ*, 9: "Dear soul, from what peril and fear you could free yourself if you lived in holy fear, mindful of your death. Apply yourself so to live now, that at the hour of death, you may be glad and unafraid. Learn now to die to the world, that you may begin to live with Christ. Learn now to despise all earthly things, that you may go freely to Christ. Discipline your body now by penance, that you may enjoy a sure hope of salvation." From Steven E. Ozment, *The Age of Reform (1250–1550): An Intellectual and Religious History of Late Medieval and Reformation Europe* (New Haven: Yale University Press, 1980), 85: "From Jerome to Bernard of Clairvaux, the monastic life was praised as a 'second baptism.' According to Bernard, becoming a monk so reformed the divine image in man and conformed him to Christ that he was more like an angel than like other men." From Bernard's explanation of how the monk becomes increasingly Christlike (quoted in Ozment, *Age of Reform*, 88): "At first, (1) man loves only himself and for his own sake . . . knowing nothing beyond his own desires. But when he discovers that he cannot stand by himself alone, he begins to seek and love God by faith. In this second state, (2) he loves God, not for God's sake, but for his own sake. Having been forced by his need to grasp something more permanent than himself, man begins to love and worship God . . . and gradually attain an experiential knowledge of God. Consequently, God becomes sweet to him . . . and (3) he now loves God not for his own sake only, but also for God's sake. Truly man remains a long time in this stage; in fact, I doubt that anyone perfectly reaches beyond it in this life to the point where (4) God is loved only for God's sake. Let those who have come so far assert it; for my part, I must say that it seems to me to be impossible [in this life]."

"I took the vow for the sake of my salvation," Luther explained many years after the fact.[18] The monastic community provided an opportunity to prepare oneself for the inevitable judgment that would come with death. To be with God in eternity, one had to become like God; and monasticism fostered this transformation. As athletes train their muscles and hone their skills in preparation for competition, so the monks engaged in retraining hearts, minds, and wills, in preparation for heaven. This was achieved through a process called sanctification—a program of self-cultivation by way of which one becomes increasingly holy—or "sanctified." As athletes increase incrementally in strength and skill, so too were the monks expected to become more Christlike through spiritual exercises aimed at training their wayward wills to submit to God's will.[19] In the face of his own death, Jesus prayed, "Not my will, but thine be done" (Luke 22:42), and it was just such perfect submission that the monks aimed to emulate. Absolute obedience to one's prior, for example, allowed one to practice, and thereby strengthen, the habit of obedience. In this disciplined, character-building process, one would be assisted and sustained by the infusion of grace provided by the church's sacramental ministry.[20] This cultivation of righteousness had its roots in the theology of Thomas Aquinas.

Drawing on both Aristotle's virtue ethics and the traditional teachings of Christianity, Aquinas created a theological synthesis that began with Aristotle's "natural" virtues, to which he then added the "supernatural" or Christian virtues—namely, those habits of faith, hope, and love (identified by the apostle Paul with the Christian life in his first letter to the Corinthians [1 Cor. 13:13]).[21] The capacity for the development of these supernatural virtues, Aquinas taught, was received exclusively through the special grace of Jesus Christ, sacramentally infused into the lives of the baptized by priests divinely ordained (and ontologically transformed) for this work. As in the case of the natural virtues, these supernatural virtues still had to be cultivated through the disciplined

---

17. Brecht, *Martin Luther*, 58–59.

18. Quoted in David C. Steinmetz, *Luther in Context* (Grand Rapids: Baker Academic, 2002), 512.

19. Thomas à Kempis, *Imitation of Christ*, 8: "You will never overcome your vices unless you discipline yourself severely." "He rules himself with strictness and endeavors to make the body subject to the spirit in all things" (ibid., 10). "Fight most manfully to overcome whatever is most difficult and distasteful. . . . For the more completely a man overcomes and cleanses himself in spirit, the more he profits and deserves abundant grace" (ibid., 11). "Oh, if Jesus crucified would come into our hearts, how quickly and fully we should be instructed!" (ibid., 12).

20. Ozment, *Age of Reform*, 35.

21. The text from 1 Corinthians reads, "For now we see in a mirror dimly, but then face to face. Now I know in part; then I shall understand fully, even as I have been fully understood. So faith, hope, love abide, these three; but the greatest of these is love" (vv. 12-13 RSV).

development of good habits (aided by grace), which incrementally increased a person's fitness for eternal life with God.[22] Aquinas thereby reconceived monastic life in the shape of Aristotle's ethics, which was then extended, through the special grace of Christ, toward its true supernatural end.[23]

THE SACRAMENT OF PENANCE AND ITS FAILURE TO CONSOLE

Life in a medieval monastery followed a daily rhythm of work and prayer, revolving around the monastic daily office, a series of noneucharistic worship services constructed largely on the framework of the Psalter, through which the monks carried out their prayer on behalf of the world. Though these "hours," as they are called, which varied across the different monastic communities, Luther's monastery followed a schedule of prayer that began in the middle of the night with Matins, followed by Prime, then Terce, and Sext at noon. In addition, Mass was celebrated every morning in the monastery community. Following the noon meal, the monks had an hour of rest, after which came Nones and Vespers. Finally, after the evening meal, there was Compline. These seven daily offices plus morning Mass, which all began promptly at their assigned times, were obligatory for every monk.[24] Luther took this monastic regimen very seriously. As with nearly everything in the monastery, the canonical hours were understood as a necessary discipline in the pursuit of saving righteousness. To neglect them was a sin; and neglect, in this context, included not only tardiness or sloppiness in execution but also a lack of authentic piety.[25] A monk was expected to attain both depth and sincerity; and this could be measured according to three levels of carefully distinguished performance. These were *simple* (the least effective), *rote* (which met the church's command), and *formal* observance of the prayers, when they were performed with right intention and full piety.[26] The problem for Luther, not surprisingly, was the difficulty of gauging the depth of his authenticity, and thus

---

22. What Aquinas called the "beatific vision." In the Beatitudes Jesus tells his followers, "Blessed are the pure of heart for they shall see God" (Matt. 5:8). Aquinas speaks of such a supernatural end—that is, an end exceeding what is possible by nature alone—as God's ultimate purpose for human beings. He describes this in his *Summa Theologica* as "the vision of the Divine Essence [which is] granted to all the blessed by a partaking of the Divine Light which is shed upon them. . . ." See the *Summa Theologica* III Q.10a.1.

23. Ozment, *Age of Reform*, 32–33.

24. Brecht, *Martin Luther*, 64.

25. Ibid., 68–69

26. Steinmetz, *Luther in Context*, 136–38. See Steinmetz for discussion of Kolde's piety.

the efficacy of his prayer life. Luther had taken the vow, as he said, "for the sake of salvation"; but despite his diligence, he found little evidence that he was proceeding in the right direction.

Luther's tendency toward perfectionism generated in him a perilous lack of certainty, which in time erupted into crisis.[27] Because Luther's teaching duties (which he took up in 1513) sometimes kept him away from community prayer, he was allowed to offer the monastic offices in private. He clearly worried a good deal about trying to keep up with his required allotment of these daily prayers; and he sometimes secluded himself on weekends to fast and pray.[28] But as time went on, he fell further and further behind. By 1520, he was not just a week or two behind. A full four months of canonical hours still awaited completion. His final exhausting attempt to fulfill his prayer obligations nearly resulted in physical collapse.

In his book *Luther in Context*, David Steinmetz summarizes Luther's ongoing spiritual anxieties. Luther, he writes, "suffered from periods of depression and acute anxiety . . . that he referred to as *Anfechtungen*, or 'spiritual trials.'"[29] These were experienced as the "fear that God had turned his back on [Luther] once and for all, had repudiated his repentance and prayers, and had abandoned him to suffer the pains of hell." None of his prayers, Steinmetz writes, "could penetrate the wall of indifferent silence with which God had surrounded himself. Condemned by his own conscience, Luther despised himself and murmured against God."[30] These *Anfechtungen* continued throughout Luther's life, though the object of his fear shifted over time, from terror before a wrathful God to recurring doubts about the dangers associated with his teachings. In these earliest days of monasticism, however, it was his fear of God's ultimate rejection that apparently elicited the kind of experience

---

27. In later years, Luther looked back on his monastic career with the following judgment. "Ask one who has most diligently observed his canonical hours of prayer, celebrated Mass and fasted daily, whether he is also sure that this is pleasing to God. He must say he does not know, that he is doing it all as a risk: 'If it succeeds, let it succeed.' It is impossible for anyone to say anything else. None of them can make a boast and say: 'God gave me this cowl, He commanded me to wear it, He ordered me to celebrate this Mass.' Until now we have all been groping in such blindness as this. We performed many works, contributed, fasted, prayed our rosaries; and yet we never dared to say: 'This work is pleasing to God; of this I am sure, and I would be willing to die for it'" (Martin Luther, *Luther's Works*, vol. 21, *The Sermon on the Mount and the Magnificat*, ed. Jaroslav Pelikan, Hilton C. Oswald, and Helmut T. Lehmann (Saint Louis: Concordia, 1999), 38.

28. Others actually paid substitutes to stand in for them, though Luther's conscientious desire to pray earnestly and authentically apparently prohibited him from turning to this solution.

29. Steinmetz, *Luther in Context*, 1.

30. Ibid.

Luther identified with his *Anfechtungen*—an experience he would later describe in 1518.

> I knew a man who said that he had often suffered these pains . . . so great and infernal that "no tongue nor pen can show" nor can those believe who have not experienced [them]; . . . so that if they . . . lasted half an hour, or even the tenth part of an hour, he would utterly perish, and his bones be reduced to ashes. Then God appears horrifyingly angry and with him the whole creation. There can be no flight, no consolation, neither within nor without, but all is accusation.[31]

Luther's focus on the work of contrition resulted in scrupulous self-examination and his regular use of confession. "Once I confessed for six hours," he wrote.[32] And though he found some solace in the act of contrition and confession, it remained for him highly problematic. Since perfect contrition was required before the official absolution could become effective (i.e., the priest's declaration that one's sins were forgiven), it was impossible to know when enough was enough. Luther could never be sure that his contrition met the standard required for the absolution to "take." Were his sins in their entirety really forgiven? Was he thus saved, or was he still bound to his sins and destined for hell?

It was the teaching on sacramental efficacy that caused Luther the greatest problem; for it contradicted his own experience of persisting sin, which continued to haunt him even after his absolution had been declared. Some years later in his lectures on Romans, trying to explain his difficulty, Luther would distinguish what he called the "tinder" of sin (also called *original sin*)[33] from "active" sin (the consequences of original sin). "Either I have never understood," he wrote, "or else the scholastic theologians have not spoken sufficiently clearly about sin and grace, for they have been under the delusion that original sin, like actual sin, is entirely removed, as if these were items that can be entirely removed in the twinkling of an eye."[34] Of course, by the time Luther wrote

---

31. Ibid., 8 (WA 1:557.33).

32. Brecht, *Martin Luther*, 68.

33. "Original sin" is the church's teaching that the failure to trust and love God faithfully is inborn in all humans. The doctrine takes its traditional form in the writings of St. Augustine, where the disobedience of Adam and Eve in Genesis 2 is believed to have initiated this situation. Ultimately, Augustine teaches, the "original" sin of Eve and Adam infects the whole human race.

34. *LW* 25:261.

these words, he had established in his own mind what he took to be the church's misunderstanding on these matters of sin and grace. "In my foolishness," he recalled, "I could not understand [how] . . . I should regard myself as a sinner." For, believing that all his sins had been removed, including his inward sin, Luther still did not experience the righteousness that the sacrament promised. "Thus I was at war with myself," he complained. "I felt that [my] past sins had not been forgiven."[35]

In later years, Luther would recall how he and his fellow monks "exhausted the confessors" with their careful enumeration of each tiny lapse of discipline. "No confessor wanted anything to do with me," Luther admitted.[36] Once a priest called a halt to Luther's endless list of indiscretions with the admonition that "God has commanded you to trust in his mercy." Another tried to recall him from his quest for reassurance, saying, "God is not angry with you, but it is you who are angry with God."[37] Johann von Staupitz, Luther's "good and reverend father in Christ,"[38] and his much-beloved confessor, told him to come back when he had something really sinful to confess.[39] But how could Luther distinguish a big sin from a little one? Both kinds separated him from God. Luther's conviction, that he was forever failing God, accosted him at every turn. No matter how disciplined or contrite he was, Brother Martin could never trust that he had done enough.

Under the papacy, Luther writes, "Christ was depicted as a grim tyrant, a furious and stern judge who demanded much of us and imposed good works as payment for our sins."[40] "I almost fasted myself to death; for again and again I went for three days without taking a drop of water or a morsel of food.[41] Like so many others, Luther envisioned Christ as a divine judge and depended on Mary and the saints to intercede for him.[42] "Oh, how many kisses we bestowed on Mary!" Luther later remarked.[43] She was the one who received every sinner as a generous and ever-forgiving mother. She gathered them up and then, taking her place between these penitents and her son, she pled with Jesus to accept

---

35. *LW* 25:261.
36. *LW* 54:94.
37. *LW* 25:69.
38. *LW* 14:283.
39. *LW* 54:94; *LW* 54:94, 133.
40. *LW* 23:57.
41. *LW* 54:339–40.
42. *LW* 22:146. "Christ in His mercy was hidden from my eyes. I wanted to become justified before God through the merits of the saints. This gave rise to the petition for the intercession of the saints."
43. *LW* 22:146. John 6:38.

them on her behalf. Given Luther's inability to find the reassurance he sought, it is no surprise that he loathed a form of prayer referred to as "the contemplation of Christ." Instead of mercy, Luther found only God's judgment addressing him from the cross. Many years later, he told a story from those early days as a monk. "I was once terrified by the sacrament which Dr. Staupitz carried in a procession in Eisleben, on the feast of Corpus Christi. Afterward I made confession to Dr. Staupitz, and he said to me, 'Your thought is not of Christ.' With this word he comforted me well. [But] this is the way we are. Christ offers himself to us, together with the forgiveness of sins, and yet we flee from his face."[44] In time, of course, Luther's Christology changed dramatically; but in these earliest days, and despite Staupitz's good counsel, this earnest young monk could not escape the divine condemnation he found at every turn.[45]

Thus the traditional penitential system failed to provide Luther with the certainty he sought. And this problem was exacerbated in the context of the Mass; for priests were expected to celebrate the Mass with a clean conscience—purified through contrition, confession, penance, and finally the sacrament of absolution.[46] But since Luther understood this sacrament as dependent for its efficacy on the quality of contrition brought by the penitent, the certainty needed to enter into the mystery of the Mass was impossible for him to achieve. He celebrated his first Mass almost paralyzed with fear. "When at length I stood before the altar and was to consecrate," Luther later recalled, "I was so terrified by the words *aeterno vivo veto Deo*[47] that I thought of running away from the altar."[48] And when Luther's father, visiting on this celebratory occasion of his son's first Mass, suggested that perhaps not God but Satan had dragged young Martin away from his duty to father and mother, Luther's

---

44. *LW* 54:19–20.

45. "I tried to live according to the Rule with all diligence, and I used to be contrite, to confess and number off my sins, and often repeated my confession, and sedulously performed my allotted penance. And yet my conscience could never give me certainty, but I always doubted and said, 'You did not perform that correctly. You were not contrite enough. You left that out of your confession.' The more I tried to remedy an uncertain, weak and afflicted conscience with the traditions of men, the more each day found it more uncertain, weaker, more troubled." Steinmetz 2, in *The Righteousness of God: Luther Studies*, trans. Gordon Rupp (London: Hodder and Stoughton, 1953). 104. See also WA 40.II.15.15.

46. Brecht, 73. "A priest conscious of having committed a mortal sin, even though he considers himself to have true contrition, may not celebrate Holy Mass without first availing himself of sacramental confession; if, in the absence of a confessor and [simultaneously] in a case of necessity, and after having made a perfect act of contrition, he has indeed celebrated, he will go to sacramental confession as soon as possible" (Canon 807 of the *1917 Code of Canon Law*).

47. "To Thee, the eternal, living and true God"

48. *LW* 54:156.

despair only deepened.[49] Maybe his father was right. How could he be sure? Was it Satan or was it God who had appointed him to this monastic life and to his work as a priest? Even the certainty of his calling—a certainty he had dared until then to trust—was now fraught with doubt, making his encounter with God before the altar that much more terrifying. "As a monk," he explained to his students many years later, "I experienced such horrors; [but] I had to experience them before I could fight them."[50]

GOD WHO IS WHOLLY OTHER: THE ABYSS BETWEEN HEAVEN AND EARTH

Luther desperately sought to appease God's wrath by way of an authentic piety. But it was the search for confidence that he had done enough—to succeed in producing the piety he believed was demanded of him—that he had done enough to produce the piety he believed was demanded of him that drove Luther to such excess. Certainty of salvation remained the goal of Luther's theological quest throughout this early period. But what drove Luther in particular to a desperation that set him apart from his more complacent Augustinian brothers? The answer to this, at least in part, may be found in Luther's unusually profound eagerness for heaven (and his correlative rejection of the temporal world). It was the distance—the infinite abyss—that Luther saw as separating this sinful world from God's righteousness that made any comforting certainty impossible. "The knowledge that there was an infinite, qualitative distance between Heaven and earth became an established principle for Luther as early as 1509," Heiko Oberman writes.[51] Getting from here to there was not therefore just a matter of being better; but it required becoming radically "other" than what the young monk Brother Martin already was.

The underlying issue for Luther was finding a foundation on which a true righteousness might be built. The tradition (called the *via moderna*[52]) in which Luther had been theologically educated taught that human beings had within themselves a divine spark—the residue left of the *imago Dei*, the image of God.[53]

---

49. When Luther assured his father that his calling was from God, his father replied, "Son, don't you know that you ought to honor your father? Just so it wasn't a phantom you saw!" *LW* 54:234.

50. *LW* 54:234.

51. Oberman, 160.

52. The *via moderna* refers to the "modern way" of theology, which included a philosophy known as nominalism. Nominalism challenges the existence of abstract or universal realities. This was contrasted with a *via antiqua*, or "the ancient way"—which affirmed the metaphysics of Thomas Aquinas and the scholastics.

What was this image of God if not some likeness that provided the ground on which one might build up the perfection demanded for eternal life with God?[54] Theologians called this the *synderesis*; and it was believed to provide the ground for that critical first step, so that by working with what was already present, a person might turn themselves toward God, in preparation for God's grace that would then carry them across the infinite divide. The nominalists (the teachers of the *via moderna*) taught that one had only to "do what is in one" in order to prepare effectively for the gift of divine grace, which would then empower the spiritual growth required for salvation. The way was hard, of course. In the "fall" of Adam and Eve, all humanity and the whole creation became so distorted that the way back was fraught with difficulties and dangers; but it was not impossible. Or at least, it was not impossible in the thinking of those responsible for Luther's theological training.

In Luther's experience, however, that abyss separating him from God seemed uncrossable. He found nothing within himself that he could trust as truly righteous—nothing about which he could be certain—and therefore no way to attain the reassurance that spiritual formation should have delivered. How could he take the first step toward the God he so feared? After all, the love of God was the most crucial command of them all, that from which everything else followed. But caught in the grip of his doubt, Luther could not find within himself that impulse to love the God he so feared. Thus the traditional penitential system offered by the church only exacerbated Luther's uncertainty.

Ultimately, Luther's certainty would come from Scripture. By 1521, he could confidently assure others that there "you will find truth and security—assurance and a faith that is complete, pure, sufficient, and abiding."[55] Thus it is an important part of Luther's story that his confessor, Johann von Staupitz, was himself a biblical scholar. Early on, Staupitz had noted the scholarly potential in the young novice Martin. In an early biography of Luther, written by one of his fellow monks, we learn that "Doctor Staupitz was very much impressed, and kept a special eye on [Luther] above the others."[56] In 1506, Staupitz, who was in charge of a number of monasteries, paid a visit to the community at Erfert. There he met Brother Martin, then busily at work at some menial task of the sort usually assigned to the novices. At the time, Staupitz

---

53. Gen. 1:27 NRSV: "So God created humankind in his image, in the image of God he created them; male and female he created them."

54. Matt. 5:48 NRSV: "Be perfect, therefore, as your heavenly Father is perfect."

55. *LW* 32:98.

56. Oberman, *Luther*, 136.

apparently convinced the prior to reassign Luther to a duty more appropriate to his talents. Brother Martin was to memorize the Scriptures, page by page, rather than scrub floors. It was a task Luther embraced with both zeal and talent.

What did Staupitz see in this young monk that moved him to request special consideration for Luther's training? It was a fateful request to be sure, for it opened a critical door into Luther's soul. Years later, Luther would be grateful for his ability to recall every word of the Bible with almost perfect accuracy. Staupitz continued to mentor Luther's spiritual and scholarly progress, and in the winter of 1508–1509, he summoned Luther to the new and, as yet, inauspicious university at Wittenberg to lecture on Aristotle's ethics. It was Staupitz who, against Luther's protestations, insisted that he take his doctorate in biblical studies, and Staupitz too who apparently stepped aside from his teaching duties in 1513 in part, it seems, to make room for Luther, who then assumed the chair of biblical theology at the University of Wittenberg.

THEOLOGICAL INFLUENCES FROM THE TRADITION

Other important voices from the tradition had an enormous effect on Luther's developing theology around this time as he continued to struggle toward a solution to his ongoing anxiety. Because of a remarkable discovery made in a German library about 120 years ago, we know today that in 1509 Luther was studying a collection of Augustine's writings.[57] Among the texts that came to light was a collection of Augustine's works, printed in 1489, with marginal notes written in Luther's hand. In his book *The City of God*, Augustine defines the gap between the righteous and the sinful in a way that resonated with Luther's own experience. Juxtaposing two cities, Augustine describes the City of God as that situation in which the faithful exist on the eternal side of the gap—that is to say, with God, as citizens of the "heavenly city." All the others, who are blind to the invisible spiritual realities, idolatrously worship the things of this world and therefore exist on the sinful side of the abyss, in the earthly city. The two cities provided a template for Luther's own experience of that impassable boundary between this fallen world and the righteousness of God.

Sometime around 1513–1514, Luther began a new (and possibly his first) series of lectures on the Bible. He began with the Psalms, carefully working his way through each and adding his commentary alongside.[58] Idolatry, or the danger of fixing one's heart on the wrong god, is a danger that Luther

---

57. Ibid., 158. The books were discovered at the Ratschul Library in Zwickau in 1889 and 1890.
58. Brecht, *Martin Luther*, 128.

lifts up here. Most people, Luther warns, "fix [their] heart[s] on created things . . . and not on the reality, which is God alone."[59] Luther points to those who "cannot grasp God and divine things."[60] In these lectures, he characterizes people according to their relationships. We "subside" in that which we ultimately trust. We depend upon it, or "stand" on it, as St. Augustine writes in his *Confessions*.[61] Luther likewise refers to a person's "foothold or settled ground, on which a man can stand with his feet, so that they do not slip into the deep."[62] It is by way of one's trust in that "foothold," or ground, that one becomes the kind of person she or he is. "The rich man subsists by riches, the healthy man by health, the honored man by honor, [and] the pleasure-seekers by pleasure." But Christ "did not have such a foothold on life that would keep him from falling altogether into death."[63] Thus "the pauper, the despondent, [and] the self-afflicter are without substance [too],"[64] and like the saints are characterized by a "faith [in] the substance of things hoped for" (rather than things that already are).[65]

In the spring of 1516, While Luther was lecturing on Romans, he received some sermons by John Tauler (d. 1361) from his friend Johann Lang. Luther found there a kindred spirit; in addition, he found that the theology he and his colleagues at Wittenberg studied had a German precedent.[66] His enthusiasm bubbles over the theology he and his colleagues at Wittenberg in a letter to Spalatin in mid-December 1516. If it pleases you to read "pure and solid theology, which is available in German and is of a quality closest to that of the fathers . . . then get for yourself the sermons of John Tauler. . . . I have seen no theological work in Latin or German that is more sound and more in harmony with the Gospel than this."[67] The theology of Tauler, who was a mystic, included a process of dying to the self that resonated with Luther's

59. *LW* 10:39.
60. *LW* 10:93.
61. "Why do you stand on yourself, and thus stand not at all? Cast yourself on him. Have no fear. He will not draw back and let you fall. Cast yourself trustfully on him: he will receive you and he will heal you" (*The Confessions of St. Augustine* [New York: Doubleday Bantam, 1960], 201).
62. *LW* 10:355.
63. *LW* 10:355.
64. *LW* 10:355.
65. *LW* 10:355.
66. Brecht, *Martin Luther*, 141: "This is proof for him that the Wittenberg theology, which was already being attacked, could appeal to a significant tradition, even though it was not a university tradition. . . . Luther is critical not only of Latin scholasticism, but already there also is a mistrust of humanism brewing within him."
67. *LW* 48:35–36.

reading of Augustine and Paul. It also allowed him to reinterpret his experience of *Anfechtungen* as a mark of God's election rather than of divine abandonment. In Tauler, the love for God results in suffering, death, and rebirth. But the work is done entirely by God (rather than through self-chosen spiritual exercises). Salvation lies in resigning oneself to God, who rejects every human work. Here God destroys in order to re-create. Steven Ozment summarizes the key point succinctly. "In medieval theology, only like could truly know like."

> This was the underlying rationale of monastic practices; through rigorous physical and intellectual exercises to replace one's own false self with a God-like self. It was the precondition of mystical union. . . . Love bound together the persons of the Trinity, the soul with God, and man with his neighbor. [But] . . . as early as his first lectures on the Psalms, Luther distanced himself from this fundamental medieval belief. . . . He was . . . struck by the way the righteous man confessed his utter dissimilarity from God. . . . Recognition and confession of sin actually brought God and man together. In this sense "unlikeness" was the unitive principle in religion: To be conformed with God meant to agree with his judgment that all men are sinful and still believe his promise to save them nonetheless.[68]

It is precisely in this opposition that God works. "Whoever casts one's self completely upon the will of God cannot remain outside God. . . . Whoever offers himself up for hell will not be judged by God, but God rather will free him," writes Martin Brecht, summarizing Luther's embrace of Tauler.[69] In December of 1516, Luther published an anonymous fragment of a piece, calling it simply *The German Theology*.[70] Though "only God knows who actually wrote it," Luther notes in his Introduction, "if we should try a guess, the material almost resembles the style of the illumined Doctor Tauler of the Preaching Order. Be that as it may, here we have the true solid teaching of Holy Writ."[71] The parallels here with Luther's own thinking are clearly visible in his Psalms lectures and in his more fully developed lectures on Romans.

In his early lectures, Luther understands Christ's redemption as a revelation of the human predicament. Those who grasp this revelation, writes Luther, "look and point [toward Christ] as if they were saying, 'Look, He is the One who is in reality, but we are not; we are only signs."[72] The faithful, Luther teaches, are those who steadfastly imitate Christ, dying to the things of this

---

68. Ozment, *Age of Reform*, 243.
69. Brecht, *Martin Luther*, 138 (Brecht cites WA, *Br* 12:403–5).

world that are, in reality, "nothing," and faithfully staking their lives on God instead. Redemption thus rests on a new understanding of how things really are between God and human beings. Christ's crucifixion was made necessary by human sin, thus demonstrating the depth of human depravity for those who have eyes to see. Redemption begins, not out of some residual inner goodness or spark that functions as the ground of similarity, but rather by acknowledging just how profoundly alienated human beings are from God. He then interprets the crucifixion as "the judgment by which God condemns and causes [us] to condemn whatever we have of ourselves, the whole old man, with his deeds."[73] This "*whole* old man" leaves no opening for some divine remainder or *synderesis*.[74] A faithful piety, and (Luther hoped) an effective one, thus requires that one stand with God in the condemnation of the entire self, righteously demonstrating solidarity with God's judgment.

David Yeago calls this Luther's "strategy of contrariety."[75] The death of the self requires a prior identification with God's judgment, which in turn moves God to mercy. It is cultivated in a way that reflects Luther's early approach to the attainment of a good contrition. On the basis of Paul's remark "for I

---

70. *LW* 48:36. The anonymously written *German Theology* that Luther embraces and presents to the public—first by publishing a fragment of the text sent to him in 1516, and then again in its complete form in 1518—teaches a theology that emphasizes the necessary death of the self as a prerequisite to the experience of God's inner presence, referred to as *sapientia experimentalis*, or the present knowledge (experience) of God. This phrase suggests a mystical union with others in the one body of Christ that transcends time and place, and notably, Luther includes this phrase—*sapientia expermentalis*—in his description of justification. Probably written by someone of the Friends of God movement in the mid-fourteenth century, it presents a paradoxical understanding of the mystical experience whereby the absolute otherness of God is retained even as one is drawn into friendship with God through Christ. Thus it rejects another form of mysticism contemporary with it, practiced by the Brothers and Sisters of the Free Spirit, who taught a form of mysticism in which the lines between what is divine and what is human are blurred. As Bengt Hägglünd notes in his introduction to a modern translation of the 1518 text, this distinction can be tracked back to a difference in the mysticism of Eckart and Tauler, with Tauler's paradoxical form being embraced by Luther via the *German Theology*. This form of mysticism practiced by the Friends of God does not adopt a dualistic tension between the spiritual and the created orders but affirms creation and the call to ethical engagement focusing on the tension between God and Satan, a form of mysticism suggested in Luther's *Freedom of a Christian* of 1521. The call to transformation—or the crucifixion of unredeemed nature (the extinction of pride and self-will)—becomes that "death of the self" emphasized in Luther's early theology. See the Introduction by Hägglünd and the text of *German Theology* in *The Theologia Germanica of Martin Luther*, trans. Bengt Hoffman, Classics of Western Spirituality (New York: Paulist, 1980).

71. Ibid., 42.

72. *LW* 10:311.

73. *LW* 27:406.

could wish that I myself were accursed" (Rom. 9:3), Luther is still teaching that "to those who truly love God . . . these words are most beautiful, and testimonies of a perfect example. For such men freely offer themselves to the entire will of God, even to hell and eternal death, if that is what God wills."[76] Under Tauler's influence, Luther had by this time embraced the mystical death of the self. Thus he could say with some confidence that "if it should please God [I] would not desire even to be saved." Something approaching certainty, he believed, could thereby be assured; for when a sinner can truly seek his own damnation, a person "knows whether he loves God with a pure heart." Yet it seems an odd sort of self-defeating certainty that Luther had devised, since it rests on the denial of the very end that "certainty" originally sought to secure. And even were this a faithful model of piety, Luther's ability to exercise it remains dubious. His declaration in the very same lecture that "it is impossible that [one who wills his own damnation] should remain in hell; [and] . . . he [who] wills what God wills therefore . . . pleases God, is loved by him, and [is thereby] . . . saved" suggests that Luther was not quite prepared to swallow the bitter medicine that he himself had concocted. Luther was, by this time, teaching that the distance between sinful humanity and the righteousness of God is one of absolute contradiction. In his gloss on Rom. 9:3, Luther writes, "What is good for us is hidden, and that so deeply that it is hidden under its opposite. [Thus] our life is hidden under death, love for ourselves under hate for ourselves, glory under ignominy, salvation under damnation, our kingship under exile, heaven under hell, wisdom under foolishness, righteousness under sin, [and] power under weakness."[77]

In March of 1545, when Luther was an old man, he recalled the scriptural breakthrough that provided a critical turning point in his theology and in his piety. However, writes Lewis Spitz, "While Luther's account of the early years . . . is a priceless historical document it is not without chronological difficulties."[78]

---

74. *Synderesis*, or *synteresis*, was understood by the scholastic theologians to refer to those first principles of conscience, out of which right moral behavior can be discerned and generated through practice and habituation. This capacity was understood to be derived from the "image of God," which, according to the Genesis account of creation, is characteristic of all human beings. (It is also the ground, or point of contact, central to Eckhart's mysticism, which Luther rejected. See note 72 above.) Luther's difficulty was that he could find no such reliable first principles within himself, out of which authentically righteous choice and action could be generated with any certainty. It was not that Luther had no conscience but rather that he believed it to be unreliable, given the distortions to reason imposed by sin.

75. David S. Yeago, "The Catholic Luther," in *The Catholicity of the Reformation*, ed. Carl E. Braaten and Robert Jenson (Grand Rapids: Eerdmans, 1996), 13–34.

76. *LW* 25:381.

77. *LW* 25:382f.

Thus the dating of this "event" is a matter of debate. Indeed, Luther's critical "breakthrough" appears to have come over a period of time. Nevertheless, some particular moments clearly stand out. One of these is surely Luther's novel, and breathtaking, reinterpretation of a text from Romans. Nevertheless, the idea gained clarity and strength in the dispute over indulgences, which provided the crucible that would form Luther's doctrine of "justification by faith alone."

"I felt that I was a sinner before God," Luther recalled in 1545, as he wrote about his career in the prologue for a collection of his Latin works that was being prepared from publication.

> Though I lived as a monk without reproach . . . I could not believe that [God] was placated by my satisfaction. I did not love . . . [but rather] I hated the righteous God who punishes sinners; and secretly . . . I said, "As if . . . it is not enough, that miserable sinners, eternally lost through original sin, are crushed by every kind of calamity . . . without having God add pain to pain . . . threatening us with his righteousness and wrath!" . . . I had already . . . been captivated with an extraordinary ardor for understanding Paul in the epistles to the Romans. But up till then . . . a single word in Chapter 1[:17] . . . stood in my way. For I hated that word "righteousness of God," which, according to the use and custom . . . I had been taught to understand [as] . . . the formal or active righteousness . . . [by] which God is righteous and punishes the unrighteous sinner.
>
> [But] . . . at last, by the mercy of God, [and by] meditating day and night, I gave heed to the context of the words, namely, "In it the righteousness of God is revealed," [understood now, in combination with another text] . . . "He who through faith is righteous shall live." [Thus, by linking the two] I began to understand that the righteousness of God is that by which the righteous live by a gift of God, namely by faith. [This means that] . . . the righteousness of God is revealed by the gospel, namely the passive righteousness with which merciful God justifies us by faith; [for] it is written, "He who through faith is righteous shall live."
>
> [Thus] I felt that I was altogether born again and had entered paradise itself through open gates. [In light of this new understanding] a totally other face of the entire Scripture showed itself to me. [So] I ran through the Scriptures from memory [and] I

78. *LW* 34:325f.

also found in other terms [a similar] analogy, as [for example], the work of God . . . is what God does in us, the power of God . . . makes us strong, the wisdom of God . . . makes us wise, the strength of God, the salvation of God, the glory of God. And I extolled my sweetest word with a love as great as the hatred with which I had before hated the word "righteousness of God." Thus that place in Paul was for me truly the gate to paradise.[79]

Luther had discovered in Paul's letter to the Romans a critical reversal. Instead of sinners needing to achieve a God-like righteousness in order for God to accept them, "the righteousness of God" meant that God makes sinners righteous, just as "God's wisdom" means that God makes people wise. Instead of trying to get to God by becoming like God, God has come to those who are most unlike God—those who are characterized by sin rather than righteousness—until, by faith, the sinner receives the righteousness that God gives as a gift. It was not, Luther understood, that the actual "substance of sin" suddenly disappeared, but that sin is no longer "imputed" or counted against the sinner.

Thus Luther arrived at an understanding that holds both sin and the negation of sin together. Having abandoned the penitential system and instead embraced Paul's theology of justification, Luther assures us that sin does not go away with confession and absolution; but in God's mercy, sin "is not imputed as sin" to those who call upon God. This paradoxical simultaneity of sin and the nonimputation of sin he likened to a sick man who is "both sick and well at the same time"—"sick in fact, . . . [yet already] well because of the sure promise of the doctor, whom he trusts and who has reckoned him as already cured."[80] And so, Luther explains, "This life . . . is a life of being healed from sin . . . not a life of sinlessness; . . . [and] the church [is the] . . . infirmary for those who are sick and in need of being made well."[81] But of course, a person is unlikely to call on the doctor unless that person knows she is sick. "It is not the one who regards himself as humble that is righteous," writes Luther, "but the one who considers himself detestable and damnable in his own eyes . . . he is righteous. . . . 'He who is dead is justified' (Rom. 6:7)."[82]

---

79. *LW* 34:336.
80. *LW* 25:262.
81. *LW* 25:262f.
82. *LW* 25:260.

THE REFORMATION BREAKTHROUGH

Though it would seem that Luther had by this time solved his central problem by integrating Tauler's mystical negation of the self (like the end of hope when one realizes he is dying from an incurable disease) with Paul's theology of justification (the totally unexpected and undeserved cure), Luther's old penitential theology continued to play a role in his thinking for some time. Even with Paul's theology of the nonimputation of sins, faith is still a requirement; and the achievement of that faith continued to prove problematic for Luther. Yeago has argued that it was between 1518 and 1519 that Luther decisively shifted his focus from the achievement of a given inner disposition (a self utterly condemned and destroyed) to a focus on the external work of God. It is in the sacraments, writes Yeago, that God's acceptance is finally made certain. During the spring of 1518, "Luther worked through (and published) three different and mutually exclusive solutions" to the question: "What is the sacrament good for, anyway?"[83] Eventually, focusing on Matt. 16:19 ("Whatever you loose on earth is loosed in heaven"), Luther settled on the sacramental act as "the concrete, external, public act of Jesus Christ in the church."[84] In his search for the true God, Yeago concludes, Luther had discovered a very Catholic solution. "When we come to the sacrament, we run into Jesus Christ."[85] Where the critical point in his earlier theology of grace is God's crucifying contradiction of sinful human nature, "here the point on which everything hinges is the authority of Christ the Savior, exercised concretely in the sacramental signs in the church."[86]

Luther's new idea was to trust God rather than the quality of his own piety. If God says your sins are "loosed" (i.e., gone), then all you have to do is trust that God means what God says.[87] Luther juxtaposed this trust in the external promise with the teaching by "recent theologians" who "contribute entirely too much to this torment of conscience by treating and teaching the sacrament of penance in such a way that people learn to trust in the delusion that it is possible to have their sins cancelled by their contritions and satisfactions."[88] Luther obviously believed by then that he had left the penitential system behind. Likewise, he rejects those "certain intellectuals, [who] by their contritions, works, and confessions, endeavor to find peace for themselves but do nothing

---

83. Yeago, "The Catholic Luther," 25.
84. Ibid., 26.
85. Ibid.
86. Ibid.
87. *LW* 31:100.
88. *LW* 31:103.

more than go from restlessness to restlessness because they trust in themselves and their works."[89] Luther had grasped Paul's theology of justification, believing that the nonimputation of sin is nothing we can achieve ourselves; but, until now, he had not found a reliable way to make this promise one that applied particularly to himself.

Yet even with his discovery of the external (and therefore reliable) promise of God in the sacrament, we still find traces of Luther's old theology of penance at work. "One is right," he concedes in his 1518 *Explanations of the 95 Theses,* "in asking how [the remission of sins] can take place before the infusion of grace . . . for man cannot have his guilt forgiven or the desire to seek remission without first of all having the grace of God which remits."[90] But, he suggests, a few lines on, "If the remission of guilt takes place through the infusion of grace before the [absolution] of the priest, this infusion is . . . so hidden under the form of wrath that man is more uncertain about grace when it is present than when it was absent."[91] Even as late as 1518, faith functions as a kind of pious work, presumably requiring something of the believer; for Luther feels compelled to exhort his reader "to guard himself very carefully from any doubt."[92] "The remission of sin and the gift of grace are not enough," he writes; there is still work left to be done, even after the remission of sins is received. For "when they have been strengthened by confidence and joy of heart over the compassion of Christ, [they will] . . . become contrite and make satisfaction." Penitential contrition and satisfaction are still part of a process on the way to heaven. In the end, Luther admits that he is "still trying to understand."

It was during the brief period between February 15 and March 28, 1518—shortly after Luther wrote the words above—that the mature theology of justification emerges in his work. Martin Brecht, in an interesting and persuasive argument, traces this theological turn, comparing a letter from February with a sermon written in March. In the letter, written by Luther to his friend George Spalatin on February 15, we discover the penitential technique required to achieve the inner self-loathing necessary for the reception of God's mercy. "You should be your own judge," Luther writes to Spalatin, "and with your works accuse yourself and confess that you are guilty and sinful."[93] But in the sermon of March 28,[94] Luther, for the first time, *joyfully* identifies Christian

89. *LW* 31:103.
90. *LW* 31:99.
91. *LW* 31:101.
92. *LW* 31:101.
93. Brecht, *Martin Luther,* 222.
94. *LW* 31:297–306.

righteousness with the self-emptying Christ who comes down from heaven for the sake of sinners. Faith is here described as a marriage that joins God's righteousness with the sinner, so that sin is covered. Referring the congregation back to a text from the Song of Solomon, Luther exuberantly describes the kind of freedom and joy that is possible as faith seals the bond of marriage. "Righteousness arises [with] the voice of the bridegroom who says to the soul, 'I am yours,' . . . [and in response] comes the voice of the bride who answers, 'I am yours.' Then the marriage is consummated; it becomes strong and complete in accordance with the *Song of Solomon* [2:16]: 'My beloved is mine and I am his.' Then the soul no longer seeks to be righteous in and for itself, but it has Christ as its righteousness and therefore seeks only the welfare of others."[95]

Here grace is no longer the medicine of immortality for the healing of sins. The action engages the sinner in her entirety–a whole, rather then a partial effect. Saving faith is now a *relationship* that replicates the union between husband and wife. The two become one and thus share everything between them. This reflects Luther's notion of subsistence in the early Psalms lectures, where one is characterized by that on which one "stands" or has a "foothold." Here Christ is that foothold; and his mercy is received via his promise—the Word spoken. This Word comes to address the sinner—the bridegroom seeing his bride. It is God's word made flesh—Christ—who gives himself to the bride, even as she gives herself to the bridegroom. In the consummation of the marriage, the two become one; and Christ's righteousness now characterizes the whole. Thus the abyss was bridged, the boundary breeched. But this was only after Luther realized there was no way for him to get to God that it was possible for God to get to him. The boundary between heaven and earth is absolute; but now a gate that was hidden has appeared. It is seen only by those who are broken; and it swings open in one direction only. And it is a gate that only God can unlock.

THE PASTORAL BATTLE AGAINST COMPLACENCY

Given the level of Luther's education and the frequency with which Masses were said at the Augustinian monastery, it is not surprising that his superiors called the young monk into the priesthood immediately upon his completion of the probationary year.[96] Originally, Staupitz assigned Luther to preach in the monastery; but at some point, probably around 1513, Luther began preaching

---

95. *LW* 31:300.
96. Brecht, *Martin Luther*, 71. This would probably have been sometime in early 1507.

regularly, if sporadically, at the Wittenberg church as well.[97] "[I] was chosen to preach against my will,"[98] Luther announced in the first of his sermons upon his return to Wittenberg in 1522,[99] and "I was called by the council to preach . . . in spite of my reluctance."[100] While Luther might not have chosen the priesthood for himself, it is clear that he took his pastoral responsibility to heart. Scott Hendrix, for example, argues that it was Luther's calling as a pastor that best explains his resistance to papal claims of authority.[101] Where God's Word was withheld from the people, Luther thought the pastoral office was not being properly exercised; and he saw it as his calling to do what he could to free God's Word from captivity. "The first and only duty of the bishop," he wrote to Archbishop Albrecht in 1517, "is to see that the people learn the gospel and the love of Christ." Christ "forcefully" commanded the gospel to be preached. "What a horror, what a danger for a bishop to permit the loud noise of indulgences among his people, while the gospel is silenced. . . . For all these souls," he warns ominously, "you have the heaviest and a constantly increasing responsibility."[102]

One of the ways Luther exercised his pastoral responsibility was through his vocation as a teacher of the Bible. In his *Heidelberg Disputation*, Luther makes it clear that the theologian's work, like the pastor's, is to serve as a soldier in God's battle against Satan for the salvation of sinners. This means that "a theologian of the cross [should call] the thing what it actually is."[103] It is not the job of theologians to think about temporal questions and to indulge in "sophistical" debate. "The whole of Aristotle is to theology as darkness is to light."[104] Most importantly, the theologian serves God's Word; and Luther was convinced that in his context it was God's word of judgment that needed to be spoken without reserve. Adopting Augustine's understanding of sin as the prideful refusal to acknowledge God as God,[105] Luther was devoted to breaking open this fortress of the devil, which alienated sinners from God's mercy. Luther believed that if he faithfully preached (and taught) God's judging and freeing

---

97. Ibid., 151.
98. Ibid.
99. Ibid., 150.
100. *LW* 51:73.
101. Scott H. Hendrix, *Luther and the Papacy: Stages in a Reformation Conflict* (Philadelphia: Fortress Press, 1981), 16–17.
102. *LW* 48:46.
103. *LW* 31:40.
104. *LW* 31:12.
105. *LW* 31:10. *Disputation against Scholastic Theology*, thesis 17, reads, "Man is by nature unable to want God to be God. Indeed, he himself wants to be God, and does not want God to be God."

word, it would be set free to do its saving work. Thus Luther argued, "The law of God [is] the most salutary doctrine of life. . . . "[It] brings the wrath of God, kills, reviles, accuses, judges, and condemns everything that is not in Christ"; but this "is not to be evaded" because "it is certain that man must utterly despair of his own ability before he is prepared to receive the grace of Christ."[106] Public disputations provided public venues for the Word to be set free to do its work. Even as Luther was engaged in making sure his star student, Bernhardi, could defend the theology Luther was teaching, Luther was at the same time preparing Bernhardi to preach the saving Word of God.

WITTENBERG THEOLOGY, AND HUMANISM

Early on in its life as an institution, the University of Wittenberg integrated the teachings of humanism[107] into its curriculum. Prince Frederick, in appointing Staupitz to help establish the new university, had already set the stage for the adoption of the new humanist curriculum, since Staupitz, with his humanist leanings, had a considerable influence on Luther's educational development. Both were biblical scholars, and both cared deeply about the new opportunities offered by humanism for the study of Scripture. After 1516, Luther adopted Erasmus of Rotterdam's newly annotated Greek New Testament; he used the newly available teachings of Jerome as well; and we have already noted the central place Augustine's theology played in Luther's development. But Luther had more in common with the humanists than his love of the ancient texts. He also shared their rejection of scholasticism, though, as Martin Brecht reports, Luther's "rejection of scholasticism had reasons different from that of the humanists, and his distance from them is unmistakable."[108] Luther's early concern with Erasmus's commentary on the biblical texts, which he revealed

---

106. *LW* 31:39ff.

107. Humanism developed out of the discovery and study of ancient or classical texts, spawning interest in the acquisition of language skills necessary to read these in their original languages. Initially associated with the Italian Renaissance, the movement quickly spread north; and by the time Luther took up advanced studies in the early sixteenth century it had established itself within many of the German university faculties. Given Prince Fredrick's desire that his new university at Wittenberg should look toward the future, it is not surprising that a humanist curriculum quickly began to replace the traditional scholastic approach to the teaching of theology. Staupitz, who was instrumental in shaping the fledgling institution, was himself interested in humanist ideas; under Staupitz's direction, Luther's interest in the Bible quickly spawned a determination to read and study it in its original languages. This meant that, added to the Latin Luther had learned as a boy, he now acquired a facility in New Testament Greek and worked hard to similarly acquire reading skills in Hebrew.

108. Brecht, *Martin Luther*, 163.

to Spalatin in a letter of 1516, already heralds what would later be a public distancing between the two scholars. At stake for Luther, and ultimately the key issue that distinguished the Wittenberg theology from the humanism being taught at other universities, was the Augustinian rejection of pride that played such a central role in Luther's thought. There was also an important, and unique, pastoral component of the Wittenberg program. In their focus on the ultimate matters related to salvation, Luther and his colleagues took a dim view of the philosophy so central to the teaching of the scholastics. Luther thought not only that the enormous importance of Aristotle and Aquinas in the scholastic project missed the point, but also, and worse, that the reliance on human nature built into its teaching had the devastating effect of increasing the very human arrogance and complacency that Luther rejected. In his view, scholastic teaching only exacerbated human beings' alienation from the saving work of Christ—saving work that could only be appropriated by a faith beginning with the recognition that "we are all beggars." Initially, some of Luther's colleagues—in particular Karlstadt, who was dean of the faculty—resisted the Augustinian influence. But after carefully reading Augustine, Karlstadt was converted to Luther's position.

Initially, Luther said, the only student interested in his theology was a man named Bernhardi; but by the time Bernhardi was ready to graduate, Luther thought the time was right for a public presentation of his new theological ideas. He decided to do this via the disputation Bernhardi was required to hold on the occasion of his completion of the degree.[109] The theses Bernhardi prepared, under Luther's watchful eye, were designed to challenge the semi-Pelagian[110] views of the *via moderna*—the branch of scholasticism in which Luther had been trained. Apparently, Bernhardi did a fine job of "cit[ing] Augustine's anti-Pelagian writings in a sharp rebuttal of Gabriel Biel."[111] It was Berhnardi's task to introduce Luther's new understanding of God's law as Luther was then teaching it in his Romans lectures; and it seems that this public debut of Luther's "theology of the cross" succeeded in effectively supplanting whatever resistance still remained among the faculty.

Almost exactly a year later, as Luther was working on a commentary of Aristotle's *Physics* "for the purpose of dethroning the god of the scholastics,"[112]

---

109. *LW* 31:5–7. Bernhardi was awarded the degree that made him a *sententiarius* on September 25, 1516.

110. Ozment, *Age of Reform*, 39–42.

111. As we learn from Bernhard Lohse, Berhardi "bluntly presented the new, radical view of sin advocated by Luther in his Romans lectures" (Lohse, *Martin Luther's Theology*, 98). Biel was the primary authority of the *via moderna*.

he wrote a set of theses for another ceremonial disputation. Again, his aim was to both teach and deliver God's judgment against the optimistic assessment of human powers then being heralded among the scholastics. The theses of the *Disputation Against Scholastic Theology* (September 1517),[113] went well beyond the standard arguments that humanists had been bringing to bear on scholasticism. Luther's early debates reveal the growing distance between himself and the humanists with whom he, and most of the Wittenberg theological faculty, had earlier aligned themselves.

Luther's Attack on Scholasticism

A sinful and self-deceptive rebellion against God, Luther believed, was endemic among those scholars who delighted too much in reason—these being first and foremost the scholastic theologians who made frequent use of Aristotle's philosophy in their scholarship and teaching. The Wittenberg curricular reforms reflect this conviction. In a letter to Spalatin in March of 1519, Luther wrote, "I think that the [lectures on Aristotle's *Physics*] should be continued only until they can be abolished—and this had better be soon. . . . It is . . . unworthy of [Melanchthon's] intellect to wallow in that mire of folly."[114] In Luther's view, the scholastic approach to revelation served only to obscure Christ. "It is better," he exclaimed, "that [Aristotle and the others] be read [poorly] and misunderstood, than that they be understood."[115] Aristotle's writings, which were revered among scholastics, thus became a particular target of Luther's. An important book of Aristotle's, titled *Nicomachean Ethics*, had excited the interest of scholastic theologians for centuries; but under the impact of Luther's developing theology of justification, it excited in Luther only his most scathing condemnation. "Briefly," he wrote in the fiftieth proposition of the *Disputation against Scholastic Theology*, "the whole of Aristotle is to theology as darkness is to light." The biblical stories describing Jesus' life, death, and resurrection; a last judgment; and the promise of life eternal had shaped Christian expectations for well over a millennium before Aristotelian ethics were woven into the Christian narrative. Luther's complaint was that, under Aquinas's logical and creative mind, philosophy and theology had been merged into one all-encompassing system of thought that made the Christian life into a self-improvement project

---

112. *LW* 31:6.
113. *LW* 31:5–6.
114. *LW* 48:112.
115. Ibid.

that ultimately served only to entice sinners into a demonic complacency that would lure them away from salvation in Christ.

We have already noted the importance of Augustine's writings in Luther's struggle toward a faith that provided him with certainty of salvation. Luther was convinced that Augustine's analysis of sin was correct. In Augustine's view, sin is not simply a problem of bad habits that can be overcome by reason's discipline. Rather, sin runs all the way down, permeating the whole created order in such a way that reason is itself in bondage to the disordered will, and worse, it is blind to its own rebellion against God. "Anyone's will hates it that the law should be imposed upon it," Luther argued.[116] Indeed, reason's hostility toward God is exercised so consistently and so cleverly that it succeeds in hiding this fact even from itself. Though we pretend otherwise in our pious protestations, "what the law wants the will never wants, unless it pretends to want it out of fear or love."[117] This sinful quest for autonomy from God ultimately defines the human predicament, according to Augustine and Luther. And, as already alluded to, it was precisely this desire for independence from God that St. Augustine identified with "original sin." Picking up on Augustine's notion of the diseased will, Luther insisted that "everyone's natural will is iniquitous and bad."[118] How do we know this? God's "law is good," but our will is "hostile to it."[119] Reason, Luther insisted, could not therefore be so easily wed to revelation, as Aquinas had attempted to do with his synthesis of Aristotle and Augustine. "It is an error to maintain that Aristotle's statement concerning happiness does not contradict Catholic doctrine," Luther wrote.[120] Scripture does not promise that Christians will be happy. In fact, Luther cautioned, Jesus teaches his disciples to take up their cross and follow him into death. "Whoever would save his life would lose it" (Mark 8:35). The suggestion that what pleases reason also pleases God defies both Jesus' teaching and his life. Instead, Luther argues, the faithful, with Christ, should expect to suffer and die at the hands of this world, even as Jesus suffered and died on a cross.

"Let no one think that we who are Christians shall have peace on earth."[121]

---

116. *LW* 31:15.
117. *LW* 31:14.
118. *LW* 31:15.
119. *LW* 31:15.
120. *LW* 31:12.
121. *LW* 13:259

> ". . . Christendom is a small group that must submit to, suffer, and bear more than all other people whatever grief the devil and the world can inflict on it."[122]

> "He who does not die willingly should not be called a Christian."[123]

Agreement with the powers of this world—worldly success—insisted Luther, indicates that one has abandoned God, not that one has triumphed over sin. The cultivation of virtue and the pride it encourages threatens to lead those most successful into the worst possible danger. Alternatively, under the received penitential system, the failure to achieve such confidence threatens a despair that is likely to drag one away from God. Either way, Luther thought, one fails to find Christ's gift of salvation. Luther's personal experience with this theology had, in his mind at least, proven its existential weakness. We recall that it was precisely in his earnest attempt to please God that Luther realized certainty of salvation was impossible to attain. And even if there were some point of righteousness upon which one could build, it would never be possible to know when one had built high enough. The lingering threat of damnation had led Luther inexorably to fear, and finally to hate, God. In fact, he insisted, the scholastic tradition had become over time the very antithesis of faithful theologizing. A brilliantly designed tool of reason, this program, which encouraged the faithful to engage in the acquisition of virtue, succeeded not in pleasing God but in driving those most successful straight into the arms of Satan.[124] Since the goal of theology, as Luther defined it in the *Heidelberg Disputation*, is to "call a thing what it actually is," he pulled no punches in his assault on human pride. From the Bernhardi theses of 1516 through the disputations against indulgences and scholastic theology, and then, on into 1518 in the disputation in Heidelberg, Luther single-mindedly attacked the prevailing theological tradition of his day with prophetic zeal. Having first been assigned to the teaching of Scripture, and then having discovered there God's judgment against human presumption, Luther was convinced that God was using him to turn things around—to recall sinners to God.

As Erasmus grasped early on, the initial reforms applauded by humanists everywhere—the replacing of Aristotle's philosophy with the intensive study of the church fathers and a new focus on Scripture—did not exhaustively describe the Wittenberg curriculum. The program there was distinctive in its

---

122. *LW* 24:358
123. *LW* 29:138.
124. Hendrix, *Luther and the Papacy*, 27.

theocentric focus. This was not only for the sake of "calling a thing what it actually is."[125] The Wittenberg theologians also pastorally sought to provide a better delivery system for God's work of redemption and salvation. They hoped to work as God's conduits, helping the baptized to discover the saving work of Christ that was theirs already. "The issue here is the future and eternal life," Luther insisted.[126] Bringing God's saving Word out in the open was, for the Wittenberg theologians, a matter of infinite importance—a fact that helps to explain Luther's absolute rejection of anything remotely linked to pride or self-love during this period of his work. For, "the proper subject of theology," wrote Luther in his reflections on the Psalms, resides exclusively in "man [understood as] guilty of sin and condemned, and God [understood as] the Justifier and Savior of man the sinner. Whatever is asked or discussed in theology outside this subject is error and poison."[127] Luther and his colleagues on the theological faculty at Wittenberg were aiming, not at a moral reformation of the church (as were many of the humanists), but at the rebirth of faithful Christians. Their pastoral emphasis on a theology of the cross, calculated to drive sinners to Christ, distinguished Wittenberg from other universities that had embraced humanist reforms.

THE INDULGENCE CONTROVERSY: PASTORAL CONCERNS

It was just this pastoral concern for the salvation of human beings, "guilty of sin and condemned," together with Luther's experience of a God who alone was the "Justifier and Savior" of sinners, that led him to propose another disputation against indulgences; and it was at this juncture that the Wittenberg theology launched a political and religious reformation that turned the face of Western Europe toward the future.

"It happened, in the year 1517, that a preaching monk called John Tetzel . . . made his appearance." So Luther begins his story, looking back from the vantage point of 1541, eager to tell his version of events. "Tetzel," he continues, "went around with indulgences, selling grace for money as dearly or

---

125. *LW* 31:40. Steinmetz expands on this: This is a theology that "deals with a God who stands in a relationship to me and who lays claim to my life, whether I acknowledge that relationship or not. Where I am not included in my reflections about God, there is no Christian theology but only philosophical speculation. Only as God reveals himself to me through his Word, only insofar as I am confronted by this God and my faith is awakened, can theology be engaged in at all. Everything which stands outside the circle of light cast by revelation is impenetrable darkness" Steinmetz, *Luther in Context*, 26.
126. *LW* 12:311.
127. *LW* 12:311.

as cheaply as he could."[128] "The whole world [in those days] complained about indulgences, and particularly about Tetzel. . . . That was the beginning. Indeed, it all goes back . . . to Tetzel's blasphemous preaching."[129]

Blasphemous or not, Tetzel, who was an experienced and effective preacher of indulgences, easily succeeded in selling his indulgences to many of Luther's own parishioners.

Indulgences were viewed as a special "kindness" bestowed upon the faithful by the church. The practice arose in response to the church's penitential system. As it had developed over time, this approach to sin taught that guilt could be sacramentally absolved (or removed) by the priest; but the punishment for sin still had to be paid.[130] In Luther's day, these "satisfactions" often took the form of prayers, pilgrimages, or fasting—works assigned by the penitent's confessor. Prescribed works that remained unfulfilled at the time of death were believed to carry over into purgatory, where imperfect souls were believed to be purged of any remaining sin before entering into eternal life with God. The piety of Luther's day focused largely on the avoidance of these purgatorial punishments; and indulgences, issued by the church, were one way to shorten the sentence, reducing or even eliminating it. Thus many eagerly sought indulgences in a world gripped by fear of divine condemnation.

---

128. *LW* 41:231. In 1506, Pope Julius II proclaimed what was called a *plenary indulgence*—that is, a general indulgence, covering the penance of sins committed and even those not yet committed. Originally conceived as a reward for Crusaders, plenary indulgences, in Luther's day, were often instituted for specific purposes. In 1515, Pope Leo X renewed Julius's indulgence for the purpose of raising money to help pay for the Church of St. Peter in Rome. Archbishop Albrecht, who was to get a cut of the money raised, in order to help fund his new ecclesiastical position (which he had to purchase from Rome), enlisted a man named John Tetzel, an experienced indulgence preacher. It was Tetzel's job to set things up and make sure the indulgences were sold. The reason these were not being sold in Wittenberg appears to be because Prince Frederick, who owned an enormous collection of relics, did not want any competition. Viewing the relics of saints (for a fee) also provided a way to increase one's accumulated merits and thereby decrease one's expected time of suffering in purgatory. Tetzel came as close to Wittenberg as he could, however—close enough so that the people of Wittenberg could easily cross the border to purchase the indulgences. Albrecht, eager for the sales to successfully raise the money he needed, and being no theologian, prepared a book of instructions for the preachers who would be selling the indulgences. They were these instructions that most infuriated Luther; for they exaggerated even the claims made by Rome. See also Hendrix, *Luther and the Papacy*, 24–25.

129. *LW* 41:234.

130. Before the rise of private confession, sinners were absolved of their sin and restored to fellowship with the community only after they made their sorrow visible by way of prescribed penitential acts. After the introduction of private confession, the priest's absolution normally preceded the works of penance that were prescribed after the sin had been forgiven.

How was it that the church could issue such pardons on behalf of God? Patterned after the banking system, the church's "treasury of merits"[131] provided a kind of account upon which the pope could draw.[132] Merits, which accumulated as the consequence of good works, could be used to satisfy sin, thereby replacing assigned punishments. The accumulated unused merits of Christ and the saints (unnecessary for those already perfected) provided the official tender of this treasury. But cash also played a role, since the sale of indulgences transferred these merits from the church's treasury to those individuals able to pay for them. By 1517, when Luther posted his infamous Ninety-Five Theses, the church was regularly turning to the sale of indulgences to fund its many political and ecclesiastical projects.[133]

Given the important role indulgences played in sixteenth-century Christian piety, it is not surprising that Luther feared his parishioners would confuse the power of papal indulgences with God's gracious work in Christ. The remission of purgatorial punishment (from an experiential standpoint) was closely related to the remission of sin and death associated with Christ's crucifixion; and when preachers like Tetzel embellished the benefits of indulgences, they encouraged the laity to trust the pope's promises more than the promises of God. In addition, Christ called on his followers to bear their crosses faithfully, whereas indulgences seemed to provide a way to avoid Christian suffering.[134] In fact, indulgences eliminated the punishment that Luther believed was necessary, both for the perfection of souls and as a sign of unity with Christ. Like many of his monastic brothers, Luther thought that suffering was to be piously sought rather than avoided. For Luther, who in 1517 was still struggling himself to make peace with God, righteousness seemed possible only by way of a self-condemnation that demonstrated solidarity with God's judgment;[135] but the vast majority of the population, Luther knew,

---

131. Hendrix, *Luther and the Papacy*, 24–25. Also see Janz, *Reformation Reader*, 57.

132. It was not until the scholastics codified these procedures during the High Middle Ages that control of indulgences was linked with the papacy. The treasury of merits was under the control of the pope because, as the heir of St. Peter, Catholics believe he is to be the earthly head of the church universal.

133. Luther did not know at the time when he wrote his Ninety-Five Theses that the money raised was to be divided—one half going for the announced work on St. Peter's and the other half to Archbishop Albrecht himself. The later discovery that this was the case only infuriated Luther all the more. Archbishop Albrecht had been granted a special dispensation from Rome that permitted him to hold several bishoprics simultaneously—a practice normally not allowed. See note 123 above.

134. Janz, *A Reformation Reader*, 59; see also *LW* 31:28. "They who teach that contrition is not necessary on the part of those who intend to buy souls out of purgatory or to buy confessional privileges preach unchristian doctrine."

preferred a free pass if they could arrange it. "Indulgences teach people to fear and flee and dread the penalty of sins," Luther wrote, "but not the sins themselves."[136] Trusting in indulgences rather than in Christ, he thought, would lead his parishioners not to heaven but instead straight to hell.[137] As the pastor of these souls, Luther felt the weight of their eternal well-being on his conscience. "Many thousands [have] died," he later recalled, by "relying on [indulgences] as though they were God's grace."[138] Remembering the early days of the indulgence controversy, Luther wrote in 1541, "I was a preacher here in the monastery and a fledgling doctor fervent and enthusiastic for Holy Scripture. . . . When many people from Wittenberg went to Jutterbock and Zerbst for indulgences . . . I began to preach very gently that one could probably do something better and more reliable than acquiring indulgences."[139] As early as February 1517, on the occasion of St. Matthew's Day (and a full eight months before his Ninety-Five Theses was posted), Luther preached on the need to take up one's cross. "They are slaves," he said; "they hate, not the sin, but the penalty."[140] Indulgences, he argued, teach us to dread the cross."[141]

Indulgences were available to people in a number of ways. The papal indulgence that Tetzel was selling was particularly popular because of the extensive—and, as Luther believed, wholly excessive—promises associated with it; but there were other ways that indulgences could be procured. Penitential prayers in the presence of saintly relics provided another way to satisfy the debt of sin. Luther's prince, Frederick the Wise, had gathered a great collection of such relics in Wittenberg, hoping to attract visitors to his territory (and one supposes, the revenue generated by their piety). Perhaps, on that particular All Saints' Day in 1517, Luther was inspired to release his Ninety-Five Theses as he gazed out at the gathering of people who had come to Wittenberg in order to escape purgatorial suffering by viewing the prince's relics.

Luther was not the only one concerned about the sale of indulgences. "The whole world [in those days] complained about indulgences," Luther reports.[142] Late medieval developments had caused many theologians to worry about the

---

135. The crucifixion of Christ is understood by the church to be God's way of atoning for the sin of all people, thereby freeing human beings from the sin that separates them from God.

136. *LW* 51:31.

137. Hendrix, *Luther and the Papacy*, 27.

138. *LW* 41:237.

139. Hendrix, *Luther and the Papacy*, 26

140. *LW* 51:30.

141. *LW* 51:31

142. *LW* 41:231–36.

enlarged claims associated with these pieces of paper, so eagerly sought by the laity. A practice that had begun as a special kindness, limited in scope to the relaxation of particular, assigned penances, had expanded to include the plenary indulgence of the sort being sold by Tetzel.[143] This amounted to a free pass, covering all temporal punishment and forgiving all sin, including even those sins not yet committed. Luther, along with others, worried about the effects of such claims on Christian piety. The extension of indulgences to cover those souls already in purgatory was especially problematic. Given these concerns, and in the absence of official papal teaching,[144] Luther's call for a formal debate on the topic was wholly in line with his responsibilities as a teacher of the church.[145] Besides, Luther was eager to learn more. Though the character of his language in the theses on indulgences is undeniably bold, Luther repeatedly claimed that he wanted to understand the indulgence practice better. In 1541, he recalled, "I did not know what indulgences were, as in fact no one knew . . . [and] I did not want the fame."[146]

Quite clear, however, about what indulgences were not, Luther did not mince words in his letter to Albrecht Archbishop of Mainz on that All Souls' Day of 1517. Luther held the archbishop responsible for the exaggerated promises that Tetzel was preaching to Luther's parishioners; for it was Archbishop Albrecht who had provided the instructions for Tetzel's sale of indulgences. "I bewail the gross misunderstanding among the people which comes from these preachers and which they spread everywhere among common men," Luther began.[147] He then went on to challenge the claims that

---

143. Janz, *A Reformation Reader*, 58–59. Quotations from the *Instructions* issued by Archbishop Albrecht and used by Tetzel: "In the confessional the following concessions are made for those who pay for it: the right to choose . . . a suitable confessor . . . [who] can absolve them once in the course of their lives and also in *articulao mortis* from certain of the gravest of sins as often as death threatens, even if the threat does not materialize. . . . The fourth principal grace is the plenary remission of all sins for the souls that exist in purgatory, which the pope grants and concedes by means of intercessions, so that a contribution placed by the living in the repository on their behalf counts as one which a man might make or give for himself. There is no need for the contributors to be of contrite heart or to make oral confession. . . . "

144. Though there had been a number of statements from Rome on the matter of indulgences, no formal declaration, or "bull," had yet been issued. Toward the end of 1518, Pope Leo would release such a bull, apparently in response to the widening controversy that followed on the heels of Luther's Ninety-Five Theses.

145. Brecht, *Martin Luther*, 127: "Precisely at Luther's time, expert scholars were beginning to claim an independent, rival authority over against those who possessed ecclesiastical and secular power. The doctor's degree and his professorship were a binding commission and a sworn obligation for Luther."

146. *LW* 41:231–232.

147. *LW* 48:46.

Albert's instructions authorized. "Evidently the poor souls believe that when they have bought indulgence letters they are then assured of their salvation. They are likewise convinced that souls escape from purgatory as soon as they have placed a contribution into the chest. Further, they assume that the grace obtained through these indulgences is so completely effective that there is no sin of such magnitude that it cannot be forgiven."[148]

THE NINETY-FIVE THESES

The theses themselves,[149] proposed for the sake of debate, were provisional, as were all theses presented for public disputation. Though stated as a matter of fact, they were formulated as claims precisely so they might be challenged. Nevertheless, these 1517 theses on indulgences still reveal a good deal about Luther's real concerns at that time. Beyond that, and of particular interest here, is the fact that in and through his sense of pastoral responsibility, Luther's two-kingdom distinction was beginning to emerge. This key insight draws a boundary between the limited, temporal reach of human works on one hand and the power of God on the other. As Luther begins his list of debating points, this idea quickly emerges. In thesis 5, for example, he argues that "the pope neither desires nor is able to remit any penalties except those imposed by his own authority or that of the canons."[150] After all, he continues in 34, "the traces of [papal] indulgences are concerned only with the penalties. . . . established by man."[151] Luther thereby eliminates the suffering in purgatory (a penalty established by God) from those things over which the pope has control. At the same time, the pope can and should act as a kind of mask for God's work, making visible what God has already made real. "The pope [himself] cannot remit any guilt," Luther writes; but he does affect the outcome "by declaring and showing that it has been remitted by God."[152] Thus Luther is careful to limit the pope's effective authority to the lifting of punishments imposed by the institutional church on earth. When the pope uses the words "plenary remission of all penalties," Luther concludes, he "does not actually mean all penalties, but only those imposed by himself."[153] The domain of the pope is restricted to penultimate judgments having to do with this life; ultimate judgments belong

---

148. *LW* 48:46.
149. *LW* 31:17.
150. *LW* 31:26.
151. *LW* 31:28.
152. *LW* 31:26.
153. *LW* 31:27.

to God alone. The distinction between the penultimate limit on human efficacy and the ultimate or infinite reach of God is crucial.

Though Luther is often accused of attacking the authority of the pope in these theses, his goal was not so much to diminish the power of the temporal church as to reassert the ultimate authority of God. Once again, we see Luther attempting to remap the theological landscape; his pastoral objective in these theses was to restore a proper "fear of God."[154] This pastoral concern is at the fore as he offers a series of theses (42–51) that begin, "Christians are to be taught . . . " For instance, in thesis 49, he writes, "Christians are to be taught that papal indulgences are useful only if they do not put their trust in them, but very harmful if they lose their fear of God because of them." And again, pointing to God's majesty, Luther speaks of the "inestimable gift of God by which man is reconciled to him." The celebration of the gospel, Luther argues, should be one hundred times as impressive as the celebration of indulgences; for ultimately the "true treasure of the church is the most holy gospel of the glory and grace of God" (thesis 62).

Luther's growing theological clarity on the distinction between realms was forged historically in the context of his challenge to indulgences, providing a foundation for the faith that he was experientially still struggling to articulate. This much was already clear—that true faith begins with a recognition of the living God, whose power and righteousness is beyond all human manipulation. Luther's emphasis on the inability of human beings to influence the spiritual domain of God would quickly come to function theologically from the opposite direction as well. If human beings have no jurisdiction over God's judgments, neither do they have any effective power over God's saving grace. The agency in such spiritual matters is all God's. The same distinction between the realms that works here to limit papal intervention in divine judgment would also come to protect salvation from the dangers of human interference.[155]

The pastoral concern Luther demonstrates in his Ninety-Five Theses was directed toward the church for the sake of the laity. Just as faithful Christians

---

154. *LW* 31:206. From his *Explanations* (for thesis 49): "I have said that indulgences are most harmful if people rejoice over such liberty without fear of God" (see also 205). Luther quotes from Job 9:28: "Blessed is the man who fears the Lord," and from Ps. 112:1: "Blessed is the man who fears the Lord always." "A saint is afraid that he might work less or suffer less than he should. Where does that put the sinner who has his sin remitted when he does less than he could do?" (*LW* 31:206).

155. *LW* 32:94. "Those who are involved in sins are not free but prisoners of the devil. . . . It is neither right nor good to play tricks with words in matters of such great importance. A simple man is easily deceived by such tricks and teachers of this kind." Also, from *LW* 33:35, "If I am ignorant of what, how far, and how much I can and may do in relation to God, it will be equally uncertain and unknown to me, what, how far, and how much God can and may do in me. . . . "

should expect the sting of purgation from sin, so too Luther thought a faithful church would welcome the challenges his theses offered. It is notable that Luther did not hold Pope Leo responsible for the false and dangerous promises he associated with the sale of indulgences. These impious practices were simply the work of charlatans, Luther thought—people ignorant of the associated dangers, and in need of correction. As a loyal member of Christ's church, and as one ordained and appointed to teach, Luther presented his theses against indulgences in the spirit of loyal service, confident that he stood alongside those in authority. "If the pope knew the exactions of the indulgence preachers," Luther declared confidently, "he would rather that the basilica of St. Peter were burned to ashes than built up with the skin, flesh, and bones of his sheep" (thesis 50). Thus Luther's Ninety-Five Theses reflected theological opinions he thought were widely shared throughout the church. Convinced that most theologians, and certainly Pope Leo, would agree that Tetzel's preaching was both incorrect and dangerous, Luther expected the pope, once informed, to quickly silence Tezel and other overzealous indulgence preachers. Thus it was for the sake of the people, for the honor of the papacy, and for the good of the whole church that Luther felt himself called to invite his colleagues to a disputation on indulgences. The dispute he provoked exceeded his wildest expectations.

THE CHURCH'S RECEPTION OF LUTHER'S PROPOSAL

No one was more shocked than Luther when he discovered what a hornet's nest he had stirred up. The "theses against Tetzel's articles," he recalled in 1541, "went throughout the whole of Germany in a fortnight."[156] Still, on the day they were posted, Luther had not an inkling of the controversy they would incite; and as the dispute spread rapidly, he assumed that the matter was but another manifestation of tensions already existing between the humanists and traditionalists at competing universities.[157]

---

156. *LW* 41:234.

157. Hendrix, *Luther and the Papacy*, 37. "[Luther] was aware that he was contradicting the teaching of Thomas Aquinas and other medieval theologians, but there was no reason for him to equate this theological disagreement with an attack on the papacy. . . . The entire program of curricular reform at the University of Wittenberg was shaped around the replacement of an Aristotelian-based theology with the study of the Bible, biblical languages, and the church fathers. This reform had been underway for some time in Wittenberg and no one had thought to challenge it as an attack on the papacy. . . . Luther regarded the issue as another encounter between the theology of the schoolmen on the one side and the Wittenberg theology of Scripture and the church fathers on the other."

Initially the controversy was limited to those scholars and churchmen already known to Luther. Archbishop Albrecht sent Luther's theses on to the faculty at the University of Mainz for their opinion. The theologians there refused to comment; interpreting Luther's theses as a challenge to papal authority, they reminded Albrecht that canon law forbade disputation on such questions. They suggested he refer the matter to Rome. Albrecht had, in fact, already done just that, including with the theses a warning that this Augustinian monk from Wittenberg was "spreading new teachings."[158] Tetzel, the indulgence preacher who had so offended Luther, is reported to have announced, "In three weeks I will throw the heretic into the fire."[159] Instead, in late January, he debated a set of theses that countered Luther's, claiming for the papacy all the authority Luther had rejected.[160]

With the aid of the newly invented printing press, the news of Luther's theses continued to spread rapidly.[161] Tetzel's published reply to Luther reached the Wittenberg bookseller in early March. Only four and a half months had elapsed since Luther had released the theses, and the dispute had already become so public that students loyal to Luther seized and burned some eight hundred copies of Tetzel's booklet. In an effort to quiet things down, Luther published *A Sermon on Indulgences and Grace* several days later, which he wrote in German rather than Latin. Luther's decision to address the wider public in a language they could understand suggests the considerable impact his theses were having on public opinion. Over the following two years, Luther's *Sermon on Indulgences and Grace* was reprinted at least twenty times; apparently, he had a message people were eager to hear.[162]

Posted at the end of October, the theses had been in the hands of the curia since January. Initially Pope Leo chose to handle the matter gently, requesting Luther's superiors to persuade him to withdraw his objections. When this produced no result, the curia, in early June of 1518, began to prepare for a heresy trial against Luther. On August 7, Luther received the official summons, requesting his presence for a hearing in Rome in just sixty days.

The summons to Rome, which arrived in Wittenberg on August 7, must have come as a shock to Luther, given his confident expectation that Leo

158. Brecht, *Martin Luther*, 206.
159. Ibid.
160. Hendrix, *Luther and the Papacy*, 34–35. Hendrix's book provides a thorough discussion of the controversy over indulgences. See also Brecht, *Martin Luther*.
161. Brecht, *Martin Luther*, 208.
162. Ibid. "Without the new medium of the printing press," Brecht adds, "Luther's thoughts would never have achieved such a rapid and wide distribution."

would agree with and support him.[163] Despite the local firestorm that his theses had ignited, and since the curricular reforms at Wittenberg had not been challenged, Luther did not initially believe himself to be in any serious trouble. In Luther's view, his theses on indulgences were simply a particular application of the same theology that had been openly taught for some time at Wittenberg. Why, he reasoned, would the church allow the Wittenberg professors to challenge scholasticism (with its reliance on papal authority) and at the same time deny Luther the freedom to question that authority in relation to the narrower issue of indulgences? With the arrival of the summons, however, it became clear that the church was treating the indulgence dispute as a serious challenge to its authority. Luther's anxiety in the face of the papal summons is revealed in his immediate attempt to forestall the dangerous journey he was being required to make to Rome.

LUTHER'S HEARING BEFORE CARDINAL CAJETAN

Prince Frederick, who wielded significant political power, was able to negotiate a change in venue. Rather than Rome, Luther was to be "heard" by Cardinal Cajetan, a theologian of repute, who was already in Germany to represent Rome at the Diet of Augsburg. Having secured Cajetan's agreement to treat Luther gently, and having made all other arrangements for Luther's safety as he could, Frederick summoned Luther to Augsburg sometime in mid-September. On October 7, he arrived in Augsburg; and by Tuesday October 12, Luther was finally ushered into the presence of the cardinal, where he dropped to the floor in an act of obeisance as he had been instructed to do. Though Cajetan began in a gentle manner, his promise to treat Luther "in a fatherly way" faltered once their differences became apparent.[164] Luther had come expecting to engage in a real debate; but Cajetan had been instructed by Rome to refrain from all discussion with Luther. Apparently he was to offer Luther nothing more than the opportunity to retract his errors and refrain from further provocation. Thus the meeting was not only difficult but also decisive, as each hardened his position in reaction to the other.

---

163. *LW* 41:235: "I [had] hoped the pope would protect me," he later recalled, "because I had so secured and armed my disputation with Scripture and papal decretals that I was sure the pope would damn Tetzel and bless me."

164. "Both sides entered the discussion with completely different expectations and objectives. [In addition] they did not like each other very much. . . . Under these conditions the proceedings were bound to be difficult" (Brecht, *Martin Luther*, 253).

Cajetan would neither allow Luther to reply to the allegations against him in a public disputation, nor, Luther lamented, "did he want to debate with me in private." Frustrated, Luther complained to his friend that Cajetan had only one thing to say; and he apparently said it over and over. "Recant, acknowledge that you are wrong; [for] that is the way the Pope wants it."[165] In fact, despite Luther's frustration, Cajetan did respond to some real issues in Luther's argument. First, with regard to the indulgences, Cajetan focused on Luther's refusal to acknowledge the critical link between Christ's merits, the pope's treasury, and the effective power of papal indulgences.[166] Since, according to church teaching, the forgiveness promised in the pope's indulgences was ultimately guaranteed by Christ's work, the claim that Christ's merits were the exclusive property of the pope to distribute as he saw fit was a key element in the logic of indulgences. But this suggested to Luther that the pope was presuming to control God's judgments. Indulgences, thus understood, obligated God to honor human decisions as to who should be forgiven—a situation that seemed to turn things upside down. And worse, Luther thought, was the fact that these human tickets into heaven were being sold to the highest bidders in order to fill the coffers of the church at Rome. The availability of the necessary funds for the purchase of an indulgence rather than the character of one's righteousness thus seemed to determine a person's ultimate destiny. Faith, good works, and the obligation to honor God set forth in the First Commandment were, in Luther's view, dangerously overturned in the exorbitant claims being made by the sale of indulgences.

But even more difficult from Luther's perspective was Cajetan's rejection of Luther's teaching that faith rested on the certainty of God's truthfulness. Such a certainty of salvation, insisted the cardinal, is a teaching both "new and erroneous."[167] But having only just begun to escape his own paralyzing fear of God on the basis of this newfound confidence, Luther could hardly relinquish the very heart of his new theology. For Luther, the question of certainty was

---

165. *LW* 48:84.

166. Written by Clement VI in 1343, it was also called *Extravagante* because it was published only as an appendix to canon law. (See n3, *LW* 31:260.) Luther's dispute with (and ultimate rejection of) the *Extravagante* is summarized in his *Proceedings at Augsburg*: "If [indulgences] convey an actual gift, they do so not as a treasury of indulgences but as a treasure of life-giving grace. Then they are given formally, actually, directly, without the office of the keys, without indulgences, alone by the Holy Spirit" (*LW* 31:269). Note that if these words are taken literally (and out of context), the church, as the conduit of God's grace, appears to become redundant—presumably a legitimate matter of concern to Cardinal Cajetan.

167. *LW* 31:270.

no longer a debatable point; and complicating things still further was Luther's conviction that it is the devil who tries to tear the faithful away from their confidence in God's truthfulness. "With your doubt you make of Christ a liar," he told the cardinal.[168]

Cajetan's insistence that human beings are, at least in part, responsible for their own salvation threatened to pry open the door that Luther had with such difficulty finally closed.[169] As suggested earlier, Luther's Ninety-Five Theses drew an absolute boundary between the efficacy of human and divine activity—a distinction clearly related to Luther's experience of the abyss and his appreciation of Augustine's two cities, and ultimately central to his belief that salvation is entirely a free gift of God. Luther had carefully substantiated these claims with biblical texts. Now Cajetan's assault on this assertion made it impossible for Luther to acquiesce. "I beg your most reverend highness to . . . have compassion," Luther pleaded, "and not to compel me to revoke those things which I must believe according to the testimony of my conscience. As long as these Scripture passages stand, I cannot do otherwise, for I know that one must obey God rather than man."[170] "Show me," Luther begged, "how I may understand the doctrine differently."[171]

But, for Luther, to be "shown" meant that Cajetan would have to demonstrate Luther's errors with a convincing argument from Scripture. It was a predictable demand from Luther, but impossible for Cajetan to honor. To give such priority to the scriptural evidence, Cajetan would have had to abandon the very foundation upon which his arguments rested—namely, that the pope's

168. Luther had by now discovered that his faith could rest with certainty on God's promise rather than on his own state of contrition—a subjective foundation that was inherently unreliable. "With your doubt," Luther now taught, "you make of Christ a liar, which is a horrible sin. . . . Thus it is clearly necessary that a man must believe with firm faith that he is justified and in no way doubt that he will obtain grace" (*LW* 31:271). It was God's word revealed in the reliable writings of the Bible that finally provided the certainty (and the peace with God) that Luther had so desperately sought. And it was just this certainty that the cardinal rejected.

169. In the written statement Luther had prepared for Cajetan, Luther appended to his biblical argument supporting texts from both St. Augustine and St. Bernard, thus demonstrating his use of a "consensus of sources." Augustine writes, "When the Word is coupled with the element, it becomes a sacrament, but because it is believed." Cited in *LW* 31:274. See note 24: In *Joannis evangelium*, tract. 80, cap. 3 (Migne 35, 1840). From Bernard, "You must above all believe that you cannot have forgiveness of sins except through the mercy of God." And Luther continues, "Add to this that you must believe that your sins are forgiven by God" (*LW* 31:274). The term "consensus of sources" is helpful in describing Luther's epistemology. It is a term introduced and defended by Scott Hendrix in his book, *Luther and the Papacy*, 41.

170. *LW* 31:274.
171. *LW* 31:274.

interpretation of Scripture was absolute. For Cajetan, faith meant submission to the authority of the church; for Luther, it was the authority of Scripture that determined whether the church was being faithful to God.[172] Given this basic difference in their theological method, there was simply no way for them to move ahead toward agreement.

The third and final day of Luther's hearing at Augsburg offered no new possibilities. Luther's written response to Cajetan began by rejecting any claim to papal authority that does not conform to Scripture. Then, arguing again for the necessity of certainty in the reception of the sacrament as well as in the reception of Christ's "justifying" presence, Luther insisted that he could not, nor should he be asked to, recant what he believed to be true on the basis of Scripture. The cardinal finally dismissed Luther, shouting "Go, and do not come back to me, unless you want to recant." "When I heard this," Luther later wrote in his report to Spalatin, "and realized that he was firm in his position and would not consider the Scripture passages, and since I had also determined not to retract, I left with no hope of returning."[173] In a dramatic gesture at once prudent and poignant, Staupitz (who had come along to support his protégé) absolved Luther from his vows as an Augustinian monk, thereby freeing himself from any responsibility to imprison or silence Luther should the pope press him to do so. Much later, Luther spoke of this as his first "excommunication."

Luther slipped out of Augsburg by night, on a borrowed horse, arriving in Nuremberg exhausted and ill on October 22. It was there, for the first time, that Luther was faced with the hard evidence of Pope Leo's opposition to his Ninety-Five Theses, though at the time Luther refused to believe it. While he was resting in Nuremberg, Luther received a copy of a letter that had been addressed to Cardinal Cajetan from Pope Leo. Sent in late August, the letter bore instructions regarding Luther's scheduled hearing. It directed the cardinal to simply seize Luther and hold him until he could be brought to Rome for a trial. Should Luther not appear, Leo instructed Cajetan to declare Luther a heretic, to summarily excommunicate him from the church, and to place Luther under the ban.[174] Every civil and ecclesial institution was to be informed that harboring Luther would result in similar excommunication from the church.

Luther read the letter with shock and disbelief, and then declared it a forgery. It suggested a pope so different from the Leo that Luther thought he knew—the Leo he had for so long defended—that he simply would not, could not, believe that this harsh judgment came from Leo's hand. "It is unbelievable,"

172. Brecht, *Martin Luther*, 253.
173. *LW* 31:275. See also *LW* 48:90–91.
174. *LW* 31:286–89. For information on the ban, see Hendrix, *Luther and the Papacy*, 287.

he wrote to Spalatin, "that such a monstrosity should have been released by a pope, especially by Leo X."

Luther believed that the cardinal was somehow behind this "forgery," and while this was not the case, Cajetan did want Luther silenced, and for good reasons. The cardinal's grasp of the underlying implications of Luther's theology was astute; and Cardinal Cajetan was guarding church dogma with the same zeal Luther brought to the protection of Scripture. Not only was he assiduous in his refusal to succumb to Luther's insistence on a debate of the scriptural arguments, but ultimately it was Cajetan who probably authored the bull excommunicating Luther from the church. If there was a defender of the Roman Church who is to be celebrated in this historical contest, it is surely Cardinal Cajetan. And, true to form, even before Luther had arrived back in Wittenberg, Cajetan had sent Prince Frederick his report of the hearing. Assuring the prince that he had treated Luther in a "fatherly way," the cardinal went on to soundly denounce Luther's teachings as heretical, demanding that Frederick arrest Luther and send him to Rome immediately, or at least expel him from Saxony.[175]

Things were not looking good for Luther in the wake of his Augsburg hearing; but he continued to trust that God would use him in defense of the gospel, even if this entailed a heretic's death. Luther was prepared to follow where God led him. As with the *Anfechtungen*, Luther now saw God's hand hidden behind the growing dangers. "I daily expect the condemnation from the city of Rome," Luther wrote to Spalatin; "therefore I am setting things in order and arranging everything so that if it comes I am prepared and girded to go, as Abraham, not knowing where, yet most sure of my way, because God is everywhere."[176] Luther assured his friend that he would "of course leave a farewell letter." "See to it," he cautioned, "that you have the courage to read the letter of a man who is condemned and excommunicated. Farewell for now," he concluded, "and pray for me."[177] Luther also bid his congregation farewell; and on the evening of December 1, 1518, having made up his mind to leave, he gathered with friends for a small celebration.

It was in the midst of this gathering that a last-minute reprieve arrived—instructions from the prince informing Luther that he should not leave Wittenberg. Thus the immediate crisis was resolved.

---

175. Hendrix, *Luther and the Papacy*, 66
176. *LW* 48:94.
177. *LW* 48:94.

From Doubt To Open Rebellion

Luther's confidence in Pope Leo was soon dealt another blow. On November 9, the pope issued an official teaching on indulgences reaffirming, point by point, Cajetan's presentation of the matter at Augsburg. The document made no attempt to meet the biblical arguments Luther had raised in opposition.[178] Now Luther could no longer argue that he brought a responsible and legitimate challenge to church practices in the absence of any official doctrine.

In Luther's report of the *Proceedings at Augsburg*, which he published in late November, we see him putting a new distance between himself and the church as his anger spills over into a clear denunciation of Rome. "It has long been believed that whatever the Roman church says, damns, or wants, all people must eventually say, damn, or want, and that no other reason need be given than that the Apostolic See and the Roman church hold that opinion." The indiscretion of flatterers, he was convinced, had succeeded in replacing the sacred Scripture with the words of mere men, so that the church was no longer being fed with the word of Christ. Thus Luther concluded, "We have come to this in our great misfortune, that the people [in Rome] begin to force [Christians] to renounce the Christian faith and deny Holy Scripture."[179] Having thus framed the matter, it was clear to Luther what God was calling him to do. Whether or not Pope Leo was responsible, Luther now believed that power in Rome had been usurped by those who would prioritize human words above God's. "Divine truth is master also over the pope," Luther wrote, and so, in this situation, "I do not await the judgment of man when I have learned the judgment of God."[180]

Given the widening controversy over Luther's theses, Staupitz was eager to give Luther a chance to publicly present his new theology, and arranged for a disputation before the order as they gathered at Heidelberg for their regular meeting.[181] In this disputation at Heidelberg, which "made a great impression

---

178. Hendrix, *Luther and the papacy*, 76–77.
179. *LW* 31:276.
180. *LW* 31:277.
181. There is disagreement about the details regarding the reasons for Luther's participation in this disputation. In his introduction to the *Heidelberg Disputation*, Harold Grimm writes, "More important for the course of the Reformation, was the fact that Staupitz asked Luther and Beir to participate in a disputation at the Augustinian monastery on April 26 to acquaint the brothers with the new evangelical theology. To avoid arousing animosity against Luther, Staupitz asked him not to debate controversial subjects but to prepare theses concerning sin, free will, and grace. . . . " (*LW* 31:37). However, Martin Brecht is less confident of the historical details. "Whether Staupitz's hand was at work here, or whether Luther was given the task of presiding because he was the director of the most important *Ordensstudium*, is not known" (Brecht, *Martin Luther*, 215).

on its hearers,"[182] Luther argued again against the scholastic theology, which focused on the acquisition of virtue. As long as persons act "as they are able to do, in themselves," Luther claimed, their acts, no matter how attractive they might appear, are, before God, still entirely evil.[183] It was a strong claim, and one that would eventually distance Luther irretrievably from Rome. Nevertheless, Luther's attack on scholastic optimism was warmly received among his Augustinian brothers. Many of the younger monks were impressed with Luther's emphasis on faith, his Augustinian refocusing on God, and his ability as a scriptural scholar to ground his arguments in the biblical texts. Some of these young men eventually became Luther's staunchest defenders, devoting their lives to this theological reformation of the church then still in its infancy.[184] Thus, even as Luther's case was daily growing more serious in Rome, the new "Wittenberg theology" was enjoying a friendly reception in Germany among friends and colleagues.

Leipzig

As Rome continued to prepare its case against Luther, the growing interest in the new Wittenberg theology back in Germany culminated in another important disputation. During the summer of 1519, a disputation in Leipzig was widely advertised, and there were many who were eager to hear Luther defend his writings. The recently invented printing press played an important role in gathering the audience at Leipzig. A major new edition of Luther's Latin Works had by this time been read, studied, and debated by scholars throughout Germany and as far away as Switzerland, Denmark, and even England.[185] Word of the Heidelberg Disputation had also aroused a good deal of interest. In addition, Luther had translated a number of his pieces from scholarly Latin into the German language of the people, hoping to correct misunderstandings that might be brewing. In light of the wide dissatisfaction with the church so prevalent in Germany, Luther's writings had been eagerly embraced by many who simply appreciated his bold stance in relation to Rome. Quite apart from the prophetic responsibility he felt to protect the biblical word of God, Luther was also a man of the people. He, like so many others, felt that the wealth of Germany was being drained away by papal taxes and schemes such as the sale

---

182. Lohse, *Theology of Martin Luther*, 107.
183. Ibid., 106–7.
184. Brecht, *Martin Luther*, 216.
185. Ibid., 284 Brecht refers here to the Froben edition of Luther's collected works that was published in Basel.

of indulgences. But other factors also seem to have influenced the extraordinary interest around the Leipzig debate—in particular, Luther's increasingly open challenge to the claim of papal jurisdiction. Quite apart from the theological arguments Luther was raising, there were many who would have been intensely interested in the political ramifications of Luther's attack on Roman authority.

The initial impetus for the Leipzig debate came not from Luther but in response to a series of theses that had been published by Andreas Karlstadt.[186] Karlstadt had originally written in support of Luther's Ninety-Five Theses, which Johann Eck publicly challenged. Eck, piqued by Karlstadt's reply, sought to engage Karlstadt in a public disputation to settle the matter. In fact, while Luther was still in Augsburg,[187] he and Eck had worked out the details for this meeting at Leipzig, where Karlstadt and Eck were to face off. But that was before Luther saw Eck's theses, which turned out to include a direct attack on Luther. It was clear to Luther that Eck was using Karlstadt as a way to engage Luther publicly. Eck's unusual and unexpected attack on Luther could only be taken as a provocation; and such a bold gesture could not go unchallenged in a world where academic prowess was measured by a man's ability to rhetorically defend himself. With the reputation of the university at stake, Luther explained to Frederick that he had no choice but to respond. Late-medieval academic etiquette, while distinctive to its time and place, was surely no less important nor the fragility of scholarly egos any less volatile than they are today.

The fanfare surrounding the Leipzig Disputation in July of 1519 was extraordinary.[188] Not only were the spectators interested in the competitive events—in this case the ten days of public debates—but there was also popular interest in the contenders themselves. Comparisons were made about their reception, their accommodations, and their lives. On June 24, the Wittenbergers arrived en masse. Karlstadt, leading the way as dean of the theological faculty, rode into Leipzig in the first wagon, piled high with books. Apparently the fact that one of the wheels fell off his wagon as he paraded into town did nothing to diminish the festival atmosphere. Karlstadt was followed by Luther, Melanchthon, the rector of the university at Wittenberg, and the Duke of Pomerania in wagon number two. Alongside walked a crowd of students and other professors from Wittenberg. They had all come to support their colleagues. All told, the delegation from Wittenberg who had come to support

---

186. Hendrix, *Luther and the Papacy*, 80. See also Brecht, *Martin Luther*, 302.

187. Luther had come to Augsburg for the hearing before Cardinal Cajetan the previous summer.

188. Brecht, *Martin Luther*, 310–22. Brecht provides a close description of the Leipzig disputation and the many related events surrounding it. See also *LW* 31:310–11.

their colleagues numbered nearly two hundred men. Eck's supporters quickly closed ranks in order to organize a similar escort of honor.

The disputants were wined and dined, especially Eck, whom Luther believed was widely favored at Leipzig. It is true that Eck's lodgings were provided, while Luther and Karlstadt had to find their own arrangements. But Duke George invited all three disputants to dinner, and the city honored the debaters with gifts. Martin Brecht reports that Eck was given a stag, Karlstadt a doe, and Luther nothing except the required gift of wine—apparently the minimum that etiquette required. Luther felt slighted, and he complained that "the citizens of Leipzig neither greeted nor called on us but treated us as though we were their bitterest enemies. Eck, they followed around town . . . clung to [him], banqueted, entertained, and finally presented [him] with a robe. . . . In short," Luther complained, "they did whatever they could to insult us."[189] Eck, however, reported that most of the citizens were Lutherans. Partisanship was clearly rampant. The accusation of heresy hung over Luther like a cloud, delighting some and distancing others. "The Dominicans were already treating Luther like a heretic," writes Martin Brecht. "When he entered their church while masses were being celebrated, the monks quickly took the monstrance off into a safe place."[190]

It was at Leipzig that Luther, for the first time, publicly revealed a new—and from Rome's perspective, distinctly dangerous—ecclesiology. Luther's proposal included, among other things, a radically reinterpreted understanding of papal authority—one which made it clear to everyone that he had moved well beyond the traditional teaching of the church. But the notoriety associated with this exposure did not come about by accident. Eck apparently intended to challenge Luther publicly on this matter, and he succeeded brilliantly, seizing the opportunity presented at Leipzig to draw Luther out into the open on the question of Rome's claim to exclusive oversight of the church universal.

Luther's revolutionary new understanding of the church, like so many of his ideas, was derived from his underlying distinction between the two

---

189. *LW* 31:323.

190. The monstrance is a receptacle, often silver or gold, that holds consecrated bread from the Eucharist celebration. In Roman Catholic teaching, the consecrated bread is understood to be the body of Christ; thus the monstrance holds Christ's bodily presence in the midst of the people. Heretics are banned from participation in the Communion meal; thus the Dominican monks were "treating Luther like a heretic" by removing the monstrance from Luther's presence. Thomas Aquinas was a Dominican, and Aquinas's teachings form the core of scholastic theology. Thus, according to Brecht, the Dominicans were on the side of Eck and against Luther in this controversy. Brecht, *Martin Luther*, 311.

realms—between the realm of the old Adam (this fallen world) and the spiritual realm of the new Adam (Christ's kingdom). In this world, Luther conceded, the pope has real authority that should be honored. The fact that Rome had enjoyed jurisdiction over other local churches for centuries argued for God's intentionality. But Rome had been given this authority only for the sake of ordering the institutional church. The inner, spiritual, or "true church"—the ultimate expression of Christian unity in Christ—was, in Luther's view, rightly understood as distinct from the Roman Church, even as the spiritual realm is distinct from the temporal. Not Peter, but Christ, Luther insisted, is the universal head of the one true spiritual church. This view of the church had critical implications for Luther himself.[191] Redefined as a penultimate, human institution, the Roman Church, like all things human, would be susceptible to sin and error. Thus, Luther reasoned, Rome's official condemnation of his teaching did not necessarily represent God's judgment. The threat of excommunication from the Roman Church, therefore, and the imposition of the ban (forbidding participation in the sacraments), no longer terrified Luther as they once had. "In this matter," he could now declare, "I fear neither the pope nor the name of the pope. . . . One thing only am I concerned about, namely, that the despoiling of my Christian name does not bring with it the loss of the most holy doctrine of Christ. In this matter I do not want anyone to expect patience of me. . . . Let them terrify someone else."[192]

Luther had by now found a secure "foothold"—place to stand beyond the reach of Rome. God's word, and not the official Roman Church, provided for Luther the only reliable point of contact between heaven and earth; and it was on this ground that Luther was now prepared to stake everything.

While his developing ecclesiology, with its challenge to papal precedence, was a novel addition to the Wittenberg program, Luther's radical rejection of the Aristotelian anthropology was not. In the case of each capacity—free will, salvific cooperation, and virtuous works—God's agency is highlighted while human participation is diminished to a vanishing point. Did Luther really mean to deny every human capacity that we associate with responsible choosing and willing and doing? As noted earlier in the chapter, this does not seem to be the case; for despite his adamant public denunciation of these capacities as "nothing," Luther, in safer contexts, did admit to the existence of human agency, which he publicly repudiated. In a letter written the following spring to his friend Spalatin, for example, we find Luther explaining his position on these matters. In the Gospel of John, writes Luther, Jesus says, "Without me you

191. Ibid., 317–22.
192. *LW* 31:316.

can do nothing" (John 15:5). Here, Luther explains, "Christ totally rejects . . . the 'general influence,' or the 'natural existence . . . , because nature cannot but seek that which is its own and [thus] abuse the gifts of God. Christ," he insisted, "declares simply and without distinction that without the 'specific . . . influence' or grace of God—nothing can be done *that in the eyes of God is* not worthy of fire" (emphasis added).[193] But he adds quickly, "Who can deny that a fornicator, adulterer, murderer, or blasphemer does his deed with the help of the 'general influence'? And how can he do these things, unless he possesses being and activity [in the realm] of nature?"[194] Luther makes it clear that he is bypassing the distinction between "natural" and "acquired" freedom intentionally; and this is not because the capacity does not exist, but because, without Christ, it can accomplish, as Jesus says, "nothing" of value from God's perspective. It was not that Luther thought these natural capacities do not exist, but that they do not exist apart from God; and, from the perspective of eternity, they are, in their fallen state, ultimately worth "nothing."

Recalling his own personal struggle to find peace with God, Luther recognized the practical utility of faithfully acknowledging a divine power and eternal presence, in the light of which all human striving is reduced to "nothing." And from personal experience, Luther knew that only when all the doors were closed could God "make a way where there is no way."[195] Thus no one was spared Luther's zealous attack on that self-satisfied pride (and the complacency that attends it) which separates itself from God. Luther was

---

193. Luther continues, "Christ declares simply and without *distinction* that without . . . the grace of God—nothing can be done that in the eyes of God is not worthy [only] of fire. And so [Christ] goes on to say, 'Whoever does not abide in me will be thrown away like a branch and will wither and people will gather it up and throw it into the fire and it will burn.' Now see, the branch which is not in Christ not only does not grow and bring fruit, but it also withers (that is, weakens and perishes); not only does it weaken and wither, but it is also taken and cut off from the vine and thrown into the fire, etc. In this way he who is only supported by the 'general influence' and the strength of nature continuously gets worse and farther away from Christ; he is being prepared for the fire, no matter how much he outwardly appears to be moral and do good. Here we should realize that we cannot do anything without Christ, whether through a 'general' or a 'specific influence.' [We should see that] whatever is done only on the basis of the 'general influence,' however outstanding it may be, is rather against Christ than for Christ. . . . At this point you could say that the gift bestowed by God is good, but that its use cannot be good unless those who use it have been healed by grace. The 'general influence' (this dangerous term), which is being and activity [in the realm] of nature, if used by anyone who does not remain as a branch in Christ, is misused and of no avail. . . . Who can deny that a fornicator, adulterer, murderer, or blasphemer does his deed with the help of the 'general influence'? How can he do these things unless he possesses being and activity [in the realm] of nature?" (*LW* 48:157–59).

194. *LW* 48:159.

195. Martin Luther King Jr.

convinced that, by applying God's judgment to human pretensions, "it comes about that, if not all, some and indeed many are saved, whereas by the power of free choice none at all would be saved, but all would perish together."[196]

Courageous Faith

Luther later described the Leipzig disputation as "a tragedy";[197] and tensions escalated in the months immediately following, as each side was left to draw its own conclusions. Clearly Luther had come away believing he had not been given the opportunity to fully make his case, and many in Leipzig believed Eck was the winner.[198] Thus the disputation, which had officially ended in July of 1519, continued at a distance, as first one side and then the other published attacks, rebuttals, and counterattacks. As Luther waited for matters to take their course, he remained busier than ever. Apparently he "was keeping three printing presses busy with his writings alone, and still they could not keep up with him."[199] Luther used this time, in part, to produce a series of writings on penance, baptism, Eucharist, and good works, thus integrating his prophetic and pastoral aims. Together, this set of writings describes the whole Christian life, from death to faith to loving service. Moved by the Spirit and sustained by Christ's promise and presence at the table, the Christian life as described in these writings is a dynamic interplay of forces let loose by God. Working through the law's imperative and the gospel's promise, God acts to redeem and release sinners from the devil's clutches. Thus God penetrates the boundary separating the spiritual realm from the earthly as the Spirit moves through the lives of faithful Christians acting in God's name for the sake of the world.

During this difficult time, Luther appears to have been almost exuberant in that Spirit he describes—experiencing himself as both divinely driven and yet free. He was working with a vigor and enthusiasm that exceeded even his usual output. "God has given me a joyful and fearless spirit," he wrote.[200] The arrival of the bull in Wittenberg did nothing to stifle Luther's jubilant mood. If anything, it seemed to prove to Luther that his assumptions about Rome were correct. "Already I am much freer," he wrote upon seeing the bull, "certain at last that the pope is the antichrist."[201] Luther was fully convinced

---

196. *LW* 33:288.
197. *LW* 31:325.
198. *LW* 31:324.
199. Brecht, *Martin Luther*, 413.
200. Ibid., 346
201. Ibid., 404 See also: Hendrix, *Luther and the Papacy*, 116.

that he was being used by God to serve a much larger plan. His conviction that the words he spoke were effectively functioning as a sword in God's hand perhaps intensified and focused his writing even more sharply, thus adding to the amperage. Luther's breach with Rome appears to have been spiritually complete long before it was fully regularized through the church's official excommunication of Luther from Rome, and Luther's unofficial "excommunication" of Rome from the spiritual church of Christ.[202]

Sometime between mid-June, when the bull[203] was released by the Church of Rome, and October 10, when it was posted in Wittenberg, Luther finished work on his *To the German Nobility*. It appears that he was encouraged to issue this call for action (and assisted in its preparation) by those with a stake in its possible political consequences. Notably, this piece was aimed at the secular authorities rather than the ecclesial—a shift that reflects an important development around this time in Luther's understanding of God's work in the civil/temporal realm.[204] This plea to the German nobility is a passionate condemnation of the Roman church, in which Luther calls on the temporal authorities to act on their Christian faith in the defense of God's word. Rome's claim, Luther writes, "that only the pope may interpret Scripture is an outrageous fancied fable. They cannot produce a single letter [of Scripture] to maintain that the interpretation of Scripture or the confirmation of its interpretation belongs to the pope alone. They themselves have usurped this power."[205] Then, calling on the princes to convene a council challenging Rome's claim to authority, Luther adds,

> When necessity demands it, and the pope is an offense to Christendom, the first man who is able should, as a true member of the whole body [of Christ], do what he can to bring about a truly free council. No one can do this so well as the temporal authorities, especially since they are also fellow-Christians, fellow-priests, fellow-members of the spiritual estate, fellow-lords over all

---

202. Brecht, *Martin Luther*, 424–26. Not everyone was as confident as Luther, however. It is interesting that, given the added threats to his colleagues, some 150 students left the university at Wittenberg out of fear that they too would be subject to the ban (ibid., 414).

203. This was not the bull of excommunication, but one that preceded it by sixty days, giving Luther another chance to recant before being officially and absolutely severed from the Roman Catholic Church.

204. The two-kingdom thinking we have observed in this period of Luther's development represents an early version of a model that would grow considerably more complex in the context of changing historical circumstances.

205. *LW* 44:134.

things. Whenever it is necessary or profitable they ought to exercise the office and work which they have received from God over everyone.[206]

Luther, convinced God was using him for God's own purposes, prophetically framed the controversy for the secular rulers in such a way as to draw them into the cosmic battle, which so profoundly shaped Luther's perspective during this period.

It is intolerable that in canon law so much importance is attached to the freedom, life, and property of the clergy, as though the laity were not also as spiritual and as good Christians as they, or did not also belong to the church. . . . It can be no good spirit which has invented such exceptions and granted sin such license and impunity. For if it is our duty to strive against the words and works of the devil and to drive him out in whatever way we can, as both Christ and his apostles command us, how have we gotten into such a state that we have to do nothing and say nothing when the pope or his cohorts undertake devilish words and works? Ought we merely out of regard for these people allow the suppression of divine commandments and truth, which we have sworn in baptism to support with life and limb?[207]

Then, revealing again his ever-present sense of pastoral responsibility, Luther ends with a familiar warning: Should we fail to act, he cautions, "we should have to answer for all the souls that would thereby be abandoned and led astray!"[208]

Within two weeks of its appearance in August of 1520, Luther's *To the Christian Nobility*, with its unusually large edition of four thousand copies, had already sold out. Ulrich von Hutten (one of a group of knights who had offered Luther protection) summoned Prince Frederick to take up arms against Roman tyranny. "Let us avenge the common freedom," he wrote; "let

---

206. *LW* 44:137. Also, "Consider for a moment how Christian is the decree which says that the temporal power is not above the 'spiritual estate' and has no right to punish it. That is as much as to say that the hand shall not help the eye when it suffers pain. . . . Since the temporal power is ordained of God to punish the wicked and protect the good, it should be left free to perform its office in the whole body of Christendom without restriction and without respect to persons, whether it affects pope, bishops, priests, monks, nuns, or anyone else" (*LW* 44:130).

207. *LW* 44:132.

208. *LW* 44:132.

us free the long-oppressed fatherland."[209] The enormous interest stirred up by Luther's *To the German Nobility* suggests there was, by this time, strong secular support was aligned Luther against Rome. And this was not only the case among the powerful aristocracy; the general public, too, was caught up in the growing turmoil. Publicists on both sides were busily managing some of the first campaigns ever waged in print. As the papal bull threatening Luther with excommunication was posted in one German town after another, there were book burnings, riots, and threats of revolt. Luther argued against any use of force. God's Word alone, Luther insisted, ought to be allowed to do God's work "without [the addition of human] hands."[210]

As the rift between the "Romanists" and the "Lutherans" grew, there were others who, though in essential agreement with Luther's call for reform, sought to find middle ground. Legitimately fearful of the political and cultural upheaval threatened by what appeared ever more likely to be a schism with Rome, they realized that once Luther's excommunication was finalized (marking him as a heretic and an outlaw), any opportunity for rapprochement that might still exist would be irretrievably lost.[211] The seriousness of this threat to political stability is evidenced by Erasmus's decision to get involved. As the most respected humanist of his day, Erasmus's opinion carried a great deal of weight. In early November, he met with Prince Frederick with a proposal designed to highlight what was good on each side while repudiating all that was, in his view, irrationally extreme or polemical. Luther's writings should be judged by an impartial group of academics, argued Erasmus, appointed by the secular (rather than the ecclesial) powers. Such a gathering of scholars might save the best of Luther's writings from the fire. Perhaps even more importantly, Luther might be admonished by his peers rather than labeled a "heretic" and an "outlaw" by

---

209. Brecht, *Martin Luther*, 369–70; Hutten published a copy of the bull with his own notes appended in which he demanded action against Rome. "Through the hands of his own," Hutten wrote, "God will punish Rome."

210. "In this matter we are not dealing with men, but with the princes of hell. These princes could fill the world with war and bloodshed, but war and bloodshed do not overcome them. We must tackle this job by renouncing trust in physical force and trusting humbly in God. . . . The more force we use, the greater our disaster if we do not act humbly and in the fear of God" (*LW* 44:125–26). Luther argued that Hutten's eager recourse to violence was inappropriate on the basis of Dan. 8:23-25, which reads, "At the later end of their rule, when the transgressors have reached their full measure, a king of bold countenance . . . shall arise. His power shall be great, and he shall cause fearful destruction, and shall succeed in what he does, and destroy mighty men and the people of the saints. . . . In his own mind he shall magnify himself. Without warning he shall destroy many; and he shall even rise up against the Prince of princes; *but, by no human hand, he shall be broken*" (Brecht, *Martin Luther*, 420, emphasis added).

211. Brecht, *Martin Luther*, 405. Miltitz wrote, "If the bull goes into effect, a schism will result."

the church.[212] While Erasmus's proposal never materialized, something like it—a secular hearing—was arranged, which by its very reevaluation of Luther's work (already condemned by Rome) manifestly challenged the church's authority. Prince Frederick was instructed to bring Luther to the diet meeting at Worms where Luther would be judged by fair and reliable scholars; and he would be justly treated. In the interim, Luther was to do nothing that might complicate the situation further.

WORMS

Even before the emperor's letter arrived, Luther, who had never been a slave to political expediency, did in fact complicate things to a considerable degree. At a book-burning ceremony of his own, Luther, along with colleagues and students, ritually excommunicated the Roman Church. In his most prophetic mode, Luther consigned to the flames books of canon law and monastic piety; and then with "trembling and prayer,"[213] he stepped forward and dropped the papal bull, *Exsurge Domine*, into the flames. It was sixty days exactly from the posting of the bull; and clearly no refutation from Luther would be forthcoming. On January 3, the church issued a document officially excommunicating Luther,[214] in response to which Luther, having composed his own document, written in a style that mimics *Exsurge Domine*, "excommunicated" Rome. Their unwillingness to engage and counter any challenges, and the pope's claim to inerrancy—these summed up for him all that was wrong with the church. "I am moved most by the fact that the pope has never once refuted with Scripture or reason anyone who has spoken, written, or acted against him. . . . Nor has he ever been willing to submit to a court of justice or judgment, but at all times bawled that he was above Scripture, judgment, and authority."[215]

---

212. Ibid., 417. Note that Luther was particularly incensed at being labeled a heretic by the church (Brecht, *Martin Luther*, 338–41). It appears that Erasmus was also eager to solicit Frederick's support to use force against Luther should he refuse to accept the judgments of this panel. Erasmus's notes of this meeting also reveal his criticism of the church, something he would have preferred to keep quiet; thus he was unhappy to discover that Spalatin had published a copy of the notes entrusted to him.

213. Brecht, *Martin Luther*, 424.

214. The bull excommunicating Luther is called *Decet Romanum Pontificem*.

215. *LW* 31:394–95. Luther comments on this "main article," "These and similar articles which are without number—all of them aim at exalting the pope above God and man." "Even his disciples say he is an extraordinary creature . . . perhaps [he is] the devil himself."

Luther was convinced that Scripture was no longer normatively informing the church at Rome; rather, Rome was holding Scripture hostage. "Truth and righteousness do not shun judgment," Luther insisted. Rather they "gladly permit themselves to be examined and tried."[216] Thus, in Luther's view, everything pointed to the conclusion that Rome, which once was the bearer of Christ, had become now the seat of the "antichrist." "The greatest evil," Luther insisted, "has always come from the best."[217] "The son of God was killed nowhere else but in the holy city of Jerusalem. . . . God has also blessed no city on earth with so much grace and so many saints as Rome . . . Therefore she, too, like Jerusalem, in gratitude to God, must do the greatest harm and give the world the true and most destructive Antichrist.'[218]

Luther's unequivocal denunciation of the papacy left no room for further negotiation. Luther was ready for what he believed would be his inevitable martyrdom. "I hope the time has come," he wrote, "for the cause to move forward in [God's] name without me."[219]

Initially the emperor had acted in agreement with Prince Frederick's plan, summoning Luther to appear at the diet for what Luther and Frederick hoped would be a real debate. Somewhat abruptly, however, the summons was rescinded. Perhaps he was put off by Luther's public repudiation of Rome; perhaps, on the advice of papal representatives, he was reluctant to allow the laity to retry a case already decided by the church. Whatever had caused Charles to reconsider Luther's appearance before the diet left Luther wondering what would come next. At Worms, the various parties wrangled over what was to be done. In the end, a compromise resulted and an imperial mandate was issued requiring the sequestration of Luther's books. Luther took this as a sign that the emperor now leaned toward Rome and away from Frederick. If Luther were called to Worms only to recant (as had happened at Augsburg), he saw no reason to make the trip. He would make himself ready, instead, for a summons to his own execution. He began to worry now about how his death might affect the young emperor's ability to rule, should he begin his reign with Luther's blood on his hands.

But these worries were all for naught. Luther was not summoned to his execution; he was in fact summoned to Worms. The negotiations between the various parties, each with something to gain in relation to Luther's case, had finally resulted in the opportunity for him to appear.[220] Many wondered

216. *LW* 31:395.
217. *LW* 31:393.
218. *LW* 31:394.
219. *LW* 31:394.

whether he would go at all, given the significant danger. But as Luther was certain God had called him into this conflict as a pawn in a much larger battle, he had no fear about what might transpire.

The trip from Wittenberg to Worms was not an easy one. Luther was so ill that he had to be bled at one of the towns along the way.[221] Nevertheless, he rallied and even preached. As Luther, with his considerable traveling party, made his way toward Worms, he was wined and dined and made much of. Trumpets announced his arrival as he and his friends rode into Worms through the city gates on the morning of April 16, 1521. Despite attempts by those eager

---

220. Brecht, *Martin Luther*, 416. "Taking Luther out of the library is easy, removing him from men's hearts . . . is difficult." At Worms, Rome wanted the requirements of the bull excommunicating Luther enforced. In Germany, this was not easy to accomplish given the rising public sentiment in Luther's favor. In order to force the issue, Rome asked the emperor for an imperial mandate against Luther that would add the force of civil law to the ban already issued by the church. Though the emperor could have issued such a mandate without outside support, he would not do so. As he initiated his reign, it was imperative that he find favor with both the church and with the secular princes; thus he would not issue the imperial mandate without the support of the secular princes. The princes used their leverage to drive a bargain; they would support a compromise version of the mandate against Luther under certain conditions. It appears that these included sequestering his books rather than burning them (until after a judgment had been reached at Worms). Luther was to be summoned to appear, but not for debate. He was to renounce those articles that were against traditional church teaching—especially the more radical statements he had made about the church since the church's bull of excommunication. If he renounced these, there might be discussion on other points. All of this would be done under secular rather than ecclesial rule. The aim here was to preserve those works of Luther's that were widely regarded as good and useful for the faith of the church. The princes were also hoping to keep the peace and to get their complaints in the *Gravamina* addressed—a point they could win, by refusing to support the imperial mandate against Luther, unless their conditions were met. (The Gravamina was a list of reforms that the princes had been requesting from Rome for a long time). Thus the church was caught. Without the imperial mandate to bolster the force of their ban, they could not turn the tide of public support for Luther. Without the support of the secular princes, the emperor would not issue the mandate; since without the promise to address the complaints against Roman "tyranny" in the *Gravamina*, the territorial princes would not support it. Thus it seems that, without the leverage offered by the *Gravamina*, Luther might well have never had his moment at Worms. The summons Luther did eventually receive did not clearly spell out what was to be done with him at Worms. He was only informed that he was being summoned for an examination of his books. In the meantime, the mandate was issued, which made it clear to those in Wittenberg that Luther had in essence already been condemned by the emperor (given the new imperial mandate against him with the requirement that his books be sequestered). Though he had been granted an imperial safe passage, this might not hold if a decision were made to apply the punishments already imposed by the church. Thus there was considerable danger for Luther if he went to Worms. It seems likely that those already at the diet did not expect him to appear, in which case he would be condemned and the case could be closed. Given the agreement of the princes, the emperor and the church could (theoretically at least) count on their support. This of course never came to pass, as Luther did in fact appear.

to turn the tide of public support, Luther's fame outpaced their efforts. It was reported that some two thousand curious onlookers came out into the streets to greet him, hoping to catch a glimpse of the famous Dr. Luther.[222]

Called before the diet the following day, Luther was asked first to identify a pile of books that had been placed on a table as his own. Then, in a single question, Luther was asked whether he was prepared to retract anything (in these books) that he had written. The general nature of the question apparently took Luther off guard. He had, once again, been hoping for a debate, or at least a list of specific articles that he could respond to individually. His bearing on this first day surprised many. They had expected to hear the bold rhetoric from Luther that his writings and reputation promised. Instead, he appeared nervous, and asked for time to consider the question he had been asked. Luther was eventually told he would be allowed time to think further. Then, with a curt reprimand that he should have been prepared already, Luther was instructed to return the following day ready to respond. Though he had given

---

221. In late medieval Europe, bloodletting was used to treat a wide variety of maladies, including plague, smallpox, epilepsy, and gout. With a history spanning at least two thousand years, no medical practice has been more trusted or more widely utilized. It was a therapy originally based on the ancient theory that good health requires a perfect balance of the four "humors" (blood, phlegm, yellow bile, and black bile); but the practice continued to receive robust support from many physicians in the West even after the rise of science, and well into the late nineteenth century. In Luther's day, the procedure was as widely trusted and commonly used as aspirin is today. For Luther, bloodletting would have probably involved making a small diagonal cut in a vein that had been tied off, collecting the tainted blood in a bowl, all the while carefully measuring the correct amount according to detailed charts drawn up to treat specific disorders. Luther suffered from ill health throughout his life; and though it worsened considerably in his later years, he was by no means free from pain even while he was still relatively young. Luther frequently reports digestive disorders and kidney stones in his letters; and he seems to have suffered in later years from heart ailments and cataracts as well. Some attribute Luther's general ill health to an early and overly zealous ascetic lifestyle during his years as a monk.

222. Oberman, *Luther*, 198–99. Oberman provides an eyewitness account of Luther's arrival in Worms, written by the papal legate Aleander: "I had already concluded my letter when I gathered from various reports as well as the hasty running of the people that the great master of heretics was making his entrance. I sent one of my people out, and he told me that about a hundred mounted soldiers, probably Sickingen's, had escorted him to the gate of the city; sitting in a coach with three comrades, he entered the city [at ten in the morning], surrounded by some eight horsemen and found lodgings near his Saxon prince. When he left the coach, a priest embraced him and touched his habit three times, and shouted with joy, as if he had had a relic of the greatest saint in his hands. I suspect that he will soon be said to work miracles. This Luther, as he climbed from the coach, looked around in the circle with his demonic eyes and said: 'God will be with me.' Then he stepped into an inn, where he was visited by many men, ten or twelve of which he ate with, and after the meal, all the world ran there to see him." Oberman adds his comment, "It was neither a triumphant victor, nor a demon or miracle worker who had come to Worms; the monk who stepped down from that coach was a sorely tested man."

a disappointing first performance, Luther seemed not to worry but greeted visitors and friends that evening with a good spirit. He was reassured by his supporters that he was under their protection should there be a move to imprison him. On the second day, Luther was ushered into a room filled to capacity. It was late in the afternoon, and the torches were lit; it was a theatrical staging for what would become one of the most famous "scenes" in Western history. Luther appeared considerably more assured; and he spoke now with his usual skill,

He began by dividing his books into three categories—those widely accepted as good and useful for the piety of the people, those that were critical of the church's practices, and those aimed at individuals, which, Luther conceded, were regrettably written in a rhetorical style unbecoming to a monk and a doctor of theology. However, taking the position that in speaking on behalf of God such a tone might be warranted, these too he could not retract. Having spoken his piece first in German, he went through it a second time in Latin. Ultimately, Luther refused to retract anything, and when pressed by the officer in charge to speak plainly, Luther concluded his speech with the following well known words:

> Unless I am convinced by the testimony of the Scriptures or by clear reason (for I do not trust either in the pope or in councils alone, since it is well known that they have often erred and contradicted themselves), I am bound by the Scriptures I have quoted and my conscience is captive to the Word of God. I cannot and I will not retract anything, since it is neither safe nor right to go against conscience. May God help me. Amen.[223]

Luther and those around him believed that, in this situation where everything was at stake, he had spoken well. Prince Frederick was especially pleased with the Latin version of the speech; and Luther was clearly pleased too. He had not failed God's Word, or his calling as God's prophet. Luther had demonstrated by his courage that he really was "captive to the Word of God," rather than a prisoner of his own fear. He had stood his ground. Many expected him to be arrested on the spot; but his promised "safe conduct" was still in effect, and Luther was reassured that he was in no immediate danger. Carried along by a throng of people to his quarters, he was prepared now to celebrate. Throwing his hands over his head, Luther shouted joyfully, "I've come through. I've come through!"[224]

223. Brecht, *Martin Luther*, 460.

No one would have been quicker than Luther to credit God with this triumph. Yet, in this moment of jubilation it was clear that Luther—the one who had succeeded in "coming through"—was prepared to acknowledge his part in this accomplishment. Luther's celebratory gesture and language suggest that he never doubted his own role as an effective agent in the achievement of this goal. Clearly it was a goal he believed God had assigned to him; but it was a goal that that he himself had fully embraced and enacted.[225] But what would happen now? Luther had already been excommunicated by the church; and there could be no doubt that, in his absolute refusal to retract anything, he had sealed whatever fragile opening might have still existed. There would be no question that the force of the imperial mandate would now be added to the church's ban against him. Not only had he been branded a heretic, but now he would also be identified as an outlaw. The two greatest powers in the land—the pope and the emperor—both had (or would) issue their respective condemnations. Would he be allowed to return to Wittenberg at all? As Luther pondered these questions back in his lodgings with his counselors, colleagues, and friends, the lawyers who represented the various interests mounted a hasty final attempt at negotiation. For two more days, they tried to find a way out of the impasse. Luther continued to hold his ground. Then, with no apparent compromise forthcoming, Luther was, somewhat surprisingly, allowed to leave. The emperor honored the safe passage he had promised.[226] How long this would be the case was anyone's guess. Thus there was no great surprise (though a good deal of weeping) when word arrived back in Wittenberg that Luther's traveling party had been attacked along the way, and Luther kidnapped. Several in the party had managed to get away with their lives to ride into town with the news of this calamity, which now spread like wildfire.

But of course Luther was not in fact dead; he was only in hiding. This part of Luther's story is so familiar as to need no retelling. Prince Frederick had, once again, come through for Luther—carrying him away to a hidden place of safety until the immediate danger had passed. What is not so well known is the fact that, as Luther's traveling party proceeded on their way toward Wittenberg, their numbers dwindled. Luther first dismissed the imperial herald with instructions to carry a letter back to Spalatin; and then, as the rest of the party neared Eisenach, he sent others on ahead so that he could visit some

---

224. Ibid., 461.

225. In light of Luther's frequent refusal to acknowledge effective human agency, his demonstration of joyful self-congratulation is noteworthy.

226. It is reported that the nobility supporting Luther, including the knights, sent an escort of twenty horsemen to accompany Luther out of the city with great honor.

relatives. Thus, when Luther and his two remaining companions were suddenly surrounded, there was no one left to protect them. It is also the case that neither the guard, who would have been under oath to protect Luther with his life, nor his other traveling companions, who might well have been willing to die in order to save Luther, perished in the confrontation.[227] Without his guards, Luther was defenseless; and with bows drawn against him, he submitted, while his two remaining companions (apparently in on the plan) ran off into the woods. At first, his captors made Luther run alongside the horses; but once out of sight they pulled up, so that Luther could also be mounted. Then, riding in a long and circuitous route through the forest, they came at last to the Wartburg Castle, where Luther was safely delivered up to his new home—at least for the time being. Dark, and nearly deserted, Luther would remain here in hiding—left to face the devil's onslaughts as he struggled to come to terms with his new situation. Having imagined that he would not live to see the results of his work, Luther must have wondered where all this was leading. As he would discover, there was still much to be done, and a critical role still left for him to play.

---

227. The imperial guards would have been under oath to protect Luther with their lives.

2

Freed to Serve

Rethinking the Two Realms

Luther's God-Satan dualism, which underscored his initial rendering of justification (as well as his early view of the two kingdoms), now began to undergo further development, especially following the Leipzig Disputation of 1519. Luther did not abandon the earlier model; rather, he incorporated the Augustinian dualism into a larger dynamic and dialectical framework emerging from Paul's eschatological concept of the old and new man. It was the integration of these two ideas that culminated in his mature understanding of God's twofold reign. This reworking of his earlier model would include within it a revised anthropology, allowing for the work of the indwelling Spirit to collaborate with human beings via the created ontic structures of this world. The revised anthropology both reflects and makes visible, to those under the influence of the Spirit, a new vision of the whole created order, defined and illuminated by the *Deus revelatus* rather than the *Deus absconditus*. Thus, Luther's mature theology of the two realms reincorporated the temporal anthropology so critical to sanctification, and it was this reinterpreted understanding of sanctification that, in conjunction with Luther's increasing political and social engagement from early 1522 onward, encouraged and allowed for the development of his theology of vocation.

In large part, this unfolded as Luther sought to answer the questions that were emerging. As always for Luther, his theology was for the sake of salvation, initially because he felt himself bound by his vocational vows as a priest and as a teacher. But as his initial insight regarding God's free justification in faith opened to address the many questions that his teaching logically entailed (and in fact, aroused), Luther came to understand his pastoral task as one that was secured, not only by his ordination vows as a priest, but also by his baptism into Christ.

We recall that, for Luther, "the proper subject of theology [is] man guilty of sin and condemned, and God the Justifier and savior of man the sinner. Whatever is asked or discussed in theology outside this subject," he insisted, "is error and poison."[1] The curricular changes at Wittenberg made this understanding of theology manifest in its course requirements. Courses on the Bible (which preached law and gospel) were developed alongside new courses on Augustine (and the depth of sin), replacing courses on Aristotle. These latter, Luther was convinced, only served to increase sin (understood as pride and a false confidence in human autonomy from God), whereas Augustine, in conjunction with Scripture highlighted the condemnation of the law and the gospel promise of free salvation in Christ, thus promoting faith, and the ultimate goal of salvation. It was this pastoral approach to theology that distinguished the Wittenberg program from the curricular changes that humanism inspired elsewhere. Insofar as humanist ends served the infinitely greater end of salvation, Luther and his colleagues were happy to make use of them.

This same pastoral calling shaped Luther's overall theological work, and for this reason his historical context must be understood in conjunction with his theology. For Luther, and for all those grasped by the Spirit, this new theology culminated in a sanctified secularity—visible to the faithful in, with, and under the created and fallen world. At the same time, the newly identified priesthood of all believers, by their preaching and practice through word and deed, became themselves the "mask" for God's Word let loose in the world. In this chapter, we will briefly track the development of Luther's revised theology of the two realms and then observe the effects of this on Luther's thinking as he began to unpack it in a new and challenging context.[2]

LUTHER'S MONASTIC ASSUMPTIONS REGARDING ANTHROPOLOGY: LECTURES ON PSALMS 1514–1516

In his earliest[3] lectures on the Psalms, Luther tells us again and again that the visible, tangible goods of the temporal world are ultimately nothing but signs that point toward a hidden reality. Some have described these lectures as Platonic, though the more immediate influence appears to have been

---

1. *LW* 12:311.
2. For a full scholarly examination of this development in Luther's two-kingdom thinking, see F. Edward Cranz, *An Essay on the Development of Luther's Thought on Justice, Law, and Society* (Mifflintown, PA: Sigler, 1998), 57.
3. These lectures, beginning in 1513, are the earliest lectures that are extant, though Luther may have begun lecturing sometime earlier.

Augustine's *On the Spirit and Letter*—itself a Neoplatonic reflection on Paul's remark that "the letter kills, but the spirit makes alive" (2 Cor. 3:6). This would hardly have been a surprising hermeneutic for Luther to have brought to his reading of the Psalms, even apart from his theological identification with Augustine. The entire monastic project, particularly his reformed community of Augustinian hermits, was an expression of such a world-denying piety; and it extended well beyond the cloister walls. When we consider how impressed Luther was (apparently along with the general public) in observing the piety of the young nobleman who begged in the streets, slowly starving himself to death,[4] it is clear that what impressed people then was not what we find impressive today.

Luther translates Augustine's dualism into one that describes a visible world that exists in almost perfect opposition to the truth, which remains hidden. "All the works of creation . . . are [only] signs of the works of God," Luther writes.[5] For all of them are transitory, merely symbolizing a hidden reality that endures. This world is but "shadows and works of foreshadowing."[6] The shadow of death, and the condemnation that reveals itself in Christ's crucifixion, overtakes us already, according to Luther. Nevertheless, we cling to that which we can perceive with our senses.

Luther's anthropology exhibits the same dualistic features as his reading of the created order. That which is hidden is superior to that which is visible, as the human soul is superior to the human body. Speaking allegorically about a Red Sea crossing, Luther writes, "In a mystical sense 'the sea' is mankind according to the body, which is full of salt and streams of passions, while the 'dry land' is mankind according to the soul, which, cleansed of the passions, becomes the dwelling place of Christ and the saints."[7] Our problem is that we cling to the sensual pleasures of this world; things on which we would stand rather than on the "dry land" of the soul.

As we have already noted, the false ground on which we stand ultimately characterizes us; so that "the rich man subsists by riches, the healthy man by health, the honored man by honor, the pleasure seekers by pleasure."[8] Indeed, Luther warns, "they will be that kind of people just as long as those things last."[9]

---

4. Brecht, 17.
5. *LW* 10:311.
6. *LW* 10:311.
7. *LW* 10:356.
8. *LW* 10:356.
9. *LW* 10:356.

To recognize one's spiritual destiny and sinful bondage to fleshly appetites that are finally "nothing" is a great gift, according to Luther.

One of the interesting things about the Psalms lectures is that, in those early days, Luther still approaches the Christian life according to the traditional view—that it is a life of incremental growth in righteousness, progressing day by day, always focused on the eternal goal, climbing rung by rung up the ladder toward heaven; but here, perhaps under the influence of Tauler's mysticism, Luther has reversed things. The penitent is identified with Christ in his suffering and dying (rather than in his power and glory). Sinners are "like" the crucified God at the foot of the ladder rather than like the righteous God at the top. It is in death that one finds the crucified God, not in righteousness; and this is an important theological move. Nonetheless, Luther still views the Christian life as one of progressing, or moving toward a goal. "Now I have begun," writes the psalmist. "Let the proud ideas about my own holiness, . . . be turned backward so that I may see that they are nothing."[10]

LECTURES ON ROMANS 1516–1518 AND THE ANTHROPOLOGY ASSOCIATED WITH JUSTIFICATION

In Luther's lectures on Paul's letter to the Romans, the contradictions have been intensified. Luther had grasped Paul's theology of justification as the nonimputation of sins. Since justification is tied to faith, and because faith is something one has or doesn't have, sinners are either wholly redeemed by God in Christ or wholly damned, outside of Christ. Notably, the flesh/spirit duality of the Psalms lectures (where the soul offers dry ground on which to stand, and the body is dismissed) takes on new referents in Romans. Paul's introduction of the eschatological opposition between the old and the new Adam now links these terms, "flesh" and "spirit," with old and new—sinful and redeemed in Christ (Rom. 5:12-19; 8:5-6). The whole person, body and soul, outside of faith, remains "flesh," which Paul uses to describe sin (rather than referring to the body). Notably, this means that the soul along with the body is wholly sinful outside of Christ as well—no longer the safe "dry ground" of the Psalms. The soul is vulnerable to sin and can be wholly corrupted along with the body insofar as the whole person, without faith, is outside Christ and thus identified with the "old" Adam. This is counterintuitive for Luther, who is accustomed to the Augustinian dualism that lifts up the invisible soul and rejects the body, along with all that is temporal and transient. Thus, even as

---

10. *LW* 10:392.

Luther is employing Paul's eschatological model in *The Freedom of A Christian* (1520), he gets confused. In his attempt to "make the way smoother for the unlearned,"[11] Luther writes, "Man has a twofold nature, a spiritual and a bodily one. According to the spiritual nature, which men refer to as the soul, he is called a spiritual, inner, or new man. According to the bodily nature, which men refer to as flesh, he is called a carnal, outward or old man."[12]

Note that Luther has identified the soul (spirit, or "inner self") with the "new man" and the body (carnal or outward self) with the "old man." Instead of maintaining the whole person, body and soul (outer and inner), with either the new Adam or the old Adam, as Paul does, Luther has fallen back into the old Augustinian dualism. Within the same text, however, Luther does in fact correctly employ Paul's anthropology, correctly describing a single person, both inner and outer (soul and body), as wholly righteous in Christ. While the new creation in Christ—established in the marriage that faith consummates—is the subject of the first half of this little book, the outworking of faith that is active in love provides the content for the second half. The gospel promise works on the inner man to establish faith, and thereby creates the "new Adam." This process of re-creation effected by the spiritual marriage (or what Luther also calls the "happy exchange") recalls his discussion of persons in his lectures on Psalms. There he spoke of persons "subsisting" in that which ultimately characterizes them—the rich man is characterized by his riches, the healthy man by his health, and so on. In this justifying event, as Luther now describes it, faith becomes the relationship that binds an individual to God through the spiritual marriage, so that henceforth this person is characterized by Christ. She is a Christian and bound to Christ in faith.

Because this characterizes the whole person (as the new Adam), the outer self—the visible and temporal body—now engages the world in a new way. Again, using the relational concept of *coram*—or standing before—Luther describes how this one, reborn in Christ, now engages her neighbors as Christ has engaged her. Whereas God's love is active in faith, the Christian's faith is active in love. Her works are good because she is good. Good fruit, Luther says, grows from a good tree;[13] but one cannot make a good tree in the opposite direction—by first making good fruit. She is wholly re-created in Christ, and the works of her outer self are also now characterized as wholly good. But these works are not good in themselves. They are, outside of faith, still evil; but in

---

11. *LW* 31:344.
12. *LW* 31:344.
13. *LW* 31:361.

Christ they are no longer imputed as sin. Thus these works, which may not yet appear good, Luther characterizes as "good works," nevertheless.

While Luther has used his new relational ontology to describe this entire process, he adds an important detail in his 1520 Freedom of a Christian, suggesting that the old ontic structures are still there. In a section that once again appears to mistakenly relate sin specifically to the outer body, Luther explains that "the inner man, who by faith . . . is both joyful and happy . . . and therefore [eager] to serve God joyfully . . . meets a contrary will in his own flesh." This, Luther explains, "the spirit of faith cannot tolerate, but with joyful zeal it attempts to put the body under control and hold it in check."[14] Hence, he continues, "a man cannot be idle, for the need of his body drives him and he is compelled to do many good works to reduce it to subjection. Nevertheless the works themselves do not justify him before God." And again,

> Man is abundantly and sufficiently justified by faith inwardly, in his spirit . . . yet he remains in this mortal life on earth. In this life he must control his own body and have dealings with men. Here the works begins: here a man cannot enjoy leisure; here he must indeed take care to discipline his body by *fastings, watchings, labors, and other reasonable discipline* and to subject it to the Spirit so that it will obey and conform to the inner man and faith and not revolt against faith . . . *as it is the nature of the body to do* if it is not held in check. (emphasis added)[15]

Luther's belief that the traditional spiritual exercises, including fasting and watches and other "reasonable discipline"—exercises such as were regularly prescribed by the church for the sake of cultivating virtue—imply (1) that the traditional underlying ontic structures are still part of Luther's overall anthropology, and (2) that his old Augustinian distrust of the temporal world, (and in particular the body), still remains. At the same time, Luther now turns towards the world he previously dismissed as nothing. Christians deploy their growing self-discipline in service to the world. For "a man does not live for himself alone in this mortal body to work for it alone, but he lives also for all men on earth; [or] rather [Luther corrects himself here] he lives *only* for others and not for himself."[16] "I will . . . give of myself as a Christ to my neighbor," Luther continues, "just as Christ offered himself to me."[17] For, he

14. *LW* 31:359.
15. *LW* 31:358–59.
16. *LW* 31:364.

explains, "A Christian most freely and most willingly spends himself and all that he has," responding, as did Christ, in self-sacrificial love on behalf of his needy neighbors.[18] Though one "needs none of these things for his righteousness and salvation,"[19] a Christian "cannot ever in this life be idle and without works toward his neighbors."[20] Thus Luther's theology, especially after 1522, took a practical new turn toward the temporal world as his doctrine of God's twofold reign began to find its social/political expression; and through this new outward gaze Luther came in time to "a more positive evaluation of the self, world, society, law and justice."[21]

ONLY A GOOD TREE BEARS GOOD FRUIT: LUTHER'S ATTACK ON THE ARISTOTELIAN ANTHROPOLOGY OF THE SCHOLASTICS

The year 1517 was critical for Luther. Not only is it famous because it is the year he posted his Ninety-Five Theses, but for our purposes here, it is important because it was in that year that Luther began to publicly teach his new theology. Initially he introduced it to his colleagues through one of his students, who debated a series of theses drawn up for graduation exercises within the college. Justification was his primary topic, but Luther saw that this entailed a number of other important issues he was eager to address. The Bible, Luther had come to believe, presented a very different view of human beings than did Aristotle or the scholastic theologians whose system depended on Aristotle's teachings. The church's emphasis on "good works," predicated on an Aristotelian anthropology, took people in exactly the wrong direction, Luther believed; it only encouraged the Pelagianism that he was convinced had come to infect the whole scholastic enterprise. "The whole of Aristotle is to theology as darkness is to light,"[22] Luther argued. He dismissed scholastic claims regarding human capacities for free will and good works. "Man being a bad tree, can only will and do evil."[23] Paul's eschatological pairing of the "old Adam," who is wholly sinful, with the "new Adam" in Christ posed a very different view of human beings than did Aristotle's anthropology.

17. *LW* 31:367.
18. *LW* 31:367.
19. *LW* 31:365.
20. *LW* 31:364.
21. Cranz, *Essay*, 57. Cranz provides a thorough examination of Luther's developing two-kingdom theology.
22. *LW* 31:12.
23. *LW* 31:9.

According to Aristotle, human beings, like the rest of the world, are made up of visible substances; and this includes the ontic structures of human reason and will. Adopted by Aquinas, and integrated into the Christian frame, Aristotle's teaching on virtue had acquired a central place in the process of sanctification. In contrast, given the whole/whole anthropology of Paul, human beings are entirely one thing or the other. There is no incremental cultivation of new virtues as one works to replace old vices. As we have seen, the character of one's works reflects the character of the inner self, *coram Deo*. And that character is entirely determined by one's relationship with Christ, which in turn must also be received wholly from God. The focus of this theology is all on Christ and not on the person. "If Aristotle would have recognized the absolute power of God,"[24] argued Luther at Heidelberg a year later, "he would accordingly have maintained that it was impossible for matter to exist of itself alone." Nothing in creation exists apart from God, including human beings with all their works, Luther insisted. And anyone who "believes that he can obtain grace by doing what is in him adds sin to sin so that he becomes doubly guilty."[25] It was in these early debates that Luther initially introduced the thesis that would eventually reappear on the bull of excommunication. "Free will, after the fall," he argued at Heidelberg, "exists in name only, and as long as it does what it is able to do, it commits a mortal sin."[26]

Two Strong and Secure Foundations

By 1521, however, Luther had arrived at a description of the faithful that took account of their dualistic state of faith (meaning that one is either wholly righteous in faith or wholly unrighteous in their sins apart from Christ) but now he included a different (and traditional) anthropology that allowed for the outer or temporal self to work toward (and enjoy) that increasing self-discipline that is associated with the virtue approach to ethics. Though never attaining a righteousness that saves, this disciplining of the residual flesh that Luther had already described in *Freedom of a Christian* a year earlier, he now understood as a godly process of healing. Thus, a kind of sanctification has now reappeared in Luther's overall understanding of human beings under the influence of faith and the indwelling Spirit. In a response to the attack on his theology from a theologian named Latomus, Luther presented a new

---

24. *LW* 31:41.
25. *LW* 31:40.
26. *LW* 31:40.

description of "grace and gift," a phrase Paul uses in his letter to the Romans. By 1521, Luther had originally identified these terms, in his Romans lectures, with the nonimputation of sin, both words describing this action of God on behalf of sinners. Grace is what is given, but Paul speaks of it as "gift" so as to make sure people understand just how free it really is. Now, however, three or four years later, Luther distinguishes between these two terms in a way that finally marks the endpoint of his developing anthropology. In justification, Luther writes, sinners "have *grace and* the *gift* through grace."[27] God has provided believers with

> two immensely strong and secure foundations so that the sin which is in them should not lead to their condemnation. First of all, Christ is himself the expiation . . . [and] they are safe in his grace, not because they believe or possess faith and the gift, but because it is in Christ's grace that they have these things. . . . The second foundation is the gift they have received, through which they neither walk according to the flesh, nor obey sin. . . . [That is,] they do not consent to the sin which they in fact have. . . . The first foundation is the stronger and more important, for although the second amounts to something, it does so only through the power of the first. For God has made a covenant with those who are in Christ, so that there is no condemnation *if they fight against themselves and their sin.* (emphasis added)[28]

Grace and gift are now different things. This reflects Luther's new distinction—grace *monergistically* (as the work of God alone) covers the whole person, while the gift is given to work *synergistically* (in cooperation with God) to defeat the residual *substance* of sin (which is no longer imputed against the sinner). Luther could not be more clear; this temporal sin can be incrementally diminished and held in check. While Luther does not say that some particular degree of success must be reached, he is now prepared to tie these works of self-discipline directly to the presence of saving faith. There is no condemnation, Luther warns, *only* "if they fight against themselves and their sins." When Paul says, "I do not do what I want, but I do the very thing I hate" (Rom. 7:15), "it is the gift that makes him spiritual and places him under grace. . . . Sin makes him carnal, but does not place him under wrath; for grace and wrath cannot both be present, nor do they fight with each other in such a way that

27. *LW* 32:239.
28. *LW* 32:239.

one dominates the other, as do the gift and sin."[29] God's gift, which places Paul wholly under grace and thus makes him wholly righteous (*coram Deo*), also acts against the residual sin in a process through which Paul is incrementally purified (*coram hominibus*). "[God's] will," Luther writes, "is not the sin which is in us, but rather our sanctification from that sin."[30] The passage illustrates Luther's growing appreciation of temporal reality and the actual experience of people for whom good works obviously did not "spring spontaneously."

Likewise, it is clear from Luther's discussion of persisting sin in this text that he is dealing now with a different anthropology altogether than that which defines the self in relationship with God. In the case of God's justifying work in Christ, persons are either wholly righteous by way of Christ's perfect righteousness, which is shared in faith, or they remain wholly unrighteous, characterized by their own sinfulness, apart from Christ. (Either one goes to heaven or one does not; a person cannot be partly in heaven and partly in hell.) But once in Christ by way of faith (and thus wholly righteous and secure in the knowledge that one is "saved"), persons, in their temporal or outer self, yet remain sinners, struggling to be better, and incrementally becoming so. Here, Luther writes, the "strife between the spirit and the flesh begins, here the spirit resists anger, lust, and pride, while the flesh wants to enjoy pleasure, honor, and comfort." We recall that just a year earlier, in his *Freedom of a Christian*, Luther identified the sorts of discipline he had in mind; and these appear to be forms of discipline he practiced in the monastery—fastings, watchings, and labor. One "must make a total commitment, [and] commend himself to God's governance," Luther writes.[31] Thus we find the classic Aristotelian presuppositions about how governance of the body is to be achieved—that is, through discipline of the flesh. The will's irrationally excessive (and therefore evil) appetites must be moderated through regular practice. Thus new habits are formed, and new virtues are thereby cultivated.[32] None of these serve to produce a saving righteousness, however. Salvation is the work of "alien righteousness" that comes from Christ alone, by way of the spiritual marriage formed in faith. Luther refers to this incremental increase in discipline as "proper faith." This describes those temporal works done in and through faith, including the work of "disciplining the flesh."

29. *LW* 32:246.
30. *LW* 32:254.
31. *LW* 44:73.
32. This is precisely the kind of transformation that Hampson argues is impossible given Luther's anthropology, and, indeed, it would be, if the only anthropology Luther had was that of the inner, relationally constructed self as it stands before God.

Attendant Anthropological Issues

One of the key challenges to Luther's theology that many have identified is the problematic nature of his claims about the loving works that are supposed to spring spontaneously from a person of faith, without the supporting capacities normally associated with human agency. We recall Daphne Hampson's conviction that for Luther, "God is conceived to be fundamental to the very constitution of the self in each moment . . . [such] that each moment I must anew base myself on God."[33] While this does represent one aspect of Luther's anthropology (in both its early and later formulation), it reflects the anthropology associated with his early theology of the cross and is not the whole story. There are important dimensions of his work that Hampson overlooks in her description—dimensions that have generally not been acknowledged. Most importantly, with the development of his mature model of the two realms, Luther's outer anthropology supports both persisting ontic structures and an expectation that these will be faithfully exercised in cooperative agency with the indwelling Spirit. It is this anthropology that supports the kind of transformation Hampson and others identify with the Christian life.

Theologians representing the "personalist school" have been the primary advocates of the "relational" self, which, rightly associated with Luther's theology of justification, effects the inner self. Unfortunately, when it is applied to the whole person indiscriminately, it also eclipses the underlying ontology of the outer self. These theologians have been enormously influential in the study of Luther on this side of the Atlantic and, as I have already suggested, have fostered the view of Luther that Hampson presents and criticizes.

The Relational Anthropology: Inner Self

Describing the person (or self) that is relationally "constituted," Gerhard Ebeling writes, "The person, as the existence of man in the sight of God, is *constituted* by his encounter with the word of God, which is addressed to man's conscience and sets it free."[34] "What is decisive in this relationship is that *there is a countenance which fixes its eye upon something*, looks at it, perceives it and *gives existence to it as such*" (emphasis added).[35] Ebeling argues that Luther's

---

33. Daphne Hampson, "Luther on the Self: A Feminist Critique," in *Feminist Theology: A Reader*, ed. Ann Loades (Louisville: Westminster John Knox, 1988), 217–18.

anthropology depends on his adoption of the "Old Testament understanding of reality," characterized as a situation of "*coram*" or "standing before." This "expression," Ebeling writes, "characterize(d) the very basis of Luther's mode of thought."[36]

> The preposition *coram* . . . can be translated into German by the word, "*vor*" and into English by "before." . . . Its precise meaning, which is also that of its etymology, is "before the face of," "in the sight of." Moreover, Greek and Hebrew possess equivalent expressions similar in their etymological structure. But in Hebrew, not only is the situation assumed by the expression "to be before the face of . . ." maintained in a more living form in the consciousness of the language, but the expression concerned is also far more frequent than in Latin and Greek. Thus in the fundamental significance of the Latin *coram* for Luther's mode of thought, the influence of the biblical, or more precisely the Old Testament understanding of reality is at work.[37]

Personhood, then, would seem, on this account, to depend (even as Hampson suggests) on an agency beyond and outside of itself for its existence. In Ebeling's view, the self is constituted *only* as it receives itself from another, and thus would seem to have no "being" in itself.[38] Human existence, as it is described here, *apparently* lacks just that sort of being that Hampson emphasizes—a being, that is, with some degree of autonomy and ongoing self-continuity through time.

Sammeli Juntunen, of the new Finnish school,[39] rejects Ebeling's interpretation of Luther's relational ontology,[40] while his colleague Risto

---

34. Of course, this description of the confrontation already presupposes the efficacy of God's Word in the gospel promise. Gerhard Ebeling, *Luther: An Introduction to His Thought*, trans. R. A. Wilson (Philadelphia: Fortress, 1972), 204.

35. Ibid., 194.

36. Ibid., 193.

37. Ibid.

38. This does not imply that being in itself is necessarily autonomous from God. Clearly this concept of being is excluded in Luther's thought. That there is an underlying ontic structure out of which a natural understanding of self emerges in Luther's anthropology is undeniable. Some will argue that it is precisely this self that is "killed" and re-created into a quite different relational self. While this is no doubt an accurate description of Luther's understanding of the process of justification, it need not imply that the underlying structures that sustain self-identity are thereby excluded from the re-created, relational self.

39. Carl Braaten and Robert Jenson eds., *Union With Christ: The New Finnish Interpretation of Luther* (Grand Rapids: Eerdmans, 1998).

Saarinen argues that the German personalist theologians' rendering of Luther's relational ontology owes more to the nineteenth-century German philosopher Hermann Lotze (1817–1881) than it does to Luther. Lotze's ontology, says Tuomo Mannermaa (in his synopsis of Saarinen's work), reduces being to an effect.

> The initial assumption of Lotze's ontology is that the everyday conception of reality, according to which things first must exist in themselves in order subsequently to be able to stand in relationship to other things, is false. There is no being in itself. The only sense of "being" is "standing in relationship." The world is not properly to be conceived as a space filled with things that, with their own being already assured, they take up relationship to other beings. Rather, standing in a mutually affecting relationship to other beings is the primary sense of what it means for a thing to *be*. Being is what happens in reciprocal affectings.[41]

Echoing some of the same concerns that Hampson raises, Saarinen suggests that "this interpretation [i.e., Lotze's] is linked with the claim that existence in faith does not mean for Luther a being (*Sein*). Rather, it is a becoming (*Werden*). Because faith is an 'actualistic' and external relation," he concludes, "it lacks internal being; that is, it lacks *forma*."[42]

The Finnish school has been particularly interested in arguing for an intrinsic righteousness associated with the believing self (which must therefore take some form). They are less interested in the question of persisting ontic structures as such—that is to say, those capacities traditionally associated with the *imago Dei* out of which the natural "self" (at least) is understood to be *cogenerated* through deliberation, decision, and action, in relationship with that before which it stands. Nevertheless, their conviction that there is more to Luther's anthropology than "effect" emphasizes, as I wish to here, both the inherent *forma* of increasing righteousness and the freely engaged agency of the subject in the cooperative process of sanctification. My aim in this chapter is to

---

40. Sammeli Juntunen, "Luther and Metaphysics: What Is the Structure of Being according to Luther?," in Braaten and Jenson, *Union with Christ*, 136–37.

41. Tuomo Mannermaa, "Why Is Luther So Fascinating? Modern Finnish Luther Research," in Braaten and Jenson, *Union with Christ*, 1–20. This is Mannermaa's synopsis of the work of his student at the University of Helsinki Risto Saarinen, who presented it in his dissertation, "The Transcendental Interpretation of the Presence of Christ Motif in Luther Research," 1989.

42. Juntunen, "Luther and Metaphysics," 138.

show that Luther's description of the "outer self" provides the underlying ontic structures to support such an agential self so often overlooked in the relational ontology taught by Ebeling and the other German personalist theologians. Luther explicitly identifies and appreciates these structures, as they provide for that human deliberation, decision, and action by which the self is engaged in ongoing transformation.

JUSTIFICATION: OBSCURING THE ONTIC STRUCTURES

As already noted, since the "Luther renaissance" early in this century, scholars have tended to focus on Luther's early "Reformation discovery," convinced that Luther's theology of justification is the key to interpreting every other aspect of his theology. But such a singular focus on justification will necessarily employ the radical dualisms related to the *coram Deo* whole/whole perspective; and these do in fact dominate the theology that emerges from the twentieth-century emphasis on the early Luther—an emphasis that Jaroslav Pelikan has referred to as "canonical."[43] Paying little attention to Luther's later double anthropology, with its temporal part/part description of the person *coram hominibus*, interpreters of Luther in the twentieth century viewed human beings as either wholly sinful in pride or wholly righteous in faith, thus obscuring the process of sanctification Luther considered so important.[44]

This emphasis on Luther's early inclination to undermine any and all hints of pride, in combination with the proclamation of the justifying Word has undeniably worked to free persons from bondage to legalism, as it did the young Luther; but it fails to empower those who seek redemption from the bondage identified by Saiving—a chameleon-like willingness to acquiesce to every request—a failure to make decisions—and a self-abnegating passivity emerging from the lack of an organizing center.[45] This "feminine sin" is not the sin of self-assertion that Luther (and the tradition following him) worried about (as Saiving argues); thus the traditional focus on humility and self-sacrificial service is rarely helpful in such a case. In bondage to this second form of sin, the needed redemption is a new ability to act agentally in the power of the Spirit,

---

43. *LW* 1:Introduction Referring to a study by Professor Meinhold in which Meinhold argues that the Genesis lectures are tainted by later Lutheran influences and therefore not an accurate representation of Luther's theology, Pelikan comments, "Meinhold's criteria themselves are not beyond suspicion. Taking for granted the emphasis on the young Luther that became canonical for Luther scholars in the past generation, Meinhold makes the early thought of Luther normative for his judgments about the authenticity of many passages in this commentary which are not suspect on other grounds."

44. See Luther's comments about the need for the faithful to struggle against residual flesh.

against those demons that paralyze a confident, self-initiated response to the world. Redemption in this context provides the ground for growth, promising a new hope that, little by little, an active, responsible relationship with the world will emerge, on the basis of a relationship already established by and with God.

But without the acknowledgment of this second form of sin, and with the correlative presumption that one form of sin requires one form of treatment, Luther (and the Lutheran tradition) has continued to dole out pastoral care with the ever-vigilant denial of self-interest that Luther's concern about the dangers of pride suggests. In *The Freedom of a Christian*, Luther tells a story, illustrating just how seriously he considers the threat to salvation that self-interest implies. Faith and freedom, warns Luther, are both lost if one succumbs to the temptation of turning one's gaze away from God and back onto the self, even for a moment.

> Should [a Christian] grow so foolish . . . as to presume to become righteous, free, saved, and a Christian by means of some good work, he would instantly lose faith and all its benefits, a foolishness aptly illustrated in the fable of the dog who runs along a stream with a piece of meat in his mouth and, deceived by the reflection of the meat in the water, opens his mouth to snap at it and so loses both the meat and reflection.[46]

Lutherans have learned this lesson well; and any attempt at such "self-improvement" (in the matter of self-efficacy, for example) has often been treated as suspicious. Faith, and with it God's justifying grace, are taken to be at risk where attention is focused on those ontic structures (and the self they sustain) through which faith is expressed in outward acts of love. Though Helmut Thielicke will hesitantly admit that "there is no denying an ontic structure of the *imago Dei* in man, [just as] there is no denying an ontic happening in the human subject," he concludes: "The real question is not whether there is this

---

45. Saiving, "The Human Situation," 31. "For the temptations of women as *woman* are not the same as the temptations of men as *man*, and the specifically feminine forms of sin—"feminine" not because they are confined to women or because women are incapable of sinning in other ways but because they are outgrowths of the basic feminine character structure—have a quality which can never be encompassed by such terms as 'pride' and 'will-to-power.' They are better suggested by such items as triviality, distractibility, and diffuseness; lack of an organizing center or focus; dependence on others for one's own self-definition; tolerance at the expense of standards of excellence; inability to respect the boundaries of privacy; sentimentality, gossipy sociability, and mistrust of reason—in short, underdevelopment or negation of the self."

46. *LW* 31:356.

ontic structure of the imago . . . but whether . . . we should be directing our attention to it, or whether the shift of attention thereby demanded will not cause us to miss the real thing which is here happening to me, and to which I am summoned."[47]

Any attempt, Thielicke insists, to focus on these ontic structures of the *imago* inevitably disrupts and destroys the primary relational reality of human beings as they are passively re-created before God.

> It would be inappropriate to attempt to investigate the ontic base of the ego where [the] . . . characterization [i.e., the "new being" forged in relationship with the living God] is supposed to take place, to ask concerning the ontic manner and fashion in which this characterization is thought to occur, e.g. by the imputation of a habitus or by demonstrable changes of the ego in consequence of the gift of grace. All such attempts are foredoomed to failure. For the inversion of outlook, by which this ontological analysis can proceed, compels us to see man in illegitimate isolation, as man "in himself," and in so doing to dissociate him from his personhood and consequently to overlook the true theme of his existence.[48]

Indeed, Thielicke's stature as a theologian, along with the danger he identifies, has apparently succeeded in discouraging many from this task of observing "man in himself." And reputations have suffered among those who have dared, against the advice of the tradition, to seek out an explanatory mechanism (or merely a phenomenological description of that dynamic which converts

---

47. *LW* 31:228.

48. Helmut Thielicke, *Theological Ethics*, vol. 1, *Foundations*, trans. William H. Lazareth (Grand Rapids: Eerdmans, 1979), 218. In *Against Latomus* (1521) Luther writes, "He who wishes to discuss sin and grace, law and gospel, Christ and man, in a Christian way, necessarily discourses for the most part on nothing else than God and man in Christ; and in doing so one must pay the most careful attention to predicating both natures, with all their properties, of the whole Person, and yet take heed not to attribute to this what belongs exclusively to God or exclusively to man. For it is one thing to speak of the incarnate God or of man raised up to God, and another to talk simply of God or of man" (*LW* 32:257). It is Thielicke's failure to pay "careful attention to predicating both natures, with all their properties" that is of concern here. "Christ remains central to Luther's paradignm," Edward Cranz notes, "but in a new sense. The distinction is now between God, in Godself and God incarnate. It is one thing to speak of God incarnate or of man deified. It is quite another thing to speak of God or of man as such. . . . God in himself has a different existence from that of God incarnate [and] man in himself has a different existence from that in Christ" (Cranz, *Luther's Thought*, 53f). It is this distinctive incarnate God, reflected in "man in himself" that Thielike overlooks.

faith into love). Gustaf Wingren, for example, rejects as blindly misguided two projects from the early twentieth century, by Karl Eger and Paul Heinz Schifferdecker respectively, which explore the power of faith for personal growth.[49] In response to these attempts to find a "systematic relationship" between faith and love—or a description illuminating the work of the Spirit as it empowers a growing sanctification—Wingren writes:

> If Luther had shown by logical principles how faith must express itself in love, as Eger and Schifferdecker desire, he would not have developed his view more systematically. Rather, he would have replaced the reality of God with an intellectual construction and denied the miraculous character of something which is a miracle. Luther knew very well what he was doing when he merely asserted the relationship between faith and love without proving it. . . . Why is it that faith does not stop [with the believer], but becomes love which is concerned about a neighbor? Faith is God, and God is like that.[50]

This, of course, leaves unmet the problem of a faith that has not miraculously "become [a] love which is concerned about the neighbor"—or at least a love that generates a concern sufficient to empower positive action on its own steam. Taking the whole/whole relational anthropology of justification (*coram Deo*) as definitive, it does not address the very real problem of persisting "flesh" in the part/part anthropology of the outer self (*coram hominibus*). Indeed, in the interests of protecting the monergism of justification, this approach ignores the synergistic nature of these outward acts of love, refusing to address that human agency which is called to cooperate faithfully with the indwelling Spirit.

---

49. Gustaf Wingren, *Luther on Vocation*, trans. Carl C. Rasmussen (Philadelphia: Muhlenberg, 1957), 40. Eger, in 1900, concluded that "serious consequences followed from [Luther's] theoretical lack of a systematic relationship between justifying faith and the fulfillment of vocation in the service of love." Similarly Schifferdecker, in 1932, argued that "the necessary inner unity between faith and the power proceeding therefrom for action in vocation Luther has not been able to establish." Wingren quotes from Eger's work, *Die Anschauungen Luthers vom Beruf*, published in 1900, and from Schifferdecker's *Der Berufsgedanke bei Luther*, published in 1932. That these two projects failed to discover a clearly articulated "mechanism" by which faith is transformed into the power of action does not mean, I will argue, that Luther ignored the experience of such a transition, nor that he failed to try to explain it. His own pastoral inclinations dictated that this process be made accessible to those who suffered from sloth rather than self-righteousness—a consideration frequently overlooked by much of the Luther scholarship from the post–World War II period.

50. Wingren, *Luther on Vocation*, 41.

Thus, while Thielicke agrees with the Roman Catholic teaching that affirms relationality with God as the ultimate ground of righteousness, he rejects the Roman Catholic *emphasis* on ontology. Thielicke writes:

> The very fact that [in Roman Catholicism] the whole *rectitudo* hierarchy depends ultimately on the relation to God injects a personal element. On the other hand, within this relation there are found the purely ontic components of nature. The result theologically is the question whether it suffices to say that what we have here is a combination or even synthesis, of ontological and personalistic thinking, or whether we must instead insist that the personal relation is overthrown in principle the moment ontological statements are made at any one point, whenever at any one point there are set apart spheres of being which *are neutral* with respect to the personal relation. (emphasis added)[51]

Thielicke adds: "An answer to this question from the standpoint of the Pauline and Reformation understanding of the matter would clearly have to be in terms of the second alternative. Paul said that "whatsoever is not of faith is sin," and the moment his "whatsoever" is limited in the slightest degree . . . the *sola gratia* and *sola fide* are abandoned in principle. Here it is a question of all or nothing."[52]

Indeed, he goes further, even repudiating his already hesitant agreement that "there is no denying an ontic structure of the *imago Dei* in man, [just as] there is no denying an ontic happening in the human subject." Thielicke also seems to reject any created *imago* at all. In the following text, for example, we find that there is no identity with God whatsoever—no *imago Dei*—without the presence of the indwelling Spirit, as the person is re-created in faith. Thielicke writes,

> [The *imago*] is thus not a residual condition, a property in the sense of a *habitus*, but something which actively happens in the moment. It has the quality of an event. This eventful quality consists in the fact that the relation to God which constitutes the *imago* must be constantly realized afresh. Fellowship always exists only as it is achieved, only as it is realized. God must posit it; man must realize it. The continuous aspect of the relationship lies exclusively in the

---

51. Thielicke, *Foundations*, 208.
52. Ibid.

divine promise.... To safeguard the momentary and personal aspect, and therefore to express the relational character of the *imago*, one must accept the extreme formulation: "The divine address constitutes the person." We put it thus in conscious opposition to the antithetical formulation that mere "addressability" is what constitutes the person, that the person is the object of a "contacting action."[53]

Thus, despite Thielicke's agreement in theory as to the existence of persisting ontic structures, his discussion of the *imago Dei* abandons the ontology commonly viewed as necessary for human volition and responsible agency and for the maintenance and incremental development of the self *coram hominibus*. Instead, he conflates the outer self into the "personalist" (or relational) self, with its ontology characteristic of faith (*coram Deo*). This portrayal of Luther's anthropology suggests the one Daphne Hampson has also attributed to Luther. Though it is not hard to locate the source of Thielicke's skepticism in Luther's early work, it is a skepticism that exceeds Luther's own, insofar as we consider Luther's theology as a whole.

Given what appears to be the exaggerated, and nonevangelical, approach pastorally exercised by the tradition, it seems that many have taken their cue from the early prophetic Luther who was admittedly more interested in pastoral affect than systematic precision. For, he observes, there is no harm done if people think too little of themselves; but there is the danger of infinite harm should people think of themselves too much. Notably, however, Luther moderated this application of prophetic excess once he was clearer about what he was dealing with. While Luther never identified a double version of sin (such as Saiving has observed with respect to gender), he was paying attention to the effects that the new evangelical preaching stirred up; and, unlike Thielike, Luther was always prepared to adjust his approach in differing contexts. Thielicke, as we have seen, worries about shifting our gaze from that "place to which we are summoned." Unlike Thielicke, however, Luther's pastoral

---

53. Ibid., 163. Despite what he says here, Thielicke does seem to allow some combination of relational and ontic descriptions of the person, as long as such a "combining" preserves the paradoxical form of Luther's thought. His acceptance of "essentialism" is undeniable given his own, quite clear, focus on persisting ontic structures in his book *Ethics of Sex*, where he speaks, for example, of women as having an "essential image" and "fundamental characteristics which are designed for wifehood and motherhood." Men he describes as having a "peculiar nature . . . . . . [that] comes out . . . . . . in confrontation with . . . . . . the 'hostilelife,' in which he must struggle, take risks, scheme, and hunt." Whether or not one agrees with Thielicke's description of these structures, their importance (under one description or another) for human interaction with the created order is undeniable (Helmut Thielicke, *The Ethics of Sex*, trans. John W. Doberstein (New York: Harper and Row, 1964), 80–81.

concern for the salvation of his people, together with the evangelical freedom that allowed him to remain open and responsive to changing circumstances, meant that when he failed to see the expected spontaneous acts of love breaking forth from among his parishioners, he readjusted his approach. He demonstrated none of the hesitancy Thielicke and Wingren display here, and had no fears about preaching a turn inward, toward the self, when it was a matter of addressing the residual substance of sin that continues to require attention. In fact, on any number of occasions, Luther spoke of this turn toward the self as a virtual requirement of faith. Though Luther himself appears to have never experienced the sort of problems that Saiving and so many others have identified (not surprisingly, given his gender), Luther did not ignore the concrete reality he discovered among those whose response did not meet his expectations.[54] While he consistently exhorted Christians to serve their neighbors in love, he also exhorted them, just as passionately, to attend to self-discipline. Since it was the only way to discern the appropriate sort, and degree, of discipline required in a particular context (which, Luther insisted, must be nonlegalistically gauged by the person involved),[55] Luther never feared to counsel such a turn. Indeed, it is the same turn toward self-examination that is, presumably, required in the act of confession before God. Unlike Thielicke, who warns that "the personal relation is overthrown in principle the moment ontological statements are made," because, though Luther exercises an evangelical freedom predicated on the faithful conviction that justification is God's work *alone*. Nothing could be more reminiscent of the piety that produced Luther's own tortured fear of failure (to correctly generate a "good contrition," for example) than this warning from Thielicke, that though "God posits it [the faith relationship]; man [sic] must realize it." It is just this fear—that the self may do (or fail to do) some required inner gesture that will "overthrow" the saving relationship—that Luther's theology of justification is meant to

---

54. Margaret Farley has identified "just loving" as precisely this careful and clear assessment of the "concrete reality" of the other. Margaret Farley, *Just Love* (New York: Continuum, 2006), 209.

55. "I am quite prepared to allow everybody to fast on any day he likes and choose which food and how much of it he likes, provided he does not stop there but pays attention to his own body. One must discipline the flesh with fastings, watchings, and labor only insofar as it is proud and self-willed and no more" (*LW* 44:75). And again, "The body is not given to us to kill its natural life or work, but only its wantonness . . . we are not to look upon the works themselves, or the days, or the amount, or the food, but only on the wanton and lustful Adam, that by these disciplines a man may be protected from the dominion of Adam. . . . In brief, when the lust of the flesh ceases, every reason for fasting, watching, working, eating this or that has already ceased, and there is no longer any commandment whatever that is binding. Yet on the other hand, a man has to watch himself lest a lazy indifference about killing the wantonness of the flesh grow out of this freedom" (*LW* 44:76).

address. And it is just that overturning of the fear of failure that makes possible the evangelical freedom exhibited in Luther's flexibility on this point—none of which appears to be part of the rigid piety demonstrated by Thielicke and Wingren in their fearful warnings.[56]

Luther observed and responded to the real needs of the laity, without making immediate assumptions or judgments against those who apparently were not responding to the "treatment" he had been doling out. Thus Luther, with his rational and evangelical flexibility—and in real Christian freedom—kept his eye on the neighbor's response rather than on his own. Given the virtual agreement today that Saiving's insight correlates with something real, might not a double response from the church to this double manifestation of sin better replicate Luther's own contextually derived flexibility?

While it must be acknowledged that Luther, both in his early attack on semi-Pelagianism and occasionally in his later work as well, himself provided the template for Thielicke's dismissive attitude toward the temporal anthropology, this pattern is not consistent throughout Luther's long career, as I intend to demonstrate. As Luther's theology matured, so too did his appreciation of the temporal realm and his discernment of difference in the individual reception of the gospel. Even in his most polemical moments, as he battled against human arrogance and pride, Luther, when pushed, would affirm the capacities of the *imago*. We find, for example, in his 1525 *Bondage of the Will*, a God-intoxicated theologian, frustrated with Erasmus's insistence on the autonomous power of those created capacities traditionally associated with the *imago Dei*. Just as importantly, however, Luther makes it clear here, even in the context of this debate, that he presupposes the existence of the accepted anthropology (only repudiating Erasmus's confidence in its autonomous power). Exasperated with Erasmus's misunderstanding of his description of

---

56. There is something disingenuous in being so acutely aware of that which one is determined not to notice. Or, as in the case of Wingren, there may perhaps even be a variant of the same hidden expression of pride at work in his denunciation of an impious curiosity of a colleague who has too boldly trespassed upon God's mystery. In either case, such careful neglect of what is clearly present in Luther's own growing discernment fails to reflect Luther's pastoral approach that Thielike and Wingren apparently hope to emulate. Luther observed and responded to the real needs of the laity, without making assumptions or passing judgment on those who apparently were not responding to the preaching of the gospel as he had expected. Thus Luther, with his rational and evangelical flexibility—and in real Christian freedom—kept his eye on the neighbor's response, always ready to reconsider his approach. Given the virtual agreement today, that Saiving's insight has real merit, might not a double response from the church to this double manifestation of sin better replicate Luther's own flexibility?

these capacities as "nothing," he points to John 3:27 ("A man cannot receive anything unless it is given him from heaven").

> John is speaking of a man, who already surely was something, and he denies that this man receives anything, namely, the Spirit and his gifts—for it was of this he was speaking, not of nature. For he had no need of Madam Diatribe [i.e., Erasmus] to teach him that a man already has eyes, nose, ears, mouth, hands, mind, will, reason, and everything there is in man—unless Diatribe thinks the Baptist was so raving that when he used the word "man," he had in mind Plato's chaos, or Leucippus' void, or Aristotle's infinity, or some other nothing which by a gift from heaven might at length become something.[57]

Despite his irritation, it is clear from his response to Erasmus that Luther's view of temporal anthropology did not differ significantly from his contemporaries, even as Thielicke notes. His description of the human being is meant precisely to affirm the obvious—that is, the existence of the natural human being (and all her parts) then widely accepted. But, in the context of other discussions, Luther not only affirms this double anthropology but also emphasizes it.[58] In a Christmas Eve sermon, for example, he describes the way God's presence cooperates with and even "improves and promotes" nature.

> We must stay with the gospel text which says [Mary] gave birth to [Jesus], . . . and with the article of the creed which says "born of the Virgin Mary." There is no deception here, but, as the words indicate, it was a real birth. Now we know, do we not, what the meaning of "to bear" is and how it happens? The birth happened to her exactly as to other women, consciously with her mind functioning normally and with the parts of her body helping along, as is proper at the time of birth, in order that she should be his normal natural mother and he her natural normal son. For this reason her body did not abandon

---

57. Martin Luther, *The Bondage of the Will* (1525), in *Luther and Erasmus: Free Will and Salvation*, ed. E. Gordon Rupp and Philip S. Watson, Library of Christian Classics (Philadelphia: Westminster Press, 1969), 287.

58. As we shall see, Luther's work on vocation, with its careful recognition of the various forms that vocation takes, explicitly notes that Jesus' vocation was unique to him. Luther's careful distinction between the unity of all in the one body of Christ and the diversity of forms that vocation takes in the temporal realm, once again, implies the double anthropology, such that one aspect (the temporal anthropology) is not transubstantiated into the other.

its natural functions which belong to childbirth, except that she gave birth without sin. . . . For grace does not destroy or impede nature and nature's works; indeed grace improves and promotes them.[59]

In opposition to the interpretation offered by the German personalists, The *Formula of Concord*, too, as it interprets Luther's theology, carefully rejects "those who imagine that in conversion and regeneration God creates a new heart and a new man in such a way that the *substance and essence* of the Old Adam, and *especially the rational soul*, are completely destroyed and a new substance of the soul is created out of nothing" (emphasis added).[60] Not only is the "substance and essence" of the natural person affirmed here, but it is also clear that there is continuity of this "substance" between the "Old Adam" and the new being, formed in faith. In one of Luther's own most positive statements about that collection of human capacities we refer to as "reason," he calls it "the most important and the highest in rank among all things and in comparison with other things of this life, the best and something divine."[61]

Thus we find that Luther's anthropology posits a dual reality for human beings that includes reliably persisting anthropological structures. And while, like Thielicke, Luther may reveal (especially in the early phases of his theological development) a hesitation to emphasize these, there are also many situations, particularly as Luther lives more and more into the temporal world, in which, unlike Thielicke, Luther quite willingly draws our attention to the ontic structures without thereby risking the relationally justified personhood upon which salvation rests. As we shall see, Luther's theology of vocation, with its recognition of a wide diversity of forms (including Luther's explicit recognition that Jesus' vocation was unique) parallels his double anthropology. While all the faithful participate in Christ relationally, they simultaneously participate in (and express in their persons and lives) the ontological structures (or *forma*) of the created order. This is likewise repeated in Luther's eucharistic theology, where the whole Christ, totally human and totally divine (as

---

59. *LW* 52:11–12.

60. Theodore G. Tappert, ed. and trans., *The Book of Concord: The Confessions of the Evangelical Lutheran Church* (Philadelphia: Fortress Press, 1959), 536–37.

61. *LW* 34:137. It is noteworthy that the Lutheran tradition in much of Europe has resisted the Aristotelian ontology of the Formula, presumably on the basis of Thielicke's concerns. In some countries (notably Sweden), the full *Lutheran Book of Concord* was not adopted, but only the *Augsburg Confession*. This division among Lutherans, over the role that Aristotelianism should play in the church's theologizing, has historically divided the Missouri Synod from the various Lutheran communities that are now united under the one Evangelical Lutheran Church of America (ELCA).

confessed in the Church's historic creeds), remains fully present in the bread and wine. The form of this world—the body, with its ontic structures—is not transubstantiated into spirit, but remains, fully present and fully acknowledged by the church. For Luther, his distinctive two-kingdom grasp of God's person and work—fully human and fully divine, as manifested in, with, and under the temporal and spiritual realms—finds expression appropriately in a theological anthropology that recognizes both dimensions. Persons are related both to God (or Satan) and to the world, participating in both realms in distinctive ways; while the inner self is constituted relationally, the outer, temporal self indisputably exists by way of ontic structures that are worthy of our attention, gratitude, and preservation—conceptually, and in time.

THE UBIQUITOUS CHRIST

It was Luther's work on the sacrament of bread and wine, and the associated discussion of Christ's ascension, that provided him with the occasion, Werner Elert writes, to "effect . . . the whole development of the modern world picture" in ways that are "almost incalculable."[62] "For Luther it was the story of Christ's ascension—which was cited by the Reformed opponents against the Lutheran doctrine of Holy Communion—that gave him the incentive to free the relationship between the present and the hereafter in a basic manner from the world picture of his time. . . . 'Heaven,' as God's place, is not a place in a spatial sense."[63] Pointing to the polemical statements in opposition to Luther's concept of "an unspatial heaven," Elert offers this sample from the pen of a Reformed preacher named Georg Spindler.

---

62. Werner Elert, *The Structure of Lutheranism*, trans. Walter A Hansen (St. Louis: Concordia, 1962), 415. There is not absolute agreement on whether Luther's work on the sacrament of bread and wine led to his conception of Christ's ubiquity, or whether his prior view of God's ubiquity informed his theological writings on the sacrament. Though Paul Althaus writes: "The conflict about the real presence gave his Christology its final form and has dominated Lutheran theology since then." He quotes P. W. Gennrich, who writes the following: "Luther's Christology is not a product of the controversy about the Lord's Supper. On the contrary, Luther's position in the controversy about the Lord's Supper is the necessary result of his basic Christological position. The controversy about the Lord's Supper however certainly stimulated Luther to expand and specially emphasize certain powers in his Christology; what he here develops, however is already contained within the context of his entire understanding of Christ as the basis of his theology" (Paul Althaus, *The Theology of Martin Luther* [Philadelphia: Fortress Press, 1972], 398; Althaus quotes P. W. Gennrich, *Die Christologie Luthers im Abendmahlsstreit* [Göttingen: Vandenhoeck & Ruprecht, 1929], 129).[AQ: Have I provided correct citation info for both Althaus and Gennrich?]

63. Elert, *Structure of Lutheranism*, 415.

The Father, they say, is everywhere. Now ascending into heaven and going to the Father are one and the same thing. Therefore ascending into heaven is tantamount to being everywhere, since, of course, going to the Father does not mean to come to the essence of the Father, because He always was with the Father, and the Father always was with Him, but to come where God's throne is.—In addition, they maintain that heaven, into which Christ ascended and wants to take us to Himself, is everywhere too and extends through heaven, earth, and hell, and that for this reason the Lord did not need to ascend a hairbreadth from earth in order to come to the Father with His body. For in their heaven, which is everywhere, angels and devils run around higgledy-piggledy, and the angels carry their heaven around with them, just as the devils carry their hell around with them. This is horrible to hear.[64]

Luther, from his side, argues that "it is a poor wit which says that Christ is ascended into heaven. But it is not in mundane or temporal beings. . . . [They] say," writes Luther, that "he is not in the world, [and] therefore he is not in the sacrament, in baptism, and the external word."[65] To lose the real presence in the bread and the wine vitiates the critical sacrament of baptism and (the arguably sacramental) preaching of the Word as well. " [T]he Scripture testifies that God is everywhere and fills all," says Luther in the *Bondage of the Will*. "Or are we to suppose that if I am captured by a tyrant and thrown into a prison or a sewer—as has happened to many saints—I am not to be allowed to call upon God there or to believe that he is present with me, but must wait until I come into some finely furnished church?"[66] "He is present everywhere, even in death, in hell, among his enemies, yes even in their hearts. For he has made and rules everything so that it must do his will."[67] "As little as God's being ever ceases," writes Luther, "so little does His speaking ever cease, through which all creatures came into being. But God speaks still, and without pause, since no creature exists on its own. . . . God speaks without ceasing. . . . When we see creatures we realize there is God, because all creatures are without pause driven through His word."[68]

---

64. Ibid., 416 (Georg Spindler, *Postilla, Auslegung der Evangelien* [Herborn, 1594], 2:121).

65. Martin J. Heineckin, "Luther and the 'Orders of Creation' in Relation to a Doctrine of Work and Vocation," *Lutheran Quarterly* (1952): 405–6 (WA 28:124).

66. *LW* 33:47.

67. *LW* 19:68.

68. Forell, *Faith Active in Love*, 66 (from Luther's Sermon on Genesis [1527], WA 24, 37, 24).

God's Right Hand: Divine Dynamism

In Luther's view of creation, says Elert, "God has a direct relationship even to the 'secondary causes,' that is, to the world as a combination of everything that constitutes nature; and . . . in this He is free . . . retain[ing] His identity as a Person. . . . The clue that leads to all these discussions is the Biblical metaphor 'the right hand of God.'"[69] "The word 'mighty,'" says Luther, "does not denote a quiescent power, as one says of the temporal king that he is mighty, even though he may be sitting still and doing nothing. But it denotes an energetic power, continuous activity, that works and operates without ceasing."[70] "God's 'right hand,'" says Luther, is God's "omnipotent power,"[71]

> which at one and the same time can be nowhere and yet must be everywhere. It cannot be at any one place, I say. For if it were at some specific place, it would have to be there in a circumscribed and determinate manner, as everything which is at one place must be at that place determinately and measurably, so that it cannot meanwhile be at any other place. But the power of God cannot be so determined and measured, for it is uncircumscribed and immeasurable, beyond and above all that is or may be. On the other hand, it must be essentially present at all places, even in the tiniest tree leaf. The reason is this: It is God who creates, effects, and preserves all things through his almighty power and right hand, as our Creed confesses. For he dispatches no officials or angels when he creates or preserves something, but all this is the work of his divine power itself. If he is to create or preserve it, however, he must be present and must make and preserve his creation in its innermost and outermost aspects. Therefore, indeed, he himself must be present in every single creature in its innermost and outermost being, on all sides, through and through, below and above, before and behind, so that nothing can be more truly present and within all creatures than God himself with his power.[72]

---

69. Elert, *Structure of Lutheranism*, 440 (WA 23:135; WA 26:329).
70. *LW* 21:330.
71. *LW* 24:189
72. *LW* 37:58.

This "purely dynamic view of the presence of God in the creatures," says Elert, reveals "a lively, indeed a tempestuous movement [that] makes itself felt in Luther's philosophy of life."[73] And as all creatures "are driven without pause" by God, so too are all creatures and all creation "masks" of God. For Luther, writes Martin Heinecken, "God deals with man through a medium. In this medium He must, however, be conceived as directly present and active."[74]

ORDERED RELATIONSHIPS AND OBLIGATIONS: THE FAITHFUL AS GOD'S MASKS

"It is precisely the created world in all its concreteness and materiality that provides one channel for God's revelation of himself," says Edger Carlson. "The home and family into which one has been born, the school which he attends, the local magistrate, the job which he is assigned in the community, all the instituted authorities by which his activity is governed—these are 'masks of God.'"[75]

Similarly, George Forell emphasizes this relationship with God that confronts one in the matrix of relationships and responsibilities that are "given" by way of one's historical context. Through the "orders of nature," says Forell, "life confronts man with God, the creator God. . . . By the very fact of man's calling as a father, or as a citizen, or as a teacher, he is confronted by the God who has established certain orders for the preservation of society."[76] "Divine stations and orders have been established by God," writes Luther,

> "that in the world there may be a stable, orderly, and peaceful life, and that justice may be preserved. . . . [These] are permanent and abide forever. Lawyers call it "natural law." . . . Human laws are not permanent and do not abide forever. Nor are they universal. . . . When an empire is changed, its laws are also changed. But these divine stations continue and remain throughout all kingdoms, as wide as the world and to the end of the world.[77]

Both Heinecken and Elert suggest that "the Ten Commandments presuppose the structure of the 'orders of creation.'"[78] But Elert emphasizes the distinction

---

73. Elert, *Structure of Lutheranism*, 445.
74. Heineckin, "Luther and the 'Orders of Creation,'" 397.
75. Edgar Carlson, "Luther's Conception of Government," *Church History* (December 1946): 261.
76. George Forell, *Faith Active in Love* (Minneapolis: Augsburg Publishing House, 1959) 67ff.
77. *LW* 13:369.

between the commands themselves and the underlying relationships or "orders" that they presuppose. "The orders which the Decalogue presupposes in its commands and prohibitions are orders designated as orders of creation. We belong to them by "nature" through our creatureliness. In his relation to these orders God is not so much a lawgiver as a creator and ruler. The term 'order,' however, is somewhat ambiguous and requires clarification."[79]

Rejecting Luther's use of "order" as a sort of command or law, Elert writes, "If we mean by 'creation' . . . the total reality which was brought into being by God's creative and governing activity, [then] . . . we are not concerned with what . . . *should* be, but with what . . . *is*."[80] The command which prohibits adultery presupposes an existing marriage bond. Likewise, the Fourth Commandment, which demands that we honor parents, calls me to honor my specific, already-given parents. When we encounter the commandments, we are already subject to particular orders. The law refers to whether I "use or misuse" the relationships into which I am already placed, says Elert.

Elert's distinction between "what is" and "what should be"—between "orders" and "commands"—seems to overlook an important aspect of the "givenness" of the natural orders. While it is true that, in Luther's view, the conscience (under the guidance of the "Golden Rule") is one instrument through which God calls our attention to the way parents, neighbors, and authorities ought to be regarded, it is also true that, when those commands are ignored, the ensuing chaos resulting from general noncompliance also wields a powerful effect. This effect operates outside and beyond the commands of conscience (or the Ten Commandments, which, in Luther's view, are the by-product of conscience). The given orders thus provide a form of natural law whereby God also commands by way of external effects alongside the accusing inner voice of conscience and the commandments given in Scripture. What *is* also becomes, in and of itself, what *will be* if the commands of conscience are ignored. That is to say, the disordered relations (which are the result of not honoring the "orders" as they present themselves in creation) themselves become God's punishment, quite apart from any external commands associated with them. This is so because of the particular sort of anthropological and biological ordering that God creates. If infants are neglected (that is, if parents fail to rightly express the social ordering in which they have been placed), then real social results ensue such as the death of the baby, as well as those wider social effects that accrue from neglecting infants and children. Indeed, Luther

78. Heineckin, "Luther and the 'Orders of Creation,'" 400.
79. Elert, *Structure of Lutheranism*, 77.
80. Ibid., 77–78.

articulates his thoughts on just this sort of neglect (and its consequences) in his *Sermon on Keeping Children in School*.[81] In this sense, working backward from the punishment delivered through ordered anthropological relationships, it would seem that the orders themselves constitute a command by way of their intrinsic potential, eventually made manifest in punishment or reward.

Can we then speak of the orders as a form of divine command? Given Luther's insistence on God's personal agency and activity in and through these "orders"—orders that are themselves the result of God's speaking them into creation—it seems to me that we can hardly do otherwise. Nor is anyone exempt from these obligations. "It is precisely in these places, where God has put him, that his obedience to God's command must become clear to him," writes Heinecken. "Here the directness and, at the same time, the mediacy of God's speaking to man must become clear."[82]

Christian Vocation: Interdependency

"In anything that involves action," writes Gustaf Wingren, in "anything that concerns the world or my relationship with my neighbor, there is nothing . . . that falls in a private sphere lying outside of station, office, or vocation. It is only before God, i.e. in heaven, that the individual stands alone. In the earthly realm man always stands in relation, always bound to another."[83]

While the ordering of human relations is created, sustained, and protected by God's primary agency, the expression of these ordered relationships, from the perspective of the individual, reflects human agency within and through that work Luther calls "vocation." "In the earthly realm," as Wingren says, "man always stands in relation, always bound to another." But while the work of vocation is given to all human beings by way of the relational matrix into which they are born, these ordered relations speak to, and are received by, believers in a particular way as God's address is revealed "in, with, and under" these given relationships. In Luther's view, the work derived from these ordered relationships replaces a self-chosen monastic discipline with a Christ-centered call to neighbor-love that not only promotes social stability but also builds up the temporal righteousness and faith of the believer. "We find many people who declare that they would like nothing better than to lead a godly life. . . . For

---

81. "For if the Scriptures and learning disappear, what will remain in the German lands but a disorderly and wild crowd of Tartars or Turks, indeed a pigsty and mob of wild beasts" (*LW* 46:217).

82. Heineckin, "Luther and the 'Orders of Creation,'" 402.

83. Wingren, *Luther on Vocation*, 5.

this reason God has ordained various estates in which men learn how to live and suffer for others. Whether in the estates of marriage, spiritual rule, or civil rule, all men are commanded by God to dedicate themselves in toil and labor to mortifying their flesh and dying unto self."[84]

But if "all men" are called to take up their given tasks, which serve both the common good and their own personal growth, only the faithful can see in these labors God's merciful hand, preserving and protecting a creation that is precious to God. By way of God's merciful Word in Christ, believers can see a gracious God at work everywhere, dynamically active for the good of all. "But this can be seen only with the eyes of faith," says Luther.[85] It is the *Deus revelatus* that one comes to know in faith—a different face of God. "I could find [God] in stone, fire, water, or rope, . . . but without the Word of God—without faith—the God one finds will be but an idol." For God "does not wish me to search for Him there—apart from the Word, and to throw myself into the fire or the water or to hang myself on a rope. He is everywhere, but He does not want you to reach for Him everywhere."[86]

Luther's grasp of the temporal realm was influenced over time by his faith. As his confidence in God's promise grew, so too did his realization that the "hidden" God, whose "alien" work Luther had once seen everywhere (i.e., the fire or water or rope with which to destroy himself) was not the final word. Luther had come to see the world differently, but only because he could now grasp the depth dimension—the spiritual reality in, with, and under the temporal. Faith allowed Luther to see Christ everywhere, changing the character of the world he was observing. Now the created order reflected the whole triune God—a good, but fallen, creation redeemed, and grasped by the eyes of faith. The Holy Spirit working within Luther drew him into participation with the God who is everywhere. While God's wrath still rages in the world, the fire, water, and rope are no longer dangerous, since they are now understood in the context of God's ultimate mercy. This reconciled view of the world changes one's reception of one's given obligations, says Luther. One sees the given task "to make a home," for example, not as something that "takes a lot," but as something that makes a "contribution."

> Why should we think it strange that it takes so much to make a home where God is not the head of the house? Because you do not see

---

84. William Lazareth, *Luther on the Christian Home: An Application of the Social Ethics of the Reformation* (Philadelphia: Muhlenberg, 1960), 132.
85. *LW* 13:7.
86. *LW* 36:342.

Him who is supposed to fill the house, naturally every corner seems empty. But if you look upon Him, you will never notice whether a corner is bare; everything will appear to you to be full, and will indeed be full. And if it is not full it is your vision which is at fault; just as it is the blind man's fault if he fails to see the sun. For him who sees rightly, God turns the saying around and says not, "It takes a lot to make a home," but, "How much a home contributes!"[87]

Theologians sometimes describe this new way of seeing and being as a "second use of the gospel" to distinguish Christian vocation from Calvin's idea of a faithful life lived under a "third use of the law"; for this is the work of love rather than law. Here the promise of Christ opens the eyes of the faithful so they can see the world as the domain of the *Deus revelatus*. Thus they are "pushed" into the world through gratitude, but "pulled" into a world transformed by the Word. Meeting them from without and from within, Christians are drawn into the activity of the triune God through the power of the Holy Spirit. The question raised by Hampson's description of such a response as "slavish" presses us to ask whether that which believers call "empowerment" is actually a kind of coercion, and if the self in such a response is liberated or heteronomously relinquished.

Persons as Masks of God

God's ubiquitous presence once again raises the issue of human freedom. "Christ," Luther taught in his Galatians lectures, "is not sitting idle in heaven but is completely present with us, active and living in us."[88] But how does the complete presence of God, present with and active in believers, affect the claim that the faithful are not less agential, but more truly the responsible selves they are called to be? In Luther's urgency to express the power of God everywhere present, he often prophetically reduces effective agency to its first cause, as we have already seen. Despite this, there is much in Luther's work, as we shall see, that mitigates against reading into his remarks an unorthodox view of necessitarianism. Luther's insistence that persons are "masks" of God should be read (I submit) as Luther intended it to be—never as an excuse that undermines human responsibility and active engagement but rather as a reassurance to the

---

87. *LW* 45:324.
88. *LW* 26:356.

husband, maid, or preacher that their work is nothing less than a holy revelation of God's own preserving and redeeming presence.

Admittedly, this claim is not always easy to sustain. Luther often speaks obscurely, sometimes with a prophetic purpose, and other times in an effort to describe what cannot be rationally grasped. Harry McSorley, in his definitive work on Luther and the question of free will, agrees that the two perspectives "from above" and "from below" are not open to rational harmonization. Rather, as he points out, the Catholic tradition has held, at least in the matter of *liberum arbitrium* and God's providence, that both sides must be *affirmed rather than rationalized*.[89] Luther's "on the one hand" and "on the other" way of stating things is thus not without precedent. In Luther's understanding of vocation, the Christian is the location where this integration occurs—not as habituation of love but as the outward experience of an inward gift. "And so, writes Luther, we find that all our labor is nothing more than the finding and collecting of God's gifts, quite unable to create or preserve anything."[90] However, "God wills that man should work, and without work He will give him nothing." But then again, "God will not give him anything because of his labor, but solely out of His goodness and blessing."[91]

> You are to plow and plant and then ask his blessing and pray; "Now let God take over." . . . He could give children without man and woman. But he does not want to do this. Instead he joins man and woman *so that it appears to be* the work of man and woman, and yet he does it under the cover of such masks. . . . You must work and thus give God good cause and a "mask."[92]

While Luther quite clearly speaks of the effect of human "work" here as merely illusory, it is notable that persons "must work" too, and contribute that which "give[s] God good cause and a 'mask.'" If they "must" do that work that produces the "mask," is this work not a critical contribution to a synergism between God and acting persons?

When Luther speaks of God's work producing the effective results, he often does so, as already noted, for the purpose of impressing upon his listeners

---

89. Harry J. McSorley, *Luther: Right or Wrong? An Ecumenical-Theological Study of Luther's Major Work, the Bondage of the Will* (New York: Newman; Minneapolis: Augsburg Publishing House, 1969), 235, emphasis added.
90. *LW* 45:327.
91. *LW* 45:324f.
92. *LW* 14:114.

the importance of their work and of themselves as God's own "mask." "There is . . . this great glory with which the divine majesty invests us, that he works through us in such a way that he says that our word is his word and our actions are his actions, so that he can in truth say: the mouth of the pious teacher is the mouth of God, the hand which you reach out in order to relieve the brother's need is the hand of God."[93]

And emphasizing again that it is "a most holy thing" to serve God by way of one's given vocation, Luther writes:

> You are a married man and you work in order that you can bring up your family honestly, listen to what that work of yours is: It is a most holy thing, in which God delights and through which he wishes to give you his blessing. This praise of work ought to be written upon the tools of every workman, upon the brow and the nose asweat with labor, for the world does not judge work to be a blessing and therefore, flees and hates it.[94]

Against the widespread belief that common work is less important than the "religious callings," Luther emphasizes the activity of God in and through the work of the earnest, hard-working laborers. After all, the priestly class already believed itself to be a kind of "mask" of God in the exercise of sacramental duties, whereby the temporal and spiritual are integrated in such a way as to make possible the reenactment of Jesus' joining of himself (or, from Luther's perspective, revealing himself) under the bread and wine.[95]

If the commoner or peasant experienced the priest as the manifestation of God among them—if only the "religious" were allowed to drink the wine because they were seen as somehow closer to God—then it would make sense for Luther to emphasize God's presence and purpose in his redescription of the common life. In attempting to reverse the order of preference between those tasks received by way of God-given relationships, talents, and social location, and the "self-chosen" works of monasticism, it served Luther's purposes (and, as he would insist, God's purposes) to emphasize just this aspect of God's

---

93. Heineckin, "Luther and the 'Orders of Creation' in Relation to a Doctrine of Work and Vocation," *Lutheran Quarterly* (1952): 400.

94. Heineckin, "Luther and the 'Orders of Creation'," 105.

95. As Luther insists, this is a new covenant, established by Jesus' speaking it into being—in such a way does baptism also speak an individual into a new being through a promise. It is the giving of the Spirit in this event that allows the individual, in their own faith, to eventually see with new eyes a world made new, redeemed, in Christ. But the presence of the *Deus revelatus* from all eternity is one with the triune God in all that is.

immediate power and presence in and through those who take up the tasks divinely assigned to them. It is clearly not Luther's intention to produce a kind of passive lethargy, but rather to incite his listeners to a new vigor and earnestness in their labor.

Similarly, in a pastoral effort to encourage his people to take the kinds of occupational risks he associated with the work of the faithful, Luther emphasized the relationship of faith with the courage to fail. Anxiety over the result of one's labor is misplaced, since it is God who ultimately elicits the results. "I have often said," Luther wrote, "that the office of preaching is not ours but God's; . . . it is not we but God who does whatever is God's."[96] It is likely that Luther himself found comfort in this affirmation of God's providence when he considered the vast social upheaval that resulted from his own preaching and writing. "Let God see to it, for he acts through me, since I am certain that none of these things have been sought by me, but that they were drawn from me, one and all, by a fury not my own. . . . I have done nothing; the Word has done and accomplished everything. . . . I let the Word do its work."[97]

In a considerably more dubious declaration, Luther likewise relieves soldiers and executioners from personal responsibility for their killing when he writes: "It is not man but God who hangs, tortures, beheads, strangles, and does battle. These are all his works and his judgments."[98]

Yet in all this, Luther is commending persons to God, emphasizing God's personal presence and power behind ordinary labor, synergistically at work within the will of the laborer in a process that we will presently explore in more detail. It is notable as well that nearly all of these references come from his work of the early to mid-1520s, precisely the period when Luther was developing his theology of vocation in conjunction with his attack on monasticism. It was just at this point as well that he was considering his response to Erasmus that took form in *The Bondage of the Will* in 1525. Both of these interests—the ennobling of common labor and his concern to curb the Semi-Pelagianism that he saw in Erasmus's remarks—are served in his articulation of temporal work as a form of human volition through which God's intended agency moves toward its goal.

---

96. Wingren, *Luther on Vocation*, 7 (WA 32:398).
97. Lazareth, *Luther on the Christian Home*, 56.
98. Wingren, *Luther on Vocation*, 7.

3

Luther and Self-Love

Luther's theological development did not stop with his mature articulation of God's twofold reign in 1522; neither did it stop with his initial "turn toward the world." It took Luther a long time to unpack the many dimensions of his doctrine of the two realms, which he only fully expressed anthropologically as he explored the practical application of his model in the context of ongoing pastoral demands. While never abandoning his self-annihilating theology of the cross in the *coram Deo* context, Luther's revised understanding of the self *coram hominibus* allowed for a quite different assessment of reason and self-love in the temporal context. In particular, this chapter focuses on Luther's growing appreciation of the self as his attention was drawn more and more to the temporal goods found in this world. This shift constitutes an important development, often overlooked, in Luther's theology.

The danger of imprudent self-sacrifice has often been observed by feminist theologians. As noted in the introduction to this book, women who allow themselves to be used in ways that deny their own agency have found such unboundaried behavior to be particularly troublesome. As early as 1960, Valerie Saiving identified what she called the "feminine sin of self-abnegation"—a situation in which a person, fearful of refusing any request, empties herself indiscriminately rather than carefully considering how best to use her good gifts and energies.[1] While Luther's theology of self-sacrifice has often been attacked as exacerbating such difficulties, what we see in Luther's work midcareer is an increasingly careful, boundaried response to need—one that aims at a just and loving response tempered by a clear recognition of finitude. Now "self-sacrificial emptying" is carried out in a rational way that more effectively serves the neighbor even as it derivatively serves the self.

---

1. Valerie C. Saiving, "The Human Situation: A Feminine View," in *Readings in Ecology and Feminist Theology*, ed. Mary Heather MacKinnon and Moni McIntyre (Kansas City, MO: Sheed & Ward, 1995), 3–18.

Luther's revised anthropology of the outer self, with its recognition of process and incremental growth in righteousness, emerges from the *coram hominibus* perspective, which he adopts more and more in dealing with the social and political issues of the day. Luther attends now to personal experience in a new way. While the experience of the "inner self" in the crisis of demonic temptation (what Luther calls *Anfechtung*) was from the beginning to the end of Luther's career a centerpiece of his theology, his attention to the subjective experience of the "outer self" is new. He increasingly identifies life as valuable and worthy of a God-pleasing self-acknowledgment. Luther's theology, in other words, demonstrates a growing appreciation of the whole person, including the God-ordained pleasures of the body and the joys of companionship. This expansion in Luther's thinking can be observed on at least three fronts: First, he abandons his earlier encouragement of suffering and death; second, he demonstrates a friendlier appreciation of human experience; and third, we can see a moderation in his strongly dualistic rendering of God. Luther's growing trust in the goods of this world is closely related to his growing confidence in a God ultimately characterized in and through Christ. Taken altogether then, these three indications reveal not the dismissal of self so widely associated with Luther's theology of justification, where self-love is seen as "wholly nefarious,"[2] but rather a growing appropriation of the self as a distinct, interrelated center of value, toward which self-care is obligatory.

SELF AND NEIGHBOR

Gene Outka has provided four categories by which various value judgments on self-love may be sorted out. These categories are organized according to an ascending scale of accepting and even appreciating self-love "as wholly nefarious; as normal, reasonable, and prudent; as justified derivatively from other-regard; and as a definite obligation, independent of other-regard, though for some coincident with it."[3] These categories will be helpful as we think about measuring Luther's growing acceptance and appreciation of what he eventually considered to be a proper self-love. The tradition has often taken Luther's view of self-love to be "wholly nefarious"[4] or at best "derived from other-regard";[5]

---

2. Gene H. Outka, *Agape: An Ethical Analysis* (New Haven: Yale University Press, 1972), 56–58.
3. Ibid., 56.
4. Ibid.
5. Ibid.

but Luther eventually embraced a proper self-love as "normal, reasonable, and prudent"[6]—even a "definite obligation."[7]

Particularly striking is Luther's view of self-love taken from his Romans lectures of 1516–1518 with a comparable gloss from his 1535 Galatians lectures. In the early lectures, Luther considers the "double love command,"—that is, "You shall love the Lord your God with all your heart, with all your soul, and with all your mind. . . . and you shall love your neighbor as yourself" (Matt. 22:37-40). "On these two commandments depend all the law and the prophets," Luther reminds his listeners, using Jesus' words. But then Luther adds his own addition. "I believe that with this commandment 'as yourself' man is not commanded to love himself but rather is shown the sinful love with which he does in fact love himself, as if to say: 'You are completely curved in upon yourself and pointed toward love of yourself, a condition from which you will not be delivered unless you altogether cease loving yourself and, forgetting yourself, love your neighbor.'"[8] Love of self here stands in direct tension with love of neighbor—precisely the theology we see reflected in Anders Nygren's interpretation of Luther when he notes that "love to one's neighbor has the task of completely dispossessing and annihilating self-love."[9] But by 1535, we hear from a very different Luther that self-love is the "loveliest and best of books" as he once again speaks about the double love command. "This commandment," he writes,

> express[es] beautifully and forcefully: "You shall love your neighbor as yourself." No one can find a better, surer, or more available pattern than himself. . . . Thus if you want to know how the neighbor is to be loved . . . consider carefully how you love yourself. In need or in danger you would certainly want desperately to be loved and assisted with all the counsels, resources, and powers not only of all men but of all creation. And so you do not need any book to instruct and admonish you how you should love your neighbor, for you have the loveliest and best of books about all laws right in your own heart.[10]

---

6. Ibid.

7. Outka, *Agape*, 56–74. An obligatory self-love that meets concerns raised by feminist theologians is one whereby "I can only love another justly if it does not violate the concrete reality either of myself or of the one I love" (Margaret A. Farley, *Personal Commitments: Beginning, Keeping, Changing* (San Francisco: Harper & Row, 1990), 83.

8. *LW* 25:512.

9. Anders Nygren, *Agape and Eros* (London: SPCK, 1953), 713.

10. *LW* 27:57.

That "loveliest and best of books" is the love one bears for oneself; it is a change worth noting.

SELF-LOVE AS NEFARIOUS

That there are many colorful and passionate denials of self-love, especially in Luther's early work, cannot be denied. "The most precious thing God has is death and dying," Luther writes, for example, in a Lenten sermon of 1518. "And Christ accepted [death] in love, joyfully and voluntarily." This is the "true holy relic" (rather than the relics of the saints that people paid to see in order to earn merits), Luther insists.[11] Then, exhorting those who would rather escape such suffering, Luther proclaims, "Fie on everyone who would try to get to heaven without following [Christ's] example."[12] As we know, Luther had, by 1518, already discovered Paul's theology of justification; but here he is still espousing a piety of extreme self-abnegation, as he had earlier in the Romans lectures. This suffering of Christ, Luther explains, is something that "*all His saints should imitate,* some to a less and some to a greater degree, for *the more perfect they are in their love, the more readily and easily they can do this*" (emphasis added).[13] Clearly there was a widely shared assumption among Luther and his colleagues that those who were closest to God should, and would, prove it by encouraging and engaging in suffering. Luther tells the story of the young nobleman who was so very pious that he starved himself to death. Watching him wasting away day by day, Luther was so impressed with the nobleman's pious self-denial that the young monk was inspired to a similar diligence.[14] For, as we have seen, the more perfect the faithful are in their love of God, "the more readily and easily they can do this."

"The love of heavenly things," Luther insists, "produces hatred of earthy things."[15] This too comes from Luther's early Lectures on Romans (1516–1518); and his conviction reflects a distrust of all things in this world that would appear to be good and pleasurable. It is by applying a "contrary" theology[16]—where the truth is always hidden under the form of its opposite—that one recognizes what is really good. All things stand under God's wrath. Thus all things, no

---

11. *LW* 51:40–41.
12. *LW* 51:40.
13. *LW* 25:382.
14. Martin Brecht, *Martin Luther: His Road to Reformation: 1483–1521*, trans. James L. Schaaf (Philadelphia: Muhlenberg, 1985), 17.
15. *LW* 25:382.
16. *LW* 25:382.

matter how attractive to the eye, must be cast off by the heart; and that includes oneself. For, Luther explains, "No one knows whether he loves God with a pure heart unless he has experienced in himself that . . . he would not desire even to be saved . . . if it should please God. . . ; nor would he refuse to be damned."[17] Luther nevertheless does admit that he is "seeking what is good for [my life] in the life to come. But he warns his students that love for oneself and for the goods of this world must be abandoned.[18] Thus Luther is in fact advising his students that if they *really* want to achieve eternal life, they must express this desire in a demonstration of trust that denies all that is pleasurable here and now. This approach would hardly seem to warrant the description of self-denial, however. It appears, rather, to be simply a more complex expression of the "self" looking out for its own ultimate good. While it may be debatable whether such a self-seeking approach, hidden under the form of self-denial, really measures up to a description of "self-love as nefarious," it is clear that Luther, in those days, embraced self-denial, suffering, and death, at least insofar as this world is concerned.

SELF-LOVE AS DERIVATIVE

But Luther grew clearer about Paul's theology of justification (1518–1519) when he moved beyond his early piety of self-denial. Discovering that the salvation he has been angling for is already his—given as a free gift from God—Luther is released from this need to impress God with his self-denial. Nevertheless, while he no longer seeks suffering and death, neither does he believe that he is free to choose worldly pleasures and self-care. Christ's suffering still serves as his template. In Luther's 1520 *Freedom of a Christian*,[19] he writes, "Just as our neighbor is in need and lacks that in which we abound, so we were in need before God and lacked his mercy. Hence, as our heavenly Father has in Christ freely come to our aid, we also ought freely to help our neighbor through our body and its works, and each one should become as it were a Christ to the other."[20] We know, he says, that "Christ . . . emptied himself, taking the form of a servant . . . and became obedient unto death";[21] thus, Luther concludes, "Although a Christian is . . . free from all works, he

---

17. *LW* 25:381.
18. *LW* 25:382.
19. *LW* 31:327.
20. *LW* 31:367–68.
21. *LW* 31:366.

ought in this liberty to empty himself, take upon himself the form of a servant . . . and to serve, help, and in every way deal with his neighbor as he sees that God through Christ has dealt and still deals with him."[22] Just in case anyone should miss the scope and depth of such self-emptying, Luther explains that a Christian "does not distinguish between friends and enemies or anticipate their thankfulness or unthankfulness, but he most freely and most willingly spends himself and all that he has, whether he wastes all on the thankless or whether he gains a reward."[23] Christians are to give all they have and resist the demands of no one, whether that person be evil or good. And since a Christian is to so help his neighbor, using his body and its works, "he brings his body into subjection that he may the more sincerely and freely serve others."[24] Thus a new kind of self-discipline becomes important, so that one's body and soul are disciplined and ready to obediently serve. "A man does not live for himself . . . but he lives

---

22. *LW* 31:366.

23. *LW* 31:367. This text is of particular interest in light of Luther's frequent dismissal of "his enemies"—that is, those whom he takes to be already working on behalf of the devil. Compare, for example, his response to the peasants, and his dismissal of those who have squandered the gifts of Christ in the context of the plague. The explanation for these two quite different responses to "enemies" has to do with Luther's understanding of the "self/other" distinction (as Gene Outka refers to it) that he proposes for the expression of dual citizenship in the Christian life. Insofar as one is working with the authorities, in the context of one's civil office, one is to apply the law with full force, assisting God with in the work of restraining sin and chaos. Within their personal relations, however, Christians are to live according to Christ's commands found in the Sermon on the Mount (Matthew 5–7). In particular, this results in an ethic of nonresistance on behalf of oneself, but firm and effective resistance insofar as one is authorized to take it for the sake of society. Luther's failure to make this distinction in this early description of the Christian life (between a personal and an official response to evil) surely played a role in both the Anabaptist determination to live by the gospel alone, and the peasants, who took their status as Christians (i.e., the equality Luther identifies with baptism) to be binding in both temporal and eternal affairs.

24. *LW* 31:364. See also 358–59, where we read, "Here the works begin; here a man cannot enjoy leisure; here he must indeed take care to discipline his body by fastings, watchings, labors, and other reasonable discipline and to subject it to the Spirit so that it will obey and conform to the inner man and faith and not revolt against faith and hinder the inner man. . . . While he is doing this, behold, he meets a contrary will in his own flesh which strives to serve the world and seeks its own advantage. This the spirit of faith cannot tolerate, but with joyful zeal it attempts to put the body under control and hold it in check. . . . Hence a man cannot be idle, for the need of his body drives him and he is compelled to do many good works to reduce it to subjection." It is of some interest that Luther identifies the forms of discipline that he was familiar with from his monastic spiritual training in virtue. This adds to the abundant evidence that Luther's anthropology of the outer self was essentially identical with that anthropology he was familiar with from the scholastic tradition (an anthropology, that is, that had its origins in Aristotle).

also for all men on earth." Or rather (and Luther immediately corrects himself), "*he lives only for others and not for himself*" (emphasis added).[25]

Two things, then, from this early 1520 description of the Christian life are to be noted: First, the Christian engages in a new regime of self-discipline, *not* for the personal rewards of virtue, but strictly that she may "more sincerely and freely serve others."[26] Second, neighbor-love, understood as an expression of one's love for God, takes precedent over everything else. Whereas Luther initially speaks here of serving both self *and* neighbor, he immediately reverses himself on this point. One is to take up a new self-discipline, but "only for [the sake of] others and not for himself." And this will be done, Luther adds, with a "joyful zeal. . . . For the spirit of faith cannot tolerate . . . a contrary will, which . . . seeks its own advantage."[27] Though Luther has the good of the neighbor in mind, he is still prophetically focused on God. "The works themselves do not justify [a Christian]," he writes; "the Christian considers nothing except the approval of God, whom he would most scrupulously obey in all things."[28] The process by which one actually does choose and act, as well as the neighbor one is called to serve—these engage Luther's interest not at all.

A year later, however, we find the temporal realm coming more clearly into focus. In Luther's 1521 *Judgment on Monastic Vows*, he speaks of serving the neighbor directly. "I do this [work of self-discipline]," he writes, "for the sake of disciplining my body to the service of my neighbor and meditating upon thy word."[29] Notably, the good works themselves are described ultimately as a "meditat[ion] upon thy word."[30] But where before he "consider[ed] nothing except the approval of God," now the "nothing except" is replaced by the both/and of disciplining himself (for his neighbor) and meditating (on God's word). And the emphasis has shifted; Luther apprehends the neighbor herself. He has moved beyond a mere peripheral acknowledgment of the neighbor to embrace both the neighbor and God.

By 1522, Luther's *Church Postil* has the neighbor squarely in its sights. Here we read, "The works that come after faith should have the sole purpose and intention of chastising the body and serving one's neighbor." Now the "sole purpose and intention" of a faith-inspired self-discipline is focused on serving the neighbor. Luther still acknowledges the infinite realm, as he points out that

25. *LW* 31:364.
26. *LW* 31:364.
27. *LW* 31:359.
28. *LW* 33:359.
29. *LW* 44:294.
30. *LW* 44:294.

these works for the neighbor are not to be done "for earning a lot of merit."[31] But while eternity (and the theology of justification) is still part of the picture, Luther's gaze has shifted; God is not directly mentioned here at all.

Even as Luther has by now turned his attention to the temporal realm, he still keeps the notion of Christ's self-sacrificial work at the center of Christian service. He is no longer intent on the destruction of the self, but neither is he willing to affirm the self as a legitimate goal. Nevertheless, in his call for the chastisement of the "flesh," the fruits of a growing self-discipline presumably also provide personal satisfaction.[32] Thus the self is in fact served; and just as service to the neighbor derivatively serves the self, so too does the self begin to assume a new value. Luther's emerging appreciation of a relationally defined self is an important advance over his earlier piety of self-destruction.

In a case that might be viewed as a *corporate act* aimed toward the neighbor with a similar likelihood of good derivatively enjoyed by the corporate "self," we observe Luther's enthusiastic response in 1523 to the establishment of a common fund to assist the poor by the citizens of Leisnig (*Ordinance of a Common Chest*).[33] Though Luther did not write this ordinance, he heartily approved of it when the Leisnig congregation forwarded the document to him for his comments. In fact, Luther was so taken by the proposal that he not only supported the parish in its attempt at self-governance but also appended his approval of the plan as a preface before publishing it.[34] Thus we find Luther supports those civic leaders who are vigilant in protecting the funds for which they are responsible. Of particular interest is the zeal with which they protect the truly needy by cutting off "the fictitious poor and idlers

---

31. *LW* 52:138 (CD-ROM), "The Gospel for the Sunday after Christmas, Luke 2" (from Church Postil).

32. Aristotle, whom Luther earlier rejected emphatically for his focus on such ethical development, teaches truly that *eudemonia* is an inescapable outcome of a virtuous character. And while this will never be an *aim* that Luther could embrace in his call for faithful discipline of the flesh, it is nonetheless an associated good that he is, as yet, unwilling to identify or claim for the self.

33. *LW* 45:169. Though this case reflects a situation in which governing authorities are guided by reason and the civil use of the law to serve the common good, Luther's theology of vocation calls for Christians to love their neighbors with Christ's love in every case. Where love is applied as it is here, in the service of one's public vocation, it must be justly distributed among many. Justice, then, is Christ's love fairly divided in a finite world. As God is one God loving the world through both law and gospel, so too the Christian is one person, working through a single love. This love, that is, a cooperative outworking of person and Spirit acting together, is divided justly (via public office), but delivered wholly, (in those cases where one is called to love a single neighbor in a particular instance.)

34. *LW* 45:169. Preface written by Luther. Luther's hope was that it would serve as a model for other evangelical communities seeking to take up the reins of civil authority from the Catholic Church.

who are not really in need."[35] Additionally, and of particular interest, is the claim that slackers who falsify their need must be turned away for yet another reason—because this is "a burden which only aggravates our own distressed condition."[36] And just in case it sounds a little too self-interested, the document points out that "men learned in the divine Scriptures have [so] advised us to exclude and disavow [those who exaggerate their need]." Luther, too, as one of those men learned in Scripture, likewise seems to support the self-concern identified here quite openly. Furthermore, we should note that, self-interest aside, the careful rationing of limited goods for those truly in need hardly meets the description of spontaneous agape identified by Nygren and others as constitutive of Christian love. The prudence required to manage such a fund is one that takes costs and benefits into account, including costs and benefits to the self. The ordinance thus demonstrates a considerably more restrained response to neighbor-need than that described in his 1520 *Freedom of a Christian*. There the Christian "most freely and willingly spends himself and all that he has."[37]

In a considerably later piece—*Whether One May Flee the Deadly Plague* (1527)[38]—Luther counsels individual Christians to care for themselves, both to protect others from contagion in service to the common good and because to fail to do so would be to "tempt God."[39]

Here we see Luther's focus on the whole community as the responsibility of each individual—each one called to carefully manage his or her life for the sake of the whole. "It is . . . more shameful," writes Luther, "for a person to pay no heed to his own body and to fail to protect it against the plague the best he is able, and then to infect and poison others who might have remained alive if he had taken care of his body as he could have."[40] Luther's concern for the neighbor is evident here, as he chastises those who are "tempting God"—acting foolishly as they apparently seek to demonstrate the perfection of their faith by refusing to take rational precautions. As we would expect, Luther's primary concern here lies not in the one who is acting but rather in the good of those who might be negatively affected by such foolish choices. Nevertheless, the derivative good in this case could not be clearer. One should take every possible precaution, assuming that "if God should wish to take me, he will surely find me and I have done what he has expected of me." At the same time, and as another

---

35. *LW* 45:185.
36. *LW* 45:185.
37. *LW* 31:367.
38. *LW* 43:113.
39. *LW* 43:124.
40. *LW* 43:131.

expression of that same end (i.e., to serve the neighbor), one must always take neighbor-need into account. For, "If my neighbor needs me," Luther writes, "I shall not avoid place or person but will go freely." This, he concludes, reveals "a God-fearing faith because it is neither rash nor foolhardy and does not tempt God."[41] "Tempting God" by being "rash" or "foolhardy" with regard to self-care endangers the common good even as it endangers the self. Luther's refusal to "tempt God" thus appears to provide an opposing boundary to unlimited (and irrationally ineffective) self-sacrifice. While it is a boundary aimed ultimately at effective service to others (as was the prudent management of the limited funds in the community chest), such rational self-care preserves and protects the life of the one who is intent on serving the neighbor.

Parents, too (and fathers in particular), have an ordained responsibility for their families that parallels the responsibility of the councilmen for the welfare of the city, even as it also parallels the responsibility of each individual for the common good. In an interesting admonition that reveals the priority of "special relations" over a universalized agape ethic, Luther calls on fathers to be diligent in the protection of their goods on behalf of those who are dependent on them. This adds another opposing boundary against an undifferentiated response to need.[42] In his *Introduction to the Ordinance of a Common Chest*, Luther lays out a plan for the transference of monastic properties. He writes, "If the heirs of the [monastery] founder are impoverished and in want . . . it is fair and in harmony with Christian love that the foundation revert to them. . . . It certainly wasn't the intention of their fathers—*and should not have been*—to take the bread out of the mouths of their children and heirs and bestow it elsewhere. And *even if that was their intention, it is false and un-Christian; for fathers are in duty bound to provide for their own children first of all*; that is the highest service they can render to God with their temporal goods" (emphasis added).[43]

Self-Love as Normal, Reasonable, and Prudent

We have seen that from midcareer onward, Luther considered persons to be called to protect themselves on the basis of their derivative value to their neighbor. The question is whether persons are not also called, by nature and

---

41. *LW* 43:132.

42. This is also visible in the prioritization of recipients for funds from the community chest. Nonresidents of Leisnig are specifically barred from receiving funds.

43. *LW* 45 173. "The father of a household should not only support his own but defend them" (*LW* 51:174).

prudence, to care for themselves as valuable—independent of, but coincident with, their value derived from other-regard.[44] This appears to be the case, though one is always called to sacrifice oneself on behalf of others if the situation should warrant it. For Luther, it is clear that persons are never valuable in some way that could be construed as radically independent of others. Still, as Luther's theology matures, he increasingly considers each individual as valuable in some natural, interdependent sense, both by way of one's relationship with God and by way of one's relationship with the world. "All of us," Luther writes (with regard to the plague), "have the responsibility of warding off this poison to the best of our ability *because God has commanded us to care for the body, to protect and nurse it so that we are not exposed needlessly*. In an emergency, however, we must be bold enough to risk our health if that is necessary" (emphasis added).[45] Not only is such self-regard enjoined by "nature," but, Luther argues, this attention to the self is also justified by way of historical and scriptural examples. "It is even commanded that every man should as much as possible preserve body and life and not neglect them, as St Paul says in 1 Corinthians 12[:21-26] that God has so ordered the members of the body that each one cares and works for the other."[46]

To flee from death and to save one's life is a natural tendency . . . implanted by God and not forbidden unless it be against God and neighbor. . . . Examples in Holy Scripture abundantly prove that to flee from death is not wrong in itself. . . . Jacob . . . fled from his brother Esau to avoid death at his hands. Likewise, David fled from Saul, and from Absalom. The prophet Uriah escaped from King Jehoiakim and fled into Egypt. . . . All of them fled from death when it was possible and saved their lives, yet without depriving their neighbors of anything but first meeting their obligations toward them. (emphasis added).[47]

While a neighbor in need does override the obligation to self-preservation, an underlying, naturally bestowed obligation to prudently protect oneself apparently exists prima facie. For the Luther of 1527, where no authentic need for self-sacrifice is present, one is called by God to care for one's own life. "No man ever hates his own flesh, but nourishes and cherishes it," Luther insists.[48]

---

44. Outka's distinctions are conflated here, but it would seem that value independent of (and coincident with) a value derived from other-regard can be construed as a value that inheres in each individual by way of his or her created nature and potential destiny vis-à-vis God, rather than a value that is understood as "autonomous" or exclusively intrinsic—that is, somehow cut apart from the living God.

45. *LW* 43:136.
46. *LW* 43:136.
47. *LW* 43:123-124.
48. *LW* 43:123.

And those who neglect this natural, God-pleasing tendency run the risk of tempting God. That this is so, he concludes, is obvious to all.

> I hear people say, "If war or the Turks come, one should not flee from his village or town but stay and await God's punishment by the sword." . . . By such reasoning, when a house is on fire, no one should run outside or rush to help because such a fire is also a punishment from God. Anyone who falls into deep water dare not save himself by swimming but must surrender to the water as to a divine punishment. . . . Likewise, if someone breaks a leg, is wounded or bitten, he should not seek medical aid but say, "It is God's punishment. I shall bear it until it heals by itself." Freezing weather and winter are also God's punishment and can cause death. Why run to get inside or near a fire? Be strong and stay outside until it becomes warm again. We should then need no apothecaries or drugs or physicians because all illnesses are punishment from God. Hunger and thirst are also great punishments and torture. Why do you eat and drink instead of letting yourself be punished until hunger and thirst stop of themselves? Ultimately such talk will lead to the point where we abbreviate the Lord's Prayer and no longer pray, "deliver us from evil, Amen," since we would have to stop praying to be saved from hell and stop seeking to escape it. It, too, is God's punishment as is every kind of evil. Where would all this end?[49]

Only ten years earlier, Luther himself was advocating precisely these self-abnegating activities, still mired in the hope of impressing God with his pious self-destruction. By 1527, however, in the midst of the plague, and with the tragedy of death all around him, Luther's rejection of any unnecessary self-sacrifice is unequivocal. He is now on the side of life; God is in this world as well as the next. God is not pleased with suicide or self-defeating passivity in the face of danger, advises Luther, for, "It is even commanded that every man should as much as possible preserve body and life and not neglect them."[50] No longer is Luther interested in pleasing a God of wrath through a regime of self-punishment designed to placate a fearsome judge. Christians glorify God by serving God's good creation, including that bit of creation that each individual is created to be.

49. *LW* 43:124–125.
50. *LW* 43:123.

While Luther never denies that those who insist on remaining behind in the plague-ridden city may be acting in good conscience, he clearly is not recommending it. "Very well," he writes, "do so [i.e., foolishly court death] if you can *but do not tempt God*." (emphasis added).[51] Tempting God is as great a sin "on the right" as is the sin of neighbor-neglect "on the left."[52] In this situation, where many are sick and dying, Luther rebukes those who would "tempt God" by putting their lives needlessly at risk. "They are tempting God," Luther writes, "and disregarding everything which might counteract death and the plague. They disdain the use of medicines; they do not avoid places and persons infected by the plague, but lightheartedly make sport of it and wish to prove how independent they are.... They say that it is God's punishment; if he wants to protect them he can do so without medicines or our carefulness." And that, Luther concludes, "actually ... would be suicide.... This is not trusting God but tempting him."[53]

Even ruling out the most radical claims regarding Luther's supposed rejection of a God-pleasing self-love, there still remain troubling questions from the feminist perspective. Luther rarely, if ever, speaks explicitly of "limits" imposed on one's obligation to meet the genuine need of one's neighbor. In actual historical situations, however, Luther's own actions suggest limiting principles that help illuminate just how far self-emptying neighbor-love is expected to go. His assumption, for example, that true neighbor-love always begins from the perspective of honoring God's will places important controls on the obligation Christians have toward their neighbors, as we have already seen. Beyond that, however, Luther's somewhat muted notion of what constitutes "harm" provides a further restraint against the otherwise infinite liability that Christians take upon themselves in Christ.

During that summer of 1527, when the plague was raging through Wittenberg, many people sought safety in outlying areas. Others argued that Christians ought to stay to assist those who needed them. Already we have noted Luther's caution that, in their boldness of Spirit, the faithful should not "tempt God" needlessly. Luther viewed such useless self-sacrifice as a "kind of suicide," and it was therefore forbidden. However, Luther was also quick to remind people of their responsibilities in this situation; and he called on the people to shoulder them faithfully. Governing officials were called to keep order; pastors needed to remain behind to serve the laity; masters, and servants too, were to care for one another as were parents, children, and neighbors.

51. *LW* 43:124.
52. *LW* 43:131.
53. *LW* 43:131.

Notably here, it is not only the civil nature of one's task but personal vocational relationships too that call people to risk their lives on behalf of needy neighbors. Those who could find adequate replacements for themselves were free to depart in good conscience; but despite this apparent opening for the meek, the fearful, and the prudent, Luther seemed to have cut off all escape by the time he reached the end of his list of relational obligations. Given that an extra pair of hands would presumably be helpful in such a crisis, everyone seemed to be included when he said, "Yes, no one should dare leave his neighbor unless there are others who will take care of the sick in their stead and nurse them."[54]

In fact, however, during that summer of plague, the university took up temporary residence nearby at Jena.[55] Most of Luther's colleagues and students fled the city. He and his friend Bugenhagen, along with two assistants, stayed on to minister to the people, turning Luther's home into a kind of hospital where the two families moved in together; but it is clear that they were the exception in this service to the sick and dying. In remaining behind, Luther defied the prince's order to flee the contagion along with the others.[56] What is most interesting is the fact that, in his writing on the plague, there is not a hint of disappointment or rebuke toward the many who did leave the city in fear for their lives. But if one is to do nothing that will harm the neighbor, how could Luther be so sanguine about the disappearance of his fellow colleagues and students? Surely the fact that so many able-bodied, theologically trained students left the work of ministering to the sick and dying to Luther and Bugenhagen must, at least to some degree, have affected their neighbors adversely. Thus we must try to discern what Luther has in mind when he speaks of an adverse consequence. Just what is it that constitutes "harm" to one's neighbor? Luther clearly does not intend here to chastise the many who fled the city. In fact, just the opposite seems to be true. Luther himself, then, must have taken the arrangements to be adequate ones. That is

---

54. *LW* 43:122.

55. Luther's piece on the plague was written in response to a request from the people of Breslau, who were afflicted with the disease in late August 1527, only a few weeks after it had broken out in Wittenberg. The university community, at the behest of the prince, fled to Jena in mid-August, and did not return until the following April, though the plague had dissipated in Wittenberg by November. While Luther was writing this piece, some monks in Leipzig, eager to disparage the new faith at Wittenberg, mocked the university community for fleeing in fear. It seems more than possible that Luther's harsh judgment of those who "tempt God" with a piety that injures both self and community was aimed as much at the monks in Leipzig as at any behavior he had observed in Wittenberg.

56. This was the new elector Prince John, who had succeeded his brother, Frederick. Luther's refusal to leave Wittenberg, even after being so commanded by the prince, is interesting in light of Luther's frequently reiterated emphasis on the duty of Christians to obey the governing authorities.

to say, while things might have been *better* for those who were ill had there been more people there to assist, things were in fact *good enough* to meet the criterion of "taking care." Does this then meet the call for neighbor-love in Luther's view? Do these arrangements correspond to the kind of service Luther had in mind when he spoke of the command to protect one's life insofar as one does not neglect God or neighbor? It would seem that Luther's view of neglect is somewhat restrained by the measure of our contemporary standards. Luther was no "people-pleaser"; and it would be a mistake to find encouragement in his theology for the sort of self-abnegating "service" to others that feminists have identified with sin. Luther's directives regarding his own priorities in visiting the sick and dying suggest that he did not allow himself to be exploited for any useless purpose; neither did he pander to every whim. "Those who have been careless and negligent in these matters must account for themselves,"[57] he writes. Referring here to the people who had failed to regularly attend to the preaching of God's Word, Luther declares, "That is their own fault."[58] He does not, apparently, assume that their desire for pastoral attention in the throes of death (surely a situation that we would today consider legitimate) implicated those potential assistants who were safely away at Jena and therefore unavailable to help out—and this despite the fact that "it is impossible to visit everyone . . . when there are many fatalities and only two or three pastors on duty."[59] Neither did he consider himself responsible where people had themselves failed to take reasonable precautions. "It is impossible to visit everyone," he writes, "to give instruction, and to teach each one what a Christian ought to know in the anguish of death."[60] If people failed to make the necessary preparations, denying the seriousness of the situation such that they delayed in calling a pastor, Luther did not consider himself obligated to come at the last second simply to attend to emotional needs.

> They want us to teach them the gospel at the last minute and administer the sacrament to them as they were accustomed to it under the papacy when nobody asked whether they believed or understood the gospel but just stuffed the sacrament down their throats as if into a bread bag. This won't do. If someone cannot talk or indicate by a sign that he believes, understands, and desires the

---

57. *LW* 43:134.
58. *LW* 43:134.
59. *LW* 43:134.
60. *LW* 43:134.

sacrament—*particularly if he has willfully neglected it*—we will not give it to him just anytime he asks for it. (emphasis added)[61]

In fact, Luther is quite crisp, and not at all sentimental, as he directs his readers to "prepare in time and get ready for death."[62]

Real need, in Luther's view, is constituted by an unsettled conscience—a sure sign that persons recognize the judgment under which they stand *coram Deo*. If Luther could not have a meaningful conversation with a patient before her death, he was not going to offer the sacraments, no matter what the family wanted. Clearly it was Luther who, in this situation, determined what constituted legitimate need. And even legitimate need was suspect if persons had not taken reasonable care for their eternal well-being. Thus neighbor-need, even in the context of something so dire as the plague, does not pose for Luther an unlimited responsibility.[63]

If anything, we are likely to see a callous indifference in Luther's curt denial of some. This unsympathetic behavior stands in tension with his frequent application of the Golden Rule; and it reveals an important, if uncomfortable, distinction at work in Luther's thinking that needs to be identified. This is the distinction between those with a faith that is weak but still struggling in the Spirit and those with no real faith at all. The key to Luther's somewhat surprising behavior lies in his double anthropology with its inner whole/whole dualism and its outer appreciation of residual sin. From the temporal perspective, "real Christians" are *simul iustus et peccator*, even as they are wholly righteous in Christ from a spiritual perspective; "hypocrites" (as Luther frequently refers to them) are those who remain entirely *peccator*—from both inner and outer perspectives. Though they call themselves Christian, they are wholly alienated from God; and just as Luther was prepared, during the peasants' uprising, to abandon those whom he believed to be pawns of Satan, it appears that the same "black and white thinking" is in play with those

---

61. *LW* 43:135.

62. *LW* 43:134. And also, "If someone wants the chaplain or pastor to come, let the sick person send word in time to call him and let him do so early enough while he is still in his right mind before the illness overwhelms the patient. . . . The reason I say this," Luther continues, "is that some are so negligent that they make no request and send no message until the soul is perched for flight on the tip of their tongues and they are no longer rational or able to speak. Then we are told, 'Dear Sir, say the very best you can to him,' etc. But earlier, when the illness first began, they wanted no visit from the pastor, but would say, 'Oh, there's no need. I hope he'll get better'" (*LW* 43:135).

63. Nor does Luther's sometimes adamant denial of free will appear to be pertinent here, given the degree to which he holds persons responsible for having chosen to turn their backs on God's gift; for such responsibility suggests the freedom to have chosen otherwise.

whom he so callously dismisses in the midst of the plague. While a visible struggle in the Spirit identifies some as faithfully on the side of God, a godless complacency likewise suggests to Luther that they have been lulled by the devil into a smug assurance that they have nothing to fear. Thus, as they apparently collude with the devil, Luther demonstrates little sympathy or sense of responsibility for their well-being. Luther's willingness to abandon those whom he considers already in Satan's clutches offends our modern concept of inclusivity; but, in a world where we regularly insist, "I'm okay you're okay," so too does Luther's insistence that we are all sinners. As Luther points out, Christ's redemption is for those who know they need a physician; and God's free justification in Christ makes sense only to some. If saving faith is from God alone, then, where complacency abounds, God must have "looked through his fingers" and let Satan do his work, as Luther so quaintly puts it.[64] We find Luther here making ultimate judgments on the basis of penultimate actions, trusting that observed behavior reveals reliable information about a person's spiritual disposition. More to the point, Luther is acting on the belief that he is capable of correctly analyzing the behavior he observes; and in this, he might himself agree that he is vulnerable to criticism. It would be considerably more difficult, however, to dispute Luther's deeper dualism without thereby undermining his conviction that justification is a free gift of God. When Luther interprets the events of this world as a reflection of an apocalyptic battle, his own behavior takes on a prophetic edge; and this perspective comes to the fore whenever Luther believes that the devil is attempting to stifle God's gospel. However, when Luther's attention is drawn to matters of temporal import, his naturally empathic tendencies emerge in full force. This is the Luther we see as he considers the dangers that arise when parents force their children into unhappy marriages. If during the plague we observed Luther's refusal to answer the call to neighbor-love in those cases where he considered the situation to be beyond anything he could do to help, here we see Luther allowing (and even counseling) a moderation in self-emptying love in those cases where faith is not yet up to the radicality of Christ's command.

In his piece *Parents and the Marriage of Their Children*, from the spring of 1524, Luther calls "weak Christians"[65] to struggle against their reluctance, but only as far as their faith and the Spirit will carry them. Here the danger

---

64. *LW* 54:129: "The power [the devil] uses is not commanded. Good gracious, no! But our Lord God doesn't stop him. He looks through his fingers. It's as if a great lord saw that somebody set his barn on fire, did nothing to prevent it, but merely winked at it. This is what God does to the devil." See also *LW* 13:148.

65. *LW* 45:389.

lies in pushing the weak too far, thereby providing the devil an opening. Luther is reluctant to burden consciences with absolute demands; for it is precisely the overburdened conscience that cannot stand before the devil's disputation. Luther takes Paul's remark seriously when the apostle laments, "I do not understand my own actions. For I do not do what I want, but I do the very thing I hate" (Rom. 7:15). The residual sin makes it difficult for Christians to actually live up to the loving self-sacrifice they see in Christ. There is no longer any hint, in this discussion of marriage from 1524, of Luther's earlier confidence that faith would automatically result in perfect love. As he considers the dangers of a forced marriage, Luther writes,

> A true Christian . . . would by all means neither refuse nor resist such a forced marriage. . . . But where are there such Christians? And if there be any such, where are there any hard enough, like Jacob [forced to marry Leah] to reconcile themselves to such injustice? It certainly is not my job to suggest or to teach anything but what is Christian, in this matter or any other. [But] if anyone finds he is unable to follow this advice, let him confess his weakness to God and pray for grace and help, just as the person does who dreads and shrinks from dying or suffering anything else for the sake of God (as he is obliged to do) and feels that he is too weak to accomplish it.[66]

While there is a real obligation, there is also remedial help and unlimited sympathy for those who pray for "grace and help" when they feel "too weak to accomplish" Christ's commands.

Luther again counsels love over legalistic obedience, just as he did in 1522, when he sought to ease the disorder that had erupted in Wittenberg during his absence. "When a strong man travels with a weak man, he must restrain himself so as not to walk at a speed proportionate to his strength lest he set a killing pace for his weak companion. [For] Christ does not want his weak ones to be abandoned."[67] The "killing pace" that Luther speaks of here is constituted by recriminations that burden the conscience, demonically tempting one to give up the struggle. It is the faithful striving in the Spirit that must be preserved at all costs rather than perfect results.[68] Persistence is key, since to turn away from the Spirit's call to discipline is tantamount to turning away from God.

---

66. *LW* 45:388.

67. *LW* 43:120. Notably, Christ does not want *his* weak ones to be abandoned. It says nothing here about the weak ones who belong to Satan.

It is one thing to be aroused by the flesh and not to tolerate its desires any further but to walk and to withstand by the Spirit, it is quite another thing to give in to the flesh and to do its works with a smug air, to persist in them. . . . Those who sin because of weakness, even if they do it often, will not be denied forgiveness, provided that they rise again and do not persist in their sins; for persistence in sin is the worst of all. If they do not return to their senses but stubbornly go on gratifying the desires of their flesh, this is the surest possible sign of dishonesty in their spirit.[69]

Luther's growing recognition of the process and struggle in choosing the good, is significant, even as he increasingly recognizes a Christian call to self-care. Again, in comparison with earlier writings, Luther's moderated approach to self-sacrifice is interesting. In his piece *On Temporal Authority* (1523), for example, Luther specifically calls all Christians to live according to the love Christ preaches in the Sermon on the Mount. "The true meaning of Christ's words, 'do not resist evil' (Matthew 5:39)," writes Luther, "is this: A Christian should be so disposed that he will suffer every evil and injustice without avenging himself; neither will he seek legal redress in the courts but have utterly no need of temporal authority and law for his own sake. On behalf of others, however, he may and should seek vengeance, justice, protection, and help."[70] Here of course Luther is expounding on the law in its fullness, which he continued to insist on throughout his life. What is different is his discussion of how Christians are to cope with such "hard commands." Admitting that "the

68. *LW* 27:65–66. Luther is concerned with capitulation to despair; since it is faith, and not works, that ultimately matter in salvation. In Luther's Galatians lectures of 1535, we read, "It is as though [Paul] were saying, 'When I command you to love one another, I am requiring of you that you walk by the Spirit. For I know that you will not fulfill the Law. Because sin clings to you as long as you live, it is impossible for you. . . . But meanwhile take careful heed that . . . by the Spirit you battle against the flesh and follow your spiritual [rather than fleshly] desires'" (*LW* 27:65).

69. *LW* 27:80.

70. *LW* 45:101. Luther writes, "With the utmost rigor we demand that all the articles of Christian doctrine, both large and small—although we do not regard any of them as small—be kept pure and certain. This is supremely necessary. For this doctrine is our only light, which illumines and directs us and shows the way to heaven; if it is overthrown in one point, it must be overthrown completely. And when that happens, our love will not be of any use to us. . . . Doctrine must be carefully distinguished from life. Doctrine is heaven; life is earth. In life there is sin, error, uncleanness, and misery, mixed, as the saying goes, 'with vinegar.' Here love should condone, tolerate, be deceived, trust, hope, and endure all things; here the forgiveness of sins should have complete sway, provided that sin and error are not defended. . . . 'One dot' of doctrine is worth more than 'heaven and earth,' therefore we do not permit the slightest offense against it. But we can be lenient toward errors of life" (*LW* 27:41).

governing authority should . . . protect [the Christian] too," Luther continues, "if it fails to do this [a Christian] should permit himself to be despoiled and slandered; he should not resist evil as Christ's words say."[71] This focus on the objective command stands in stark contrast to Luther's attention to the subjective experience of trying to achieve such self-emptying obedience as he counsels those pressed unjustly to marry against their wishes. "I would . . . advise those weak Christians who may be unable to comply with Christ's command to seek and gain the good offices of princes, burghermasters, or other authorities, that they may put a stop to such outrageous injustice, deprive the father of his devilish power, rescue the child from him, and restrict him to the proper use of his parental authority."[72] Luther is, again, unwilling to blunt the edge of the law because it is difficult (or impossible) to accomplish. "Although a Christian is in duty bound to tolerate injustice," he continues, "*the temporal authority is also under obligation to punish and prevent such injustice and to guard and uphold the right.* Should the government too prove to be negligent or tyrannical, as a last resort the child might flee to another land and abandon both parent and government" (emphasis added).[73] Once his attention is drawn to consider the matter, it becomes clear that Luther is neither oblivious to the horrors of temporal injustice, nor does he expect others to passively abandon every worldly hope as Jesus was able to do—even though they are called to do so. Nevertheless, the realistic task of Christians is not to achieve Christlike perfection; Christians are called instead to trust Christ's work rather than their own and to cooperate with the indwelling Spirit. This is the goal of a truly Christian life. Luther need not reduce God's extraordinary expectations for this world in order to make those demands achievable by a fallen humanity, since it is Christ and not the fulfillment of the law that restores persons to God.

Insofar as the need of the neighbor is both real and pressing, Christians are called to answer that need as fully as they can, leaning into the Spirit for courage, ever trusting that it is Christ's work that is ultimately determinative rather than the perfection of one's response. But as we have seen, Luther imposes considerable restraints on neighbor-love, suggesting that any simple recourse to unexamined compassion is excluded. We have seen that Christians are called to prioritize the needs they encounter, taking finitude into account. Life, understood as a gift, is to be protected and nurtured, including that life which is one's own. In part, this allows one to better serve others, and in part it honors the natural, inborn, and God-pleasing responsibility to protect the self.

71. *LW* 45:101.
72. *LW* 45:389.
73. *LW* 45:389.

Everyone is part of a larger community; and every life is valuable according to the relationships this entails—valuable independent of, but coincident with, one's value to others. Pride, and a failure to honor the resources of this world, drives sinners to "tempt God." Luther expects Christians to properly employ the goods of creation in service to life, and to the glory of God. In rationally calculating how love might be most justly distributed, the degree of need, the fact of special relations, and the ultimate hope of salvation are all to be taken into account. Luther's striking exclusion of those whom he considers to be past the point of redemption suggests that these people take last place when salvation is still at stake for others. Luther employed a triage approach during the plague, where the need for salvation first, and then life itself, always trumped temporal need. Perhaps Luther would have made a pastoral visit to serve the emotional needs of the dying had there been others there to cover those whose eternal salvation was still at stake. It was not that Luther lacked empathy, but rather the evidence points to his concern for eternal goods over the merely temporal. Nevertheless, he did not consider such temporal needs sufficient to endanger the lives of others (who might have stayed behind to assist with pastoral duties), which is to say that the preservation of life, even apart from concerns about salvation, was more important to Luther than the emotional needs of others—a prioritization one would be unlikely to dispute. It is likewise Luther's concern for the eternal well-being of his neighbors that limits his expectations of those who are "weak in faith."[74] Far better to struggle and fail, recognizing that one is saved by faith alone, than to despair over trying to reach too high and thereby fall away from the Spirit. Though some thought otherwise, this was never a recommendation to sloth, which, Luther insists, demonstrates a falling away from faith. Perseverance against demonic fears, conversely, is a sure sign of God's empowering presence, even if the challenges are not thereby overcome. To attempt and to fail, to seek reconciliation in Christ and try again, to keep one's conscience free in Christ and one's heart yoked to the Spirit in love—these are the marks of a Christian life lived out in faithful service to the neighbor.

Taken on the Wing: God's Good Gift of Marriage

In mid-June of 1525, a shaken and dismayed Philipp Melanchthon reported that "Luther unexpectedly and without informing in advance any of his friends of what he was doing, [has] married [Catherine von] Bora."[75] The shockwaves were palpable. As it turned out, however, the theological expansion we have

---

74. *LW* 43:120.

already seen in Luther's increasing appreciation of the temporal realm took a giant leap forward in this much-maligned event. Luther's unexpected marriage to Katie in 1525 brought him profound and unexpected joy. The marriage drove home to Luther the God-pleasing delights of this world in a way no other gift of God could.

"Nine apostate nuns, a wretched group, have been brought to me by honest citizens of Torgau," Luther wrote to his friend Spalatin on April 10, 1523.[76] Luther had received a letter from the nuns asking for his support and assistance in helping them escape the community to which they were legally bound.[77] Thus Luther had arranged with the "honest citizens of Torgau" to provide them with a wagon and a man to drive it. While the other sisters were busily preparing for the upcoming Easter celebration, the young women quietly slipped out the gates, hidden, so the story goes, in herring barrels loaded onto the wagon. Luther's many tracts and treatises in opposition to monastic

---

75. William Lazareth, *Luther on the Christian Home: An Application of the Social Ethics of the Reformation* (Philadelphia: Muhlenberg, 1960), 27 (cited there as S-J 2:325).

76. Ibid., 12 (cited there as Ta 172–73. And to Wenzel Link, Luther wrote a day earlier, "Today I took in nine nuns from the convent at Nimbschen, among whom there are two von Zeschaus and a Staupitz" (S-J 2:179).

77. Els De Paermentier, in an article exploring the construction of conceptual and physical boundaries around medieval cloisters notes that "the generally prevailing motive of churchmen behind the principle of enclosure was protection. In particular female sexuality, which evoked worship as well as contempt in the Middle Ages, turned religious women into vulnerable creatures" ("Experiencing Space Through Women's Convent Rules: The Rich Clares in Medieval Ghent (Thirteenth to Fourteenth Centuries)," *Medieval Feminist Forum* 44, no. 1 (2008): 53–68, accessed January 25, 2013, http://ir.uiowa.edu/cgi/viewcontent.cgi?article=1709&context=mff, 57. Protecting the virtuous chastity of the nuns also protected the church's reputation, so that a good deal of energy and thought, both civil and ecclesial, went into maintaining the boundary. The cooperation between the church and civil society on this matter is demonstrated by the fact that the physical walls of many cloisters, delineating this sacred, virginal space from the world, were neither particularly high nor strong. It was, rather, the tacit agreement between those inside the walls and those outside that actually protected the vulnerable nuns from the world. "Nuns were only authorized to leave their convent in dangerous and inevitable circumstances [such as fire]" (ibid., 62). Otherwise, they needed the explicit approval of the cardinal in charge. Neither could a nun leave alone; but they were always to be in one another's company. Not only did this protect their virtue, but it also served to form that corporate identity which was to replace the individual or personal sense of self. Even family visits to the nuns inside their cloister were allowed only in urgent situations. Otherwise, only those whose presence was critically necessary for the maintenance of the community were allowed to enter—the priest, doctor, or those workers whose skills were absolutely necessary—and only with explicit permission. Where these rules were broken, "not only the individual who had entered the cloister . . . but also the nun who had given access . . . was punished with excommunication" (ibid.). This ecclesial ban from all sacramental participation meant an eternity in hell—a fate feared more than death itself.

vows had produced the remarkable effect of emptying many a monastery, including his own; and now the movement had breached the walls of the sealed cloister at Nimbschen. Thus the nuns who arrived on Luther's doorstep that spring were only the latest to have followed his advice—though probably also the most vulnerable.[78] Three of the women had gone immediately to their families, but these remaining nine were afraid to return to Duke George's Catholic territory. Some, like Katie, had been dismissed by their families long ago and were not welcome back.

Luther worried about the consciences of those who had been subtly and not-so-subtly coerced to take vows of celibacy only to find they did not have the "gift."[79] Thus he was sympathetic and eager to assist these women. Nothing less than Christian freedom was at stake, Luther thought; for not only was there a question as to how freely such vows had been taken, but worse, the promise to remain celibate was for nearly everyone, Luther believed an impossible one to keep. Having observed the many sexual indiscretions of priests sworn to celibacy, as well as the struggle for chastity that tortured his monastic brothers, Luther was convinced that these vows were not only unbiblical but also counter to God's divine ordinance woven into nature itself. "Nature does not stop its work just because a man has reluctantly taken a vow of celibacy. . . . Sexual organs remain active and fulfill the purpose for which God created them."[80] "I feel very sorry for them," Luther said in his letter to Spalatin regarding the escaped nuns. "But most of all [I feel sorry] for the many others who are perishing everywhere in their cursed and impure celibacy." Quickly turning to more practical matters, Luther continued, "First I shall inform their relatives and ask them to take in the girls. If they are unwilling, then I shall have the girls provided for elsewhere. Some families have already promised to take them. For others I shall get husbands if I can. . . . I pray that you also do a charitable

---

78. To help a woman, or to take a woman out of the cloister without permission, was, under most civil law, considered a capital offense. Thus it was no small task that Luther had asked the "honest citizens of Torgau" to accomplish. Likewise, it was no small task for the nuns to risk all that such an escape implied.

79. Born of nobility, Katie had been sent to the convent when she was ten with the full consent of her father and new stepmother. There she was educated until she was fifteen, and a year later, on October 8, 1515, she was consecrated a nun, apparently destined to remain at Nimbschen for the rest of her life. Katie was then just sixteen years old.

80. William H. Lazareth, *Luther on the Christian Home* (Philadelphia: Muhlenberg, 1960), 213. "Most bishops derive a large part of their annual income from the fees collected from the priests' concubines. Whoever desires to have such a woman is obligated to pay the bishop at least a gulden a year. . . . Who would ever have thought that our spiritual fathers could permit such sexual promiscuity and deny their priests the right to marry just for the sake of money?" (Ibid., 206.)

work and beg some money for me from our rich courtiers in order that I might support the girls for a week or two."[81]

While Katie and the others moved in with families in town, Luther looked about for suitable husbands. After a suitor for Katie disappeared because he had been pressured by his family to resist such an imprudent marriage, Luther began to campaign for Dr. Kasper Glatz, who had been a rector at the university. But Katie would have none of it. In an unusually outspoken gesture for a young woman in her situation, she announced to Luther's friend Amsdorf (who had chided her for being unreasonable about the proposed marriage with Glatz) that she was not opposed to marriage. Indeed, she would be willing to marry Amsdorf, or even Dr. Luther; but a marriage with Glatz was impossible. While she might well have been making a point—simply naming these two because of their obvious unsuitability (for they were considerably older than Katie and well beyond the common age of marriage)—her words must have cracked open a door in Luther's mind that he had previously kept tightly shut.

Despite Luther's energetic and enthusiastic defense of marriage, which he taught was a good and God-pleasing estate, Luther had not included himself among the potential bridegrooms for the young women he was helping. When Karlstadt was pressing monks and priests to marry in 1521, Luther had responded with shocked surprise. "Good God! . . . They will never thrust a wife on me!"[82] And as time went on and the monasteries were increasingly emptied, Luther answered the inquiry of a friend with similar conviction, noting that marriage was only the remotest possibility, since "I daily expect death and the punishment due to a heretic.[83] Katie's refusal to consider Dr. Glatz coincided with several other things—enough to convince Luther that marriage was indeed a possibility for himself.

First, Luther's father, Hans, showed unexpected enthusiasm for the marriage when Luther (apparently) informed him that Katie had proposed the

---

81. Ibid., 14. Luther nobly issued a public letter on behalf of these women, *That Maidens May Honorably Leave Their Cloisters* (1523); and his concern for Christian freedom is clear throughout. "Truly a blessed robbery, just as Christ was also a robber when his death stole from the princes of this world their armor and fortress and he cast them all into prison. We have also liberated these poor souls from the human tyranny under which they suffered. Properly and significantly, it has taken place at Easter when we celebrate Christ's capture of his own captors. . . . Our actions have been undertaken in the Lord and we are not afraid of the light of day. . . . We wish to provide an example for pious rulers and people so that they will also help other nuns to be released without fear of conscience or consequence. . . . In time," Luther suggested, "things will be a lot better." But for the moment, "the nine nuns who have chosen to leave should be respected and held in honor by all for their courageous decision" (Ibid.)

82. Lazareth, *Christian Home*, 19.

83. *LW* 49:93.

match. Eager for grandchildren, Hans's excitement must have deeply affected Luther's earlier dismissal of marriage. Luther was only too aware that he had defied his father's wishes when he entered the monastery; and he had already published a passionate confession regarding his faithless disobedience. Now he had the opportunity to obediently honor his father's hopes for descendants; and this seems to have played an important role in freeing Luther to consider the possibility of marriage more seriously.

Another key factor behind Luther's decision to marry was the terrifying expansion of the peasants' revolt. At the end of April, Luther, who was disturbed by growing reports of violence, traveled through Thuringia to visit his parents and friends, and to try and restore peace. As he had done three years earlier in Wittenberg, Luther preached almost daily in an effort to stop the growing violence; this time, however, his efforts were without success.

Determined to "spite the devil," Luther brutally attacked the peasants in a tract that was widely read and quickly denounced.[84] In this piece, Luther defiantly renounced those who would throw the world into chaos and leave death and terror in their wake.[85] In the face of impending social chaos, Luther attacked the peasants with what many considered to be a bitter and cruel disregard. Thus, by early June, his reputation was at an all-time low, and friends and colleagues worried about the future of the great reforms that had been put into place based on Luther's ideas. Far from envisioning an unlawful marriage between a convicted heretic and a runaway nun, Luther's present reputation seemed to his friends to call for a prudent response rather than further scandal. Jerome Schurff cautioned that "if this monk marries, the whole world will join the devil in laughing at him and immediately bring to naught all that he has accomplished."[86] Likewise, Melanchthon wrote to a friend in the days immediately following the marriage, "You might be amazed that at this unfortunate time, when good and excellent men everywhere are in distress, [Luther] not only does not sympathize with them, but as it seems, rather waxes wanton and diminishes his reputation, just when Germany has especial need of his judgment and authority."[87]

Eventually Luther came to believe that his marriage to Katie would please God. Sure that God was pouring out divine wrath upon Germany, Luther grimly announced, "I am well aware the devil is angry since up to now he has

---

84. *LW* 46:49.

85. *LW* 46:50. Luther calls upon the princes to "smite, slay, and stab . . . remembering that nothing can be more . . . devilish than a rebel. It is just as when one must kill a mad dog."

86. Lazareth, *Christian Home*, 25.

87. Ibid., 27.

been unable to accomplish anything, either by fraud or force. He is set to get rid of me, even if he has to attempt the worst and confound the whole world altogether. . . . If I can manage it, before I die I will still marry my Katie to spite the devil.[88]

In fact, Luther gloried in the outcry that rose up against him, as he was convinced that it was the cry of the devil on the run. In a letter to Amsdorf during those days, Luther consoled his friend, revealing his own perspective on the situation at hand. "Rejoice that Satan is so indignant and breaks out into such blasphemies whenever I touch him. For what are these [public complaints] but the voices of Satan, by which he tries to disgrace me and the gospel? He who has thus far so often beaten Satan under my feet [i.e., Christ], and has broken to pieces the lion and the dragon, will not allow the basilisk to tread on me. So, let them roar. My conscience is certain. Let [my harsh words] be crucified, let them displease those who feel superior to our efforts and the name of the gospel..[89]

Luther believed that God had prepared him to lead the charge against Satan; and now the moment for battle seemed to Luther to have arrived. He was sure that his faith would sustain him in a showdown with the serpent. The revolt of the peasants simply added yet another front to God's war on Satan that Luther had made his own. He had long worried about those who traded in their monastic vows for the marriage bed; for a hasty choice, without a clear conscience, made them vulnerable to the devil's disputation. Just ten days before his wedding, Luther was still unclear about his own upcoming nuptials. "Though up to now . . . I have always feared that I was not fitted for [marriage], I have it in mind . . . to marry sometime before I die . . . [especially] if my own personal example would be helpful for the conscience of weaker brothers."[90] "By delay Hannibal lost Rome," he argued to Spalatin; "Scripture, experience and all creation testify that the gifts of God must be taken on the wing."[91]

Thus the events came together—Katie's need for a husband, Hans's delight at the thought of a grandson, the pastoral call to assuage bad consciences by standing himself as an example, and the prophetic call to laugh in the face of the devil. All converged in a kairotic moment, even as Satan's army streamed over the hills and valleys of Saxony in their quest to finish Luther off. As the Spirit flew past, Luther grabbed for the Spirit's wing and held on. While it has been

---

88. *LW* 49:111.
89. *LW* 49:113.
90. Heiko A. Oberman, *Luther: Man between God and the Devil* (New Haven: Yale University Press, 1989), 273.
91. Lazareth, *Luther on the Christian Home*, 22 (cited there as WA, *Br* 3:886).

customary to attribute Luther's marriage to the plight of "poor Katie," it would seem that, while neighbor-love no doubt played a role in Luther's thinking, it was a minor role in a much larger drama. Luther was marrying to spite the devil on behalf of God. "The rumor is true that I was suddenly married to Catherine," Luther insisted in a note to Spalatin just four days after the wedding; it was "God [who] has willed and brought about this step."[92] Then, by way of explanation, and as if to reassure himself that his own agency could have played no role at all, Luther added, "I feel neither passionate love nor burning for my spouse, but I cherish her."

Luther had for some time been arguing that the biblical mandate to "be fruitful and multiply," combined with a naturally implanted appetite for sexual expression, argued against the church's demand for celibacy. As early as 1520, in his treatise *To the Christian Nobility*, Luther wrote, "Before God and the Holy Scriptures marriage of the clergy is no offense."[93] "The pope has as little power to command this as he has to forbid eating, drinking, the natural movement of the bowels, or growing fat. Therefore, no one is bound to keep it."[94] "So much misery has arisen from this that tongue could never tell it."[95] Marriage, Luther taught, was ordained by God; both for the good of procreation and to assist human beings in controlling an appetite that, while created good, had been altogether corrupted by lust.[96] Having described marriage as a "hospital for incurables,"[97] and having admitted to Spalatin that he himself was "neither wood nor stone,"[98] Luther's explicit denial of sexual attraction to Katie revealed

---

92. *LW* 49:117.

93. *LW* 44:179. Luther points to 1 Tim. 3:2, 4; Titus 1:6-7. "A bishop shall be a man who is blameless, and the husband of but one wife, whose children are obedient and well behaved." Also, regarding 1 Tim. 4:1, 3, Luther explains, "There shall come teachers who bring the devil's teaching and forbid marriage. . . . You will find many a pious priest against whom nobody has anything to say except that he is weak and has come to shame with a woman. From the bottom of their hearts both are of a mind to live together in lawful wedded love, if only they could do it with a clear conscience. But even though they both have to bear public shame, the two are certainly married in the sight of God" (*LW* 44:177).

94. *LW* 44:178. "We . . . see how . . . many a poor priest is overburdened with wife and child, his conscience troubled." And again, "Whoever does not feel fitted for celibacy because he has to work at his chastity would call upon God's name and enter into marriage. A young man should marry by the time he is twenty, a young girl by fifteen or eighteen" Lazareth, *Luther on the Christian Home*, 212.

95. *LW* 44:176.

96. Lazareth, *Luther on the Christian Home*, 208. "Is it not a great thing that even in the state of innocence God ordained and instituted marriage? But now this institution and command are all the more necessary since sin has weakened and corrupted the flesh.").

97. *LW* 44:9.

98. Lazareth, *Luther on the Christian Home*, 19

that he was already alert to the likely public assumption that his marriage was the result of uncontrollable lust.[99] And in this Luther was not mistaken. His closest colleague, Melanchthon, suggested in a letter soon after the wedding, "Now that the deed is done, we must not take it too hard or reproach him. . . . [I think] that he was compelled by nature to marry."[100] Luther's enemies, making similar assumptions, were considerably less forgiving.

> How long, most insane and libidinous of apostates, will you abuse the patience, lenity, the tender forgiveness of the most learned men and the most illustrious of princes of Germany. . . . Luther, leave that seat of pestilence, Wittenberg! You have truly sinned heavily in much, most of all in this, that, as an apostate monk . . . you daily and nightly wanton and chamber with a nun. . . . Obstinate and defiant wretch, abandoned to your own desires, proceed from bad to worse. Fall into the pit of impiety, be snared in the springs of sin, be captured by the net of eternal damnation; be merry until you descend into hell, as you surely will, where infernal brand! You will burn forever, and be eaten alive by the never-dying worm.[101]

Erasmus referred to Luther as the "fallen monk" and helped to spread the rumor that Luther had married Katie because of a child she supposedly bore a few weeks after the marriage.[102]

In a letter to his friend Amsdorf, written a few days after the wedding, Luther wrote, "Indeed, the rumor is true that I was suddenly married to

---

99. Ibid., 5f. On this point, Lazareth comments, "In interpreting the young monk's struggles with the 'flesh' an area which has been marked by bitter controversy in the past, two equally false extremes are to be avoided: 1) the attacks of enemies who contend that Luther's marriage in particular and the Reformation in general can ultimately be traced back to his sexual frustration; and 2) the defense of friends who reply that Luther's monastic trials were purely religious and not at all sexual. Evidence from his own confessions would support a third position, which recognizes realistically that Luther—like his fellow monks—did, of course, suffer from some sexual frustrations; but which also contends that religious anxiety over salvation was by far Luther's primary concern, the one which was eventually to provide the driving force behind the Reformation and all of its ethical by-products" (ibid.).

100. Lazareth, *Luther on the Christian Home*, 27 (cited as S-J 2:325).

101. Ibid., 25. The author of this text is identified by Lazareth as follows: "Probably not even Luther . . . however, expected that the cruelty would reach the depths to which Lemnius, von derHeyden, and Hasenberg were capable of sinking. Luther's action had undoubtedly lanced a festering sore to the quick and the poison came gushing forth" (ibid., 24). For more, see Preserved Smith and Charles Jacobs, eds,, *Luther's Correspondence and Other Contemporary Letters*, 2 vols. (Philadelphia" Lutheran Publication Society, 1913–18).

102. Lazareth, *Luther on the Christian Home*, 24.

Catherine. [I did this] to silence the evil mouths which are so used to complaining about me. For I still hope to live for a little while. In addition, I also did not want to reject this unique [opportunity to obey] my father's wish for progeny, which he so often expressed.[103] At the same time, I also wanted to confirm what I have taught by practicing it; for I find so many timid people in spite of such great light from the gospel."[104] Then, almost as an afterthought, Luther added, "God willed me to take pity on the poor abandoned girl."[105] Heiko Oberman, reflecting on Luther's marriage to Katie, suggests that "defiance of the devil is probably the worst reason for marriage ever recorded."[106] Even in its own historical context (where romantic love was not yet part of the picture), this was not an auspicious beginning.

SURPRISED BY JOY

"It was an open secret in Wittenberg that Martin and Katie did not get along very well because of their clashing temperaments and personalities," writes William Lazareth.[107] And perhaps during these first weeks following the wedding Luther may have had second thoughts; for shortly afterward, Melanchthon remarked to a friend, "When I see Luther in low spirits and disturbed about his change of life, I make the best efforts to console him kindly."[108] Nevertheless, Luther celebrated the event publicly and with great spirit. In an invitation to the fete sent to a local *braumeister*, he wrote, "[So] that my parents and all good friends may be merry, my Lord Catherine and I kindly beg you to send us, at my cost and as quickly as possible, a barrel of the best Torgau beer. . . . I also beg you and your wife not to stay away but happily to appear." Another reads, "I beg that you will come and give your blessings. . . . [And] bring any friends!"[109] Luther appears to have been rather pleased with events despite the concerns of his friends.

There were, of course, awkward moments in the first year of marriage. Nevertheless, the couple surprised everyone with their unexpected compatibility and deepening love for one another.[110] "In this first year," Luther

---

103. *LW* 49:117. See n5: "Luther made a similar statement in his letter to John Ruhel and others, dated June 15, 1525; WA, *Br* 3, 531; S-J 2, 323."

104. *LW* 49:117.

105. Lazareth, *Luther on the Christian Home*, 23.

106. Oberman, *Luther*, 280.

107. Lazareth, *Luther on the Christian Home*, 22.

108. Ibid., 26–27 (cited there as SJ 2:325).

109. Ibid., 23.

later recalled, "my Katie used to sit down next to me while I was studying and, not knowing what to say, would begin to ask questions like: "Dear doctor, is the prime minister of Prussia the duke's brother? . . . Man has strange thoughts. . . . He suddenly thinks, 'Before you were alone, now you are two.' Or, in bed, when he awakens, he sees [a braid] lying next to him that he never saw before."[111]

Katie brought order and a new peace into Luther's life. She also made sure that he ate well and regularly. In the midst of the social chaos swirling around Luther during that summer of 1525, the orderly household that Katie quickly established must have seemed a veritable paradise. "Before I married," Luther recalled later, "the bed was not made up for a whole year and became foul with sweat. But I worked all day and was so tired at night that I fell into bed without knowing that anything was amiss."[112] Managing the Luther home was no easy task. The old cloister that was given to Martin and Katie to use as their home was in need of repair. Though they were given one hundred gulden by the prince to celebrate their marriage, all the money went into repair and renovation of the old monastery. Luther received but nine gulden a year for his preaching in the city church. In 1524, the prince instituted an annual salary for Luther's teaching of one hundred gulden a year, and this was soon raised to two hundred a year in order to give him as much as Melanchthon. But the Black Cloister[113] was often filled with guests, extended family, and students, and they all had to be fed. Luther gauged his costs to be around five hundred a year; and it was up to Katie to somehow make do. Her managerial skills were legendary; and Luther was both impressed and grateful for the extraordinary talents his new wife brought to the partnership. She took over the finances and found ways to supplement their income with the purchase of a farm that helped to keep the pantry laden and the multitude of guests fed who joined them at table. Katie also brewed her own beer, took in lodgers, and even tried her hand at breeding swine.[114] A neighbor described the Luther home as being "occupied by a motley crowd of boys, students, girls, widows, old women, and youngsters. . . . There is much disturbance in the place; . . . [and though] his house would offer you an agreeable, friendly quarter for a few days . . . I would not advise that your Grace [Prince George of Anhalt] stop there."[115]

110. Ibid., 23.
111. Ibid., 30
112. Ibid., 28.
113. The old Augustinian monastery was commonly referred to as the "Black Cloister" because of the black garb worn by the monks.
114. Oberman, *Luther*, 279–80.

A year after Martin and Katie were wed, the first of six children arrived. Whatever doubts Luther might have been harboring early on in the marriage disappeared. Whereas he had long been aware of his father's desire for grandchildren, he was unprepared for the joy he experienced at the birth of this first son. In a letter to Spalatin, Luther wrote, "I thank you in the Lord for the hearty congratulations which you have sent me. I am a happy husband and may God continue to send me happiness, for from the most gracious woman, my best of wives, I have received, by the blessings of God, a little son, Hans Luther, and by God's wonderful grace, I have become a father."[116] The pleasure Luther took in his children is legendary; in 1527, he proudly announced to Spalatin that little Hans "is in the teething month and is beginning to say 'Daddy.'"[117] In his letters, Luther regularly greeted his children in the most tender of terms. "Kiss young Hans for me," he wrote to Katie, "and keep after Hanschen, Lenehen, and Aunt Lena to pray. . . . I am unable to find anything to buy for the children in this town even though there is now a fair here. . . . Please have something ready for me!"[118] Luther mentioned having received letters from the children and then, teasing Katie, he added, "but from Your Grace I have received nothing."[119] One of his most famous letters was written to Hans, then age four. Luther tells the boy about a "pretty, beautiful, cheerful garden where there are little children wearing golden coats." There they sing and dance and romp about. They ride nice ponies with golden reigns and silver saddles and pick "fine apples, pears, cherries [and] yellow and blue plums under the trees." In closing Luther asks the boy to "Greet Aunt Lena, . . . and give her a kiss for me." He signs the letter, "Your loving father, Martin Luther."[120]

Luther took very seriously the vocation of raising up children well; and his acceptance of those temporal ontic structures required for the formation of virtue was supported by his attention to a firm, if loving, discipline of his children. "I am sending my son John to you so that you may add him to the boys who are to be drilled in grammar and music," Luther wrote to his

---

115. William Lazareth, "Testimony of Faith: The Genesis of Luther's Marriage Ethic Seen Against the Background of His Early Theological Development (1517–1525)" (Joint Committee on Graduate Instruction, Columbia University, 1958), 295 (cited as Schwiebert, E.G., *Luther and His Times* [St. Louis: Concordia, 1950], 597).

116. Lazareth, *Luther on the Christian Home*, 31.

117. Lazareth, "Testimony of Faith," 297.

118. *LW* 50:49. In another letter to Katie, Luther speaks of sending back "the silver apple which my Gracious Lord presented to me. . . . You may divide it among the children and ask them how many cherries and apples they would wish in exchange of it: give them these at once" (*LW* 50:209).

119. *LW* 50:120.

120. *LW* 49:324.

friend Marcus Crodel. "I have added the boy, Florian . . . these boys need the example set by a crowd of many boys . . . but be very strict with this one. . . . Soon, if I live, you will also have my other two sons. For I think that after you there will be no teachers as diligent . . . especially in grammar and in strictness so far as conduct is concerned."[121] Florian, one of Katie's nephews, joined the Luther family after his father's death, and apparently he required an extra dose of Crodel's diligence, at least in Luther's view. There is "no greater or nobler authority on earth," wrote Luther, "than that of parents over their children."[122] "God has done marriage the honor of putting it into the Fourth Commandment," he wrote. "Show me an honor in heaven or on earth, apart from the honor of God, that can equal this honor! . . . And if God had told us nothing more about married life than this Fourth Commandment, we should still have learned sufficiently from it alone that in the sight of God there is no higher office, estate, condition, or work (next to the gospel, which concerns God himself) than the estate of marriage."[123]

Whereas Luther's initial defense of marriage was all on the basis of its value in restraining sin—an approach that took marriage out of the church and put it squarely under the rule of civil and natural law—by 1523 he had arrived at an evangelical view of marriage that incorporated his theology of vocation.[124] Marriage, like the other vocations, provided that location where the two realms interpenetrate in the outworking of faith. The inclusion of the Holy Spirit in this mature theology of marriage became the opening for Luther's deepening appreciation and joy—his growing ability to take pleasure in such an outstanding temporal gift.

And in all of this, Katie was at the center. In a sermon from 1530 on adultery, Luther makes the Christian distinction clear. Without the Holy Spirit one lives under the law, either failing to keep it, and thereby producing a bad conscience, or congratulating oneself on one's purity, thereby producing a self-righteous distancing from God. "Christ," wrote Luther, was "the opposite of both of these ways."[125] According to Luther, the problem was that "one cannot see God's word in one's spouse[--cannot], see them as God's gift and blessing. . . . [And] the devil plays on this."[126] It is an "art to see [one's] spouse as the

---

121. *LW* 50:232.
122. *LW* 45:46.
123. *LW* 45:154.
124. Lazareth, "Testimony of Faith," 234.
125. Susan C. Karant-Nunn, *Luther on Women: A Sourcebook* (Cambridge: Cambridge University Press, 2003), 143 (cited there as *Weekly Sermons on Matthew* 5–7, 15.30/15.32, WA 32:369–75).
126. Ibid., 144.

beautiful jewel that God has made her to be."[127] I would not trade my Katie for France or Venice together."[128] What had begun as a relationship of respect between Martin and Katie eventually blossomed with time into a profoundly loving companionship that continued to deepen and grow over the years.

After 1522, Luther's health declined precipitously, and it may well be that Katie's care added years to his life.[129] The details of Luther's maladies are widely known. He showed no hesitation in sharing regular updates on his health with Katie and others in his circle; and Katie became adept at ministering to her husband. On several occasions, Luther's bouts with kidney stones and constipation nearly killed him. One of these attacks occurred while Luther was in Smalcald. He was so close to death that Katie had been summoned, and his companions were already carefully chronicling his final words for the sake of posterity. "Oh how passionately I yearned for my family as I lay at death's door,"[130] Luther would recall later.

> I thought that I would never see my wife and little children again. How much pain that distance and separation caused me! I believe that dying people must know the greatest natural love and affection of all, as when a man remembers his wife and a parent thinks of his children. Since, by God's grace, I have recovered, I now love my dear wife and children all the more. No one is so spiritual that he does not feel this natural love and affection; it provides great strength to the bond of fellowship which exists between a man and his wife.[131]

Luther's deep love for his family was especially visible in August 1528, at the death of his eight-month-old daughter. "My baby daughter, little Elizabeth, has passed away," he wrote to a friend. "It is amazing what a sick, almost woman-like heart she has left to me, so much has grief for her overcome me. Never before would I have believed that a father's heart could have such tender feelings for his child."[132] The following May, another daughter was born, and Luther rejoiced over the relatively easy birth and the healthy child. "Three hours after I had written the [last] letter," Luther wrote to a friend, Katie "gave birth to a healthy baby daughter without difficulties. The Lord has blessed us so

---

127. Ibid., 32 (cited there as WA, *Tr* 2:2350a–b).
128. Oberman, 280.
129. Lazareth, *Luther on the Christian Home*, 28.
130. Ibid., 32.
131. Ibid.
132. *LW* 49:203. This text is from a short note Luther wrote in thanks for a rattle that had been sent as a gift for his son John.

richly that she had an uncomplicated delivery. . . . The Father of all grace has graciously presented a baby daughter to me and my dear Katie."[133] Magdalene, or "my little Lenschen," as Luther fondly called her, was the youngest of their three children, and clearly a favorite, perhaps in part because she arrived so quickly after the death of her older sister. About a year later, when Luther was away in Coburg, Katie must have sent a picture of the child to Luther; for we hear from one of his companions who wanted Katie to know that "you did something very good when you sent the picture to Doctor [Luther], for the picture [helps] him to forget many troubling thoughts. He has attached it to the wall opposite the table in the . . . chamber where we eat."[134] In a letter Luther sent to Katie at this same time, it is clear just how engaged Luther was in the life of little Magdalene. After telling Katie that he had received the picture she sent, Luther took up what must have been a long-distance discussion about the baby's care and feeding. "I think it would be good if you want [to stop nursing her], [but] gradually, so that at first you omit one feeding per day, then two feedings per day, until [she] clearly stops [nursing by herself]."[135] It was apparently important to Luther that the process of weaning not be unpleasant for the child. Indeed, the discussion reflects paternal involvement that one finds among modern American couples today, but no doubt was unusual in early sixteenth-century Europe. Lucas Cranach painted another picture of Magdalene when she was about twelve years old, surely a mark of her importance within the family.

Thus the sorrow that both Katie and Martin felt when Magdalene fell ill and died at the age of thirteen is almost incalculable. The tenderness Luther expressed is noteworthy. A friend who was in the room reported that

> when she was lying in bed, he said to his daughter, "Magdalene, my little daughter, you would gladly remain here with me. . . . Are you also glad to go to your Father in heaven?" The sick girl replied; "Yes, dear father, as God wills." The father said, "Dear daughter!" [And] turning away from her, he said, "The spirit is willing, but the flesh is weak. I love her very much . . . I am angry at myself that I am unable to rejoice from my heart and be thankful to God." . . . When his wife wept loudly, Martin . . . comforted her by saying: "Remember where she is going. It will be well with her. The flesh dies but the spirit lives." When his daughter was in the agony of death, he fell upon his

133. *LW* 49:19.
134. *LW* 49:312–313, note 6.
135. *LW* 49:312.

knees before the bed and, weeping bitterly, prayed that God might save her if it be his will. Thus she gave up the ghost in the arms of her father.[136]

Three years later, in a letter written to console a friend on the death of his wife and daughter, Luther wrote again of his pain. "It may appear strange, but I am still mourning the death of my dear Magdalene, and I am not able to forget her. Yet I know surely that she is in heaven . . . and that God has thereby given me a true token of his love in having, even while I live, taken my flesh and blood to his Fatherly heart."[137]

Luther had come a great distance since he thought this world was "nothing, because it is worth nothing." When still a young monk, he had discovered God's free salvation in Christ; and it was, he said, "as if the gates of paradise were thrown open." Now that he was a grieving father, he had been welcomed inside. Even as he wept for the beloved daughter he lost, he rejoiced, because God had "taken [his] flesh and blood to his Fatherly heart." Whereas Luther was once convinced that there was no place for him in the "beautiful garden," he now saw the doors open before him and felt welcomed into God's embrace. Luther now knew intimately the love a father has for his child. The "for you" Luther insisted upon in the Eucharist became absolutely real in this gathering in of his own created body by way of his "little Lenchen"—an action Luther took as God's "true token of his love." Luther's personal experience of God by this time more nearly reflected his unique eucharistic theology; for there Luther affirmed Christ's true body and blood "in, with, and under" the real bread and wine that does not "transubstantiate" the "essence" of the bread and wine away. Rather, these bits of God's good creation are fully honored in Holy Communion. Likewise, Luther's understanding of the self as something that is worthy of God's love was confirmed.

An Expanded Vision of God

It is often said that Lutheran theology depends on a proper distinction between law and gospel.[138] Indeed, Luther himself said it frequently. Either the law accuses and kills, or a promise redeems and re-creates. These two forms of God's address are to be carefully distinguished in their work on the subject. We find in Luther's later work, however, a growing convergence between Luther's

---

136. *Luther: Letters of Spiritual Counsel*, ed. and trans. Theodore Tappert, Library of Christian Classics 18 (Philadelphia: Westminster Press, 1955), 51.
137. Ibid., 80.

early dualistic rendering of a wrathful God (condemning under the law), and its opposite, the God of mercy and love (freely redeeming in Christ). While Luther continued to articulate that love was received as wrath when it was refracted through the law (as it engages unbelievers), his growing confidence that wrath was finally an expression of God's love enlarged his rendering of the law. Luther wrote in his Genesis lectures (1535–1545): "Consider His physical blessings that the Lord has granted us this world to enjoy; that He has given us wife, home, and children; that He preserves all these and increases them by His blessing—tell me, will you not endure with a calm mind whatever physical hardships may come, and say that this is a fatherly anger and not that of a judge or a tyrant?"[139]

We can observe the meeting of wrath and mercy worked out in his discussion of Genesis 3 (that is, in Luther's explanation of the consequences of Adam and Eve's disobedience).[140] Eve would find difficulties in child-bearing and Adam, in tilling the soil; but these "punishments" are coupled with the promise that their sin would one day be overcome by way of a child born to woman. "Even then," Luther wrote, "Christ, our Deliverer, had [already] placed Himself between God and man as a Mediator."[141] Thus, "in those very

---

138. Heiko Oberman has explicitly argued that the intensity of Luther's *Anfechtungen* did not let up in his later years—if anything, it increased—and Oberman's evidence for this is compelling. (See Oberman, p. 313f.) The argument that Luther's embrace of the world shifted over time, as his confidence God's mercy (or, his grasp of the *Deus revelatus*) strengthened, does not conflict with Oberman's evidence that the devil's assaults continued to plague Luther to the end of his life. Rather, the greater grasp of God's mercy would, in Luther's thinking, be likely to result in the intensification of doubt, brought on by the devil's disputation. After all, as Luther often noted, the devil hates it when Christ gets the upper hand. This "strengthening" of faith is visible in Luther's discovery that the mercy one discovers in Christ, *coram Deo*, is also manifest in and through the created order, *coram hominibus*, experienced as a divine love that categorically expands beyond the divine mercy identified with justification. Thus, the expansion of Luther's theology, which increasingly focuses on God's creating and sanctifying work, need not be seen as a dismissal of the dramatic redemptive work accomplished in Christ, since it is in the context of God's redemptive work that the devil's *Anfechtungen* emerges most sharply.

139. *LW* 1:199–200.

140. The challenge that the Genesis lectures are not really Luther's presupposes that "the early thought of Luther [should be considered] normative for judgments about the authenticity of many passages in this commentary, which are not suspect on other grounds," notes Jaroslav Pelikan. But, he continues, "About most sections of the commentary any responsible historian of theology must conclude that if Luther did not really say this, it is difficult to imagine how Veit Dietrich or even Melanchthon himself could have thought it up." Jaroslav Pelikan is suggesting that dismissing the theology found in the Genesis lectures on the basis of Luther's early work is hardly a convincing argument; and he challenges such a judgment precisely on the basis of Luther's theological development, "taking for granted," Pelikan notes, "the emphasis on the young Luther that became canonical for Luther scholars in the past generation" (*LW* 1:Introduction).

141. *LW* 1:181.

punishments, there shines forth [the Lord's] inexpressible mercy, which encourages Eve and gladdens her heart in the midst of her misfortunes."[142] Though Eve would have pain in childbearing, "there still remains that outstanding glory of motherhood and the blessing of the womb." Vocation (in this case, motherhood) is the divinely given obligation through which both the punishment and (even more importantly) the promise are discerned by the faithful, who "delight in God's gifts and blessings and also bury the punishments, annoyances, pains, griefs, and other things."[143]

For those with eyes to see, vocational obligation beckons rather than repulses because the punishment embedded in one's God-given task no longer accuses and kills. God's wrath is now mediated through the promise; and the law becomes, for the faithful, the loving discipline of a parent who yearns for her child's health and wholeness. "It is," wrote Luther, "a very great measure of grace that after Adam's sin God does not remain silent but speaks, and in many works indeed, in order to show signs of His fatherly disposition." In contrast, "with the serpent everything is done differently. And so, although the promise concerning Christ is not yet there, it is already noticeable in the thought and counsel of God."[144]

Conclusion

There is virtual agreement that Luther moved beyond his exclusive God-versus-Satan duality, initially visible in his teaching on justification, to a later eschatological rendering of God's twofold reign, which integrated the original

---

142. *LW* 1:200.

143. *LW* 1:201.

144. *LW* 1:181. In Harry J. McSorley, *Luther Right or Wrong? An Ecumenical-Theological Study of Luther's Major Work, the Bondage of the Will* (New York: Newman; Minneapolis: Augsburg Publishing House, 1969), 356. Harry McSorley notes that Wolfhart Pannenberg also sees a new unity of the hidden and revealed God in Luther's Genesis lectures (McSorley, 356). "The resolution of doubts concerning one's own election through faith in the unity of the eternal God with Jesus Christ unavoidably destroys the deterministic scheme in which Luther earlier had thought of predestination," Pannenberg writes (McSorley, 356). (McSorley is quoting Pannenberg's "Der Einfluß der Anfechtungserfahrung auf den Prädestinationsbegriff Luthers," *Kerygma und Dogma* 3 (1957): 109–39.) "O. Ritschl [also] thought that he saw in the Lectures on Genesis an 'implicit' correction of the dualistic tension in the concept of God" (McSorley, 356). While the observations of Ritschl and Pannenberg may not rise to the full repudiation of what McSorley describes as "Luther's doctrine of necessity," but these observations do support the notion that Luther's new focus on the human being from the *coram hominibus* perspective—a focus that continued to expand after 1522—makes a significant difference in his appraisal of God and (I would add) God's creation, once again arguing for a critical shift in Luther's theology over time.

duality into the new schema. This development, however, in its early expression up through the mid 1520s, does not fully take into account Luther's mature application of this doctrine, in which God's love becomes fully visible *both* in the created order *and* in the redemptive realm. The both/and approach Luther incorporated into his outer anthropology around 1520–1521 in time became Luther's dominant descriptor, rather than the either/or vision of reality, which had earlier overwhelmed or obliterated the temporal glory of God.[145] As Luther's confidence in the presence of a single loving God at work in both realms deepened,[146] he increasingly focused on the penultimate situation of the believer *coram hominibus*, while never relinquishing the priority of the ultimate situation for each individual *coram Deo*. Thus Luther eventually reclaimed the temporal realm, as well as the temporal selves, in his theology which he had earlier dismissed as worthy only of death in their utterly self-contradicting sinfulness. Apprehended through the eyes of faith, and with a growing confidence in God's loving intentions toward himself, Luther no longer identified the temporal realm absolutely with sin, but rather began to see it more and more as the God-pleasing context for both social and individual flourishing. It is on this basis of Luther's appropriation of temporal experience that we will explore his view of human agency (and particularly his thinking on *liberum arbitrium*). Based on his mature embrace of the created world and the temporal self, we will want to consider more carefully that human capacity called "volition," by which these redeemed and beloved selves are called into active, participatory relationship with God and neighbor.

---

145. The both/and approach continues to reflect the ongoing cosmic battle between God and Satan—visible in, and necessary to, Luther's theology of justification (as well as his own ongoing experiences of *Anfechtungen*).

146. This appears to be a correlate to the lived experience of vocation in which the two realms interpenetrate under a single identity.

4

Life in the Spirit

In the summer of 1520, Luther was excommunicated in the papal bull *Exsurge Domine*, which listed forty-one propositions extracted from Luther's work, all of which were condemned *in globo*.[1] Proposition thirty-six refers to thesis 13 of the *Heidelberg Disputation* (1518) in which Luther argues, "Free will, after the fall, exists in name only."[2] My aim in this chapter is to understand better what Luther hoped to convey when he chose these words. Did Luther mean by this denial that persons are moved in such a way that the natural mental process of volition is somehow bypassed? Or, allowing for volition as a process in Luther's anthropology, does his concept of choosing and acting allow for contingency—that is, the possibility that agents have the freedom to choose and act in ways other than those ways they actually do choose and act? And, if contingency does not exist, are human beings responsible for the decisions, choices, and actions they commit or omit, given that these necessarily must occur, as they in fact do occur? Given the importance of responsible freedom in any consideration of human agency, these are questions we will need to address.

In the introduction to this book I introduced the sin of passive self-abnegation identified by Valerie Saiving, Judith Plaskow, Daphne Hampson, and others; in this final chapter, I attempt to provide a specifically Lutheran response by focusing on that Spirit-empowered agency Luther experienced personally, once he was certain that his salvation was secure in Christ. Notably, Luther gained certainty of his salvation precisely when he discovered that it was nonnegotiable. Since victory no longer depended on his own accomplishments

---

1. Harry J. McSorley, *Luther: Right or Wrong? An Ecumenical-Theological Study of Luther's Major Work, The Bondage of the Will, by a Roman Catholic* (New York: Newman, 1969), 251. An *in globo* condemnation addresses all of the propositions together, such that as a group they are "condemned either as heretical, or as scandalous, or as false, or as offensive to pious ears, or as seductive of simple minds, etc. But there is no indication as to which of these censures applies to which proposition" (ibid.).

2. *LW* 31:40.

(or failures), salvation now appeared to be 100-percent reliable because it was 100 percent the work of God. Faith simply meant trusting that God wasn't lying to him when the gospel promise of Christ's free salvation was delivered to Luther through his study of the Bible. God's reliability was now the ground of Luther's certainty; and it was this ground that transformed his crippling fear into freedom. Ironically, however, this freedom, which rests on God's agency alone, rests therefore simultaneously on human beings' lack of freedom to interfere in the process.

Thus Luther took up the radical denunciation of free will that eventually found its way into the bull of excommunication. When Erasmus suggested to Luther that he might do better to leave the subject of free will alone, Luther responded energetically, "It is not irreverent, inquisitive, or superfluous, but essentially salutary and necessary for a Christian to find out whether the will does anything or nothing in matters pertaining to eternal salvation. . . . For what we are doing is to inquire what free choice can do, what it has done . . . and what [it is in] relation to the grace of God."[3] It was not by accident that Luther so boldly denounced free will in thesis 13 of the *Heidelberg Disputation*. Theologically, the scholastic teaching on free will was an attack on Luther's central theological doctrine—justification by faith alone. Again, emphasizing the critical importance of recognizing that salvation is entirely God's work, Luther writes, "If I am ignorant of what, how far, and how much I can and may do in relation to God, it will be equally uncertain and unknown to me, what, how far, and how much God can and may do in me."[4] Recalling the vehemence with which Luther rejected Cardinal Cajetan's argument against the certainty of faith, remembering Luther's own struggle to find the ground out of which he could trust God, and considering his willingness to die a heretic's death rather than renounce this ground of certainty, we ought not be surprised to encounter his passionate rejection of Erasmus's affirmation of free will.

In fact, as we will see, the spiritual freedom that Luther's teaching on justification promises should not result in the moral sloth Erasmus feared. The acknowledgment of God's activity provides the ground for a cooperating, or theonomous, agency of the outer, temporal self, in tandem with the indwelling Spirit. Luther took this cooperative work to be effectively transformative. The turn to the world that Luther's teaching on vocation implies includes a simultaneous turn to the self, as the reluctant will is called forth in the power of the Spirit to do battle against those sinful habits that persist. The salvation faithfully and passively received by the inner self becomes cooperatively, and

3. *LW* 33:35.
4. *LW* 33:35.

freely, agential through the outer or temporal self as one engages the world through vocationally conceived relationships.

Taking Luther's intentions into account (insofar as we can discern them), it appears that, despite his denial of free will, Luther largely shared the view of human agency we find in Augustine's later, anti-Pelagian writings, though Luther neither employed the common theological language used by Augustine and others nor was he as circumspect as was Augustine about speaking his mind. Given Luther's extraordinary grasp of language and his appreciation of the power language has in constructing our understanding of the world, it is not surprising that he used language creatively to challenge old paradigms and create new ones. The condemned thesis on free will, for example, allows for multiple interpretations—a point Luther must have been well aware of.

GOD'S PROVIDENCE AND HUMAN FREEDOM: THE PASTORAL ATTACK ON PRIDE

There is a frequently quoted passage from Luther's 1525 *Bondage of the Will*, which Karl A. Meissinger suggests is usually cited "with a slight shudder."[5]

> The human will is placed between [God and Satan] like a beast of burden. If God rides it, it wills and goes where God wills. . . . If Satan rides it, it wills and goes where Satan wills; nor can it choose to run to either of the two riders or to seek him out, but the riders themselves contend for the possession and control of it.[6]

"This passage," admits Walter von Loewenich, "seems flatly to put an end to man as a personal being."[7] But, he adds, "the image ought not be pressed. . . . Even with an unfree will man remains thoroughly a person; he is not simply an instrument."[8] Harry McSorley, in his study of Luther's position on the question of free will, agrees with von Loewenich, that to focus on this text alone would surely misrepresent Luther's view of the matter. For, as McSorley points out, the text does not stand in isolation. For example, we again find Luther insisting that "if God is in us, Satan is absent, and . . . if God is absent, Satan is present,"[9]

---

5. McSorley, *Luther: Right or Wrong?*, 309.

6. Martin Luther, *The Bondage of the Will*, in *Luther and Erasmus: Free Will and Salvation*, ed. E. Gordon Rupp and Philip S. Watson, Library of Christian Classics (Philadelphia: Westminster Press, 1969), 140.

7. McSorley, *Luther: Right or Wrong?*, 339.

8. Ibid. (McSorley is quoting here from Walther von Loewenich, *Luther und der Neuprotestantismus* [Witten: Luther-Verlag, 1963], 418.)

9. *LW* 33:65–66.

and the presence of either entails the fact that "only a good" or "only an evil will is in us."[10] Thus "free will," Luther declares, "is a mere dialectical fiction."[11] In his assessment of von Loewenich's perspective, McSorley comments, "Only by re-defining 'person' to exclude the element of free decision can one agree with von Loewenich that [a human being] who is unable to choose between or to decide for God or Satan remains 'thoroughly a person.'"[12] As McSorley suggests, it is just this capacity for free will that had for centuries been associated with the unique standing of human beings over every other creature. Since to choose requires the capacity to imagine oneself in the future—to observe oneself—this capacity, apparently unique to human beings among the creatures, had become the absolute centerpiece of medieval theological anthropology. Luther seemed to be denying all of that and to be describing human beings not as creatures that stand apart and above all the other creatures in creation, but rather reducing human beings to beasts.

Clearly the Church at Rome, in 1521, agreed that Luther had overstepped a critical line when they included Luther's thesis 13 from the *Heidelberg Disputation* in the bull of excommunication.

Thesis 13 reads in full, "Free will, after the fall, exists in name only, and as long as it does what it is able to do, it commits a mortal sin."[13] One could well read this to mean that there is no choice human beings make—no matter how free it appears to be—that could actually have been decided in any other way than it was decided. In fact, as we shall see, this is not what Luther meant; rather than applying the term as it was commonly understood, Luther applied it only to those decisions that affect one's ultimate destiny. Luther could certainly have made his meaning clearer, or he could have used the term as it was commonly used, but he chose to do neither.

Texts from Luther such as those above are sometimes characterized as "necessitarian."[14] This is because it appears that whatever choice was made was in fact a necessary one, since the choice could not have been otherwise. While these texts represent only a small segment of Luther's pronouncements on free will, the confusion they generate is not the result of Luther's sloppy or

---

10. McSorley, *Luther: Right or Wrong?*, 336. (McSorley is quoting here from Karl Meissinger, *Erasmus von Rotterdam*, 2nd ed. [Berlin: A. Nauck, 1948], 309.)

11. *LW* 33:115.

12. McSorley, *Luther: Right or Wrong?*, 339.

13. *LW* 31:40.

14. McSorley writes, for example, "The radicality of the *Assertio* consists above all in the fact that Luther leaves himself clearly open to the charge of necessitarianism or theological determinism" (*Luther: Right or Wrong?*, 255).

inaccurate thinking. Luther cared deeply about this debate, as he made clear to Erasmus in 1525 (see quotations above). Notably, however, after vehemently rejecting Erasmus's suggestion that he stay away from the subject of free will, Luther reminded Erasmus that he was discussing "matters pertaining to eternal salvation."[15] This addition, of course, is key; since Luther says quite clearly here that he is not talking about free will in any other context than the spiritual; but because Luther was not using the term as it was normally understood, interpreters have consistently misunderstood him on this point.

Luther undoubtedly knew that the term "free will" (or *liberum arbitrium*) normally refers to human choice with regard to things both temporal and spiritual. Thus the fact that he did not clearly eliminate the obvious confusion arising from his novel application of the term is interesting. It is a strategy we have seen before. In the 1517 *Disputation against Scholastic Theology*, Luther defends Augustine's teaching of the will as wholly sinful, insisting that those acts that are called virtuous are in fact sins. Notably, in his characterization of these acts as sinful, Luther declared that to call them good "is the same as permitting Pelagians and all heretics to triumph."[16] This way of characterizing actions, emphasizing the breadth and depth of sin, he learned from Augustine. Nevertheless, though both Luther and Augustine worked hard to push back the human presumption that people must (and can) earn God's love and their own eternal salvation, this does not mean that either Augustine or Luther believed that every choice was of this magnitude. Given the assumptions associated with the term, however, it appeared from his usage that Luther was denying human beings any sort of natural freedom along with his denial of freedom in relation to God.

LUTHER'S AUGUSTINIAN REJECTION OF PRIDE

We know that Luther was deeply influenced by the writings of Augustine, especially during the period of his early development. Luther was intent on fighting the semi-Pelagianism in which he had himself been trained and which, he believed, pervaded the scholasticism of his day. Augustine too had defended Christian doctrine against Pelagianism in the fourth century, opposing its optimistic confidence in the undistorted character of that distinctively human quality referred to as the *image of God*. This image of God involves the will—a capacity identified by Augustine as particularly unreliable. Like Augustine, Luther highlighted the ravages of sin that makes it impossible for human beings

---

15. Luther, *Bondage of the Will*, 114.
16. *LW* 31:9 (thesis 2).

to do anything on their own behalf in the acquisition of saving righteousness. In adopting Augustine's understanding of sin, Luther also highlighted the ravages of sin that have so damaged the *imago Dei* as to utterly deform it. Thus Luther sometimes seemed to dismiss the created order as so deeply infected by Satan's presence as to be of little or no value. In a remark by Augustine that might have served as a template for Luther, we read, "Whatever good a man does that is not done because true wisdom dictates it, is a sin by the very fact that the end is not good—even though the act may seem good."[17] Augustine uses the term "true wisdom" here to refer to that sort of willing that faithfully acknowledges God. Thus any act that emerges from a nonbeliever is, in Augustine's view, sin. Luther agreed with Augustine that, without faith, no work can be considered good. "Although the works of man always seem attractive and good, they are nevertheless likely to be mortal sins," he writes in the *Heidelberg Disputation*.[18] Against the form of scholasticism associated with William of Ockham and Gabriel Biel, Luther declares, "The person who believes that he can obtain grace by doing what is in him adds sin to sin."[19] Both Augustine and Luther are distinctly hesitant to speak of any action as good outside of faith. Here is Luther's prophetic perspective at work as he attempts to remap the theological landscape. Luther's early insistence on characterizing all actions, both spiritual and temporal, from the perspective of God's condemnation means that no act can be judged according to its appearance in this world. Given the similar language and concepts employed, Luther appears to have thought himself faithfully following Augustine as he prepared the ninety-seven propositions of the *Heidelberg Disputation*.[20]

While there sometimes appear to be important differences between the two theologians, these may simply reflect Augustine's silence before a mystery that Luther felt compelled to speak about. Augustine also continued to refer to free will (or *liberum arbitrium*) according to normal usage. Harry McSorley, for example, points to a passage where Augustine characterizes the temporal aspect of an action apart from its ultimate nature, demonstrating a critical doctrinal difference from the young Luther, who was at war with the scholastic theologians of his day. Augustine agrees that an act which *appears* to be compassionate must be understood "in itself . . . [as] an act of natural compassion [that] is good."[21] Admittedly, Augustine quickly adds, "But he who uses this good work in an unbelieving way uses it badly."[22] Nevertheless, the distinction

---

17. McSorley, *Luther: Right or Wrong?*, 69.
18. *LW* 31:39.
19. *LW* 31:40.

Augustine draws here, however reluctantly, between the act in itself and the act as characterized by the faith (or unfaith) of its agent is an important one. Among other things, it suggests that the created order has its own intrinsic value. Luther, at first glance, appears to categorically refuse any acknowledgment of temporal righteousness existing in itself. Luther's approach not only reaffirms the sin that undermines all human pretense but also emphasizes the omnipotence and ubiquity of God. In thesis 34 of the *Heidelberg Disputation*, Luther makes this explicit. "If Aristotle would have recognized the absolute power of God, he would accordingly have maintained that it was impossible for matter to exist of itself alone." Thus, despite the similarities between Luther and Augustine on this matter of free will, there are also differences. While Augustine is prepared to view the same act from more than one perspective, Luther, during this early period, was describing both the character and the ontology of human works exclusively through the lens of God's judgment.

We do find in the *HD*, however, at least one case where Luther moderated his condemnation of human virtue (understood as wholly sinful outside of Christ.) He admits in thesis 5 that human works are not all "mortal sins." "We speak of works which are apparently good," Luther adds; for these apparently

---

20. In reference to Matt. 7:18, Luther writes: "In many places St. Augustine teaches that man apart from grace is an evil tree. Whatever he does, therefore, in whatever manner he may use his reason, elicit, command or do an act, he always sins when he lacks faith working through love" (McSorley, *Luther: Right or Wrong?*, 70.) This is a rendering of sin that McSorley refers to as a "broad" form of sin. "The first of these sentences," comments McSorley, "is a correct statement of Augustine's thought but the second is not. (ibid.) McSorley notes that "if the analogous character of Augustine's terminology is overlooked, he is bound to be misinterpreted. To say simply and without qualification, therefore, that, for Augustine, all actions of unbelievers are sins is to falsify Augustine's thoughts by over-simplification and by univocal interpretation of his analogous language. For Augustine, unbelievers can perform acts which are good in their '*officium*,' such as prudence and temperance. Such acts can never be called bad from the point of view of the '*officium*.'" (*Officium* is "that which is done," in contrast to *finis*, which means "that *purpose* for which an act is done," or "its *end*.") In this respect, McSorley continues, "they [i.e. prudence and temperance] clearly differ from acts of imprudence and intemperance. *Luther, already in 1516, tends to overlook the distinctions which Augustine makes concerning the good acts and virtues of infidels*" (ibid.) Ultimately, Luther came to make the same distinction using the term *proper righteousness* to distinguish an act done in faith (for God's sake), in contrast to an act viewed by the world as virtuous but not done in faith (an act he identifies with "civil righteousness"). This second sort of act is characterized from its *coram hominibus* perspective, even as Augustine can speak of an act as good in a limited sense in its *officium*. Thus Luther eventually makes the same distinction provided by *the officium/finis* distinction—that is, a distinction between acts viewed by the world as good and those viewed by the world as evil from acts viewed by God as truly good (according to their *finis*).

21. McSorley, *Luther: Right or Wrong?*, 69.
22. Ibid.

good works are not "crimes."[23] Thus we find Luther recognizing, along with Augustine, the effective reality of human agency (operating apart from the indwelling Spirit), however slight this effect might be. By moderating his description on the basis of apparent good, Luther, like Augustine, reluctantly appears to have recognized temporal existence as more than "nothing."[24]

The Heidelberg Disputation took place in the spring of 1518. In September of that same year, Luther preached a sermon on Philippians 2 in which he considered three forms of righteousness.[25] Here, Luther explicitly identifies what was only hinted at in the texts above. He speaks openly of an "apparent righteousness,"[26] which, he admits, rightly characterize some actions that are at the same time sinful from God's perspective.[27] They are what we observe when "a man is good before people, and cannot be accused."[28] Such acts "are contrary to manifest evil," writes Luther, prepared now to grant them a kind of non-Christian righteousness. The description he uses for these—*Scheingerechtigkeit*—has been translated by some theologians as "civil righteousness" [i.e. righteous in a civil sense].[29] "Such, he concedes, "were many kings of Israel and the people of Israel to whom the Lord gave good temporal things and many victories."[30] Luther includes in this group those "Christians"

---

23. *LW* 31:39 (thesis 5).

24. In part, Luther's energetic dismissal of everything human may be linked to more than his personal experience (and disappointment) with a system of penance that relies on "doing that which is in one." Luther may also be attacking himself (as we are wont to do), since he also taught this semi-Pelagian theology of the *via moderna* during his earliest lectures. We find, for example, in a passage from his lectures on Psalms (115:1), a passing moment of agreement with his teachers. "Hence, the teachers correctly say that to a man who does what is in him God gives grace without fail" (*LW* 11:396).

25. Martin Luther, "Sermon on Threefold Righteousness, Philippians 2" trans. Glen Zweck (Project Wittenberg, 1997), http://www.iclnet.org/pub/resources/text/wittenberg/luther/web/3formsrt.html. According to Zweck, in the introduction, the translation "deliberately . . . kept as close to the original Latin as possible" since, Zweck suggests, "the German translation of this sermon, in the St. Louis edition, makes Luther more Lutheran than he was at the time." For an excellent analysis of Luther's understanding of "civil righteousness," see Lazareth, *Testimony of Faith*, 124–32 (with Luther texts in original German); and Lazareth, *On the Christian Home*, 102–31. The latter is an extended discussion of Luther's view of God's two-fold reign, natural law, social justice, and civil righteousness, with English translations of the texts. A more contemporary discussion of the civil realm, social justice, and civil righteousness is included in chapter 6 of William H. Lazareth, *Christians in Society: Luther, the Bible, and Social Ethics* (Minneapolis: Fortress Press, 2001), 139f.

26. Luther, "Sermon on Threefold Righeousness." .

27. Ibid.

28. Ibid.

29. Lazareth, *Testimony of Faith*, 127f..

30. Ibid.

who have fallen away from Christ, and now live by the civil law rather than the gospel.

> Here belong [also] those who worship the saints for the sake of bodily things, and priests who serve for the sake of present things, and likewise the monks, and those who do many other such things. In short, this is the righteousness which receives its reward here, and is punished in the future, but somewhat more mildly than criminals. . . . [For] it serves not God, but itself, nor is it the righteousness of sons but of slaves, nor is it peculiar to Christians, but rather that of Jews and Gentiles. Nor are Christians to be exhorted to it, because it proceeds out of fear of punishment or love of its own comfort, not from the love of God.[31]

Applying this approach to the matter of free will, Luther, it appears, by the fall of 1518 was prepared to accept not only the existence of *liberum arbitrium* but also its capacity to accomplish something of value (even in its fallen condition). In his 1535 *Bondage of the Will*, Luther explicitly acknowledges both our temporal existence and those works that pertain to it, explaining that "human creatures are divided between two realms. In one of them they are directed by their own choice and counsel, apart from any precepts and commandments of God, namely in dealing with *things beneath* them. There they reign and are lords, having been left in the hand of their own counsel."[32] Though "free" in a limited sense, such choosing and acting are never independent of God; for as Luther quickly adds, "Not that God so leaves them as not to cooperate with them in everything, but he has granted them the free use of things according to their own choice."[33]

THE POWER OF LANGUAGE TO CONSTRUCT A WORLDVIEW

That which theologians call "free will," then, Luther appears to acknowledge, at least by 1535, though he refused to use this terminology. However, one critical difference in Luther's understanding of that capacity separated him in critical ways from the scholastics. While he acknowledged the capacity for free choice in the temporal realm, the boundary between things above and things below

---

31. Ibid.
32. Robert Kolb, *Bound Choice, Election, and Wittenberg: Theological Method from Martin Luther to the Formula of Concord* (Grand Rapids: Eerdmans, 2005), 50. (Kolb is quoting from *LW* 33:118–19.)
33. Ibid.

was absolute. He denounced any reference to free will at all in relation to the spiritual realm. The scholastics agreed that divine providence always limited any absolute freedom in relation to God; but they continued to carve out a space for free will in relation to God insofar as it did not contradict divine providence. While Luther acknowledged that the scholastics never claimed to teach a human capacity for free choice that exceeds or contradicts God's providential choosing and foreknowledge, he considered this a distinction without a difference—a claim that is both empty and dangerous.[34] "I would wish," Luther declared, "that the words, 'free will,' had never been invented. They are not found in Scripture and would better be called 'self will' which is of no use [when it comes to salvation]."[35] Indeed, Luther's failure to explain that this useless free will pertained exclusively to matters of salvation encouraged just that confusion, which led Rome to condemn his teaching as at least dangerous and possibly heretical. In light of Luther's apparent disregard for the possible misunderstanding of his own position, he, perhaps surprisingly, rejected the term "free will" for the very same reason. "It is neither right nor good to play tricks with words in matters of such great importance," he wrote. "A simple man is easily deceived by such tricks and teachers of this kind."[36] "If anyone wishes to retain these words, he ought to apply them to the newly created man, so as to understand by them the man who is without sin. He is truly free, as was Adam in Paradise, and it is of him that Scripture speaks when it deals with our freedom. But those who are involved in sins are not free, but prisoners of the devil."[37]

Yet, Luther's apparent blindness to his own lack of clarity is not without reason. There is a difference that makes one form of confusion acceptable to Luther and the other repugnant. Given the pastoral need to undermine and obliterate the self-righteous pride that separates people from God's free gift of salvation, Luther had no fear of the consequences if people thought he denied free will in every case. If people were offended by this, that was fine. If his words caused confusion that might serve God's work of slaying pride for the sake of salvation, then so much the better. Confusion from the opposite side, however, could do inestimable harm. People could well misunderstand the scholastic subtleties that protected God's providence, thinking rather that free will left them entirely free from God's interference in their quest to win a place

---

34. For an extended and nuanced argument supporting Luther's belief in *liberum arbitrium* (alongside other necessitarian texts), see McSorley, *Luther: Right or Wrong?*
35. *LW* 32:94.
36. *LW* 32:94.
37. *LW* 32:94.

in heaven. Thus their pride would either puff them up or their piety leave them hopelessly broken, even as Luther was broken before he discovered that salvation was a free gift. We have seen this linguistic concern for the salvation of souls before; and it suggests that Luther's pastoral concerns consistently trumped his desire to write and teach with systematic precision. For the Wittenberg theologians, and perhaps most of all for Luther, theology was neither an art nor a job. It was, rather, a holy vocation, intended to serve God's ends, always aiming at the eternal welfare of the neighbor. That Luther clearly loved his work and took pleasure in doing it well seems undeniable; but his pastoral instincts nevertheless usually trumped every other motive.

THE MEDIEVAL THEORY OF CONSEQUENCE

In exploring and explaining Luther's reluctance to characterize a fallen world using such terms as *free* or *good*, McSorley raises an important distinction in the Catholic tradition. This distinction makes it possible to describe the free choice and action of human beings, on one hand, and to acknowledge God's overarching power, on the other.[38] Not only does this distinction attempt to honor the free will identified with the image of God, but it also insists on a freedom that makes sense of human responsibility; for if human beings are not free to sin or not sin, then it must be God (or something else) who is responsible for the sin that human beings do. And, if that is the case, how can it be just to hold human beings responsible? Who or what is really at fault? While the *consequentiae/conequentiis* distinction, as it is called, makes no attempt to prove or explain the mechanism by way of which human free will and God's divine providence both choose, independently and effectively, the same outcome (such that it is fair or just to hold human beings responsible for their choices), it does, as Harry McSorley puts it, "state the mystery correctly."

38. Aristotle demonstrates the distinction by asking: Is the prediction that "There will be a sea battle tomorrow" necessarily true, if it is true, and does its truth entail that the sea battle is inevitable? The illicit inferential move from (1) "If there is a sea battle tomorrow then it is true that there will be a sea battle tomorrow" to (2) "If there is a sea battle tomorrow then there must be a sea battle tomorrow" illustrates the fallacy of confusing the *necessitas consequentiae* with the *necessitas consequentiis*, or the necessity of the *consequence* (if *x* is true, then *x* is true) with the necessity of the *consequent* (if *x* is true, then *x must* be true). Luther's disagreement is predicated on his conviction that salvation is entirely the work of God. Therefore, in this specific instance, where human beings do not have the freedom to choose or not choose salvation, no distinction between what *might* happen with regard to my salvation and what *must* happen with regard to my salvation can be made. This does not mean, however, that Luther rejects the distinction as it is applied to human choices about temporal things.

It presupposes the arguments for the free will based on Scripture and reason and simply seeks to respond to a difficulty arising from a [simultaneous] belief in God's infallibly certain knowledge of all human events and in . . . His will which providentially directs all things. . . . *Neither does the distinction explain the mystery* of the relation between divine and human activity. Rather, it enables us to state the mystery correctly and to retain it, affirming both God's transcendent, unfailing working and man's free will. (emphasis added)[39]

Luther's response to the scholastic explanation, however, was unequivocal rejection, at least insofar as it is applied to the matter of salvation. Not only does the distinction fail to acknowledge God's wholly effective agency in this matter, but it also runs the risk of undermining the faith that saves, as does the language of "free will" that this distinction employs. Thus, Luther insists, it is not only a false distinction (that is, a distinction without a difference), but it is also infinitely dangerous. In Luther's view, it systematically inflates human pretension by encouraging the church's failure to rightly honor God. "These are only empty words," Luther writes,

> especially since they . . . give the occasion to understand the expression "contingency of the consequent" to mean that salvation takes place or does not take place because of our own will. . . . It solves nothing to ask whether this consequence is contingent . . . inasmuch as God alone is necessary for this purpose. . . . For what else does the expression "to be contingent" mean than to be a creature and not God? . . . There is no place here for this kind of equivocation. For no one is asking or in doubt as to whether a created thing is contingent in its essence, that is, subject to change and thus not God or something immutable, but the question is concerning . . . whether what God has predestined takes place by necessity. . . . [Those] less educated [ask] . . . : Does the contingency of an event impede the sure predestination of God? . . . The answer is that with God there simply is no contingency, but it is only in our eyes.[40]

At issue is whether a particular outcome is necessary or whether it is but one possible outcome among others. A parallel case perhaps makes the application of this distinction (and the reasons why Luther rejects it) clearer. Parents may

39. McSorley, *Luther: Right or Wrong?*, 235.
40. *LW* 25:372–373.

long for a little girl, and they may "choose" to have a girl rather than a boy, but the critical combining of sperm and egg, which actually determines the sex of a given child is not a process over which human beings have choice (at least not yet). For a choice to be really free, it must also be able to actually effect a difference in the outcome. Even though this event has not yet occurred, so that either a boy or a girl might be the result of a given pregnancy, it is illusory to suppose that the parents longing for a girl will effectively make it so. This is what Luther means when he asks, "Does the contingency of an event impede the sure predestination of God? . . .The answer is that with God there simply is no contingency, but it is only in our eyes." To describe an event as "contingent" means that more than one outcome is possible. (The parents might have a boy or a girl.) But just because there is more than one possible outcome does not mean that the outcome can be changed by the parents' choosing. This is so, Luther says, because "God alone is necessary for this purpose."

"God alone," says Luther, has the power to influence (or choose) the outcome. Unlike the matter of whether a child turns out to be a boy or a girl, however, the question of whether one is saved or damned is presented in Scripture as a set of alternatives specifically related to temporal choices individuals have made. The very notion of a "Judgment Day" suggests that one is being judged or held accountable for choices one is rightly responsible for. Our assumption in such a case is that if we must make good choices, then we can in fact make them. When Jesus divides the sheep from the goats in Matthew 25, he does so on the basis of choices people have made. Did you visit the sick? he asks Did you feed the hungry? Apparently the division of some to salvation and others to perdition is based on their answers to Jesus' questions. This is what McSorley means when he says that Scripture assumes that people are responsible for, and therefore capable of, doing what they must. And though Luther agrees that people are indeed rightly held responsible, he does not admit to an effective connection between what people do and whether they wind up with the sheep or the goats. When Luther insists that "God alone is necessary for this purpose," he is saying that God alone has the power to choose who will be graced with the gift of a saving faith, which in turn determines who will wind up in paradise and who will spend eternity in hell. Logically, the connection between "justification by faith alone" and "free will" is a tight one; so we should not be surprised at Luther's grave concern over a teaching that implies people do have a choice (and the implied power that truly free choice entails). "God alone is necessary," Luther insists; God alone has the unique power to determine, without interference, the final destiny of every created thing. To faithfully "fear God" as we should, Luther thought, meant recognizing the true majesty of

God and the radical dependency of human beings (despite theological assertions about the "image of God"). The claim that human beings are ultimately free flies directly in the face of his critical Pauline doctrine that God alone justifies sinners.

Perhaps Luther did understand the *consequentiae/consequentiis* distinction, and rejected it using the language he did for pastoral rather than systematic reasons. When Luther says that contingency points to the fact that "human beings are not God" (see quotation above), he appears to have been intentionally using a familiar word in an unfamiliar way in order to make a point. This is, after all, a rhetorical technique that Luther frequently employed. (One thinks, for example, of his co-opting of the word *vocation* to suggest that the ordinary tasks of this life are holy orders—no different from the work of priests, monks, and nuns, insofar as they all serve God's ends. All Christians, Luther insisted with his novel use of the term *vocation*, are called to serve God through ordinary, secular tasks that build up and preserve the social order, in which God is present and involved, just as surely as God works through the church.) Applying the same approach, Luther seems to be suggesting that "contingent," which was commonly used to refer to "free will," should be associated instead with that which is most dramatically unfree and ungodlike—the created mutability and radical dependency of human beings on God. To use the word "contingent" in reference to a similarity between human beings and God was, in Luther's eyes, an expression of the very pride that, ironically, underscores human "contingency"—that utter lack of divine likeness—which culminates (under the power of sin) in the death and destruction of the self. What could be more in keeping with Luther's theological interests than to tackle both points (dependency and pride) simultaneously in his reappropriation of the word *contingent*?

ALTERNATE ACCEPTED INTERPRETATIONS OF *LIBERUM ARBITRIUM*

McSorley's insistence on the reality of a freedom that is truly open to more than one possible outcome in matters that include salvation is important; but it is not clear that this particular rendering of freedom and responsibility with regard to salvation represents the whole tradition. In a very interesting discussion of Augustine's teaching on the irresistibility of grace, it appears that Augustine held a position on free will that is rather more like Luther's than Aquinas'. At least in some cases, it seems that Augustine defined human freedom, not as the possibility of more than one outcome (in relation to salvation, particularly), but in terms of a volition that properly employs that given human capacity for the work of choosing. In a response to R. Seeberg's discussion of this point, McSorley writes,

> If Augustine seems to speak of the irresistibility of grace (and Seeberg recognizes that this expression is not found in Augustine), this is . . . not to be taken as a denial of free will. For as Seeberg . . . puts it, "even the divinely effected transition into this new live-condition (justice) takes place with free will in that the irresistible grace brings about the very turning of ourselves and our wills to God. . . . The good will is indeed caused or willed by God, but God wills it in such a way that the will itself wills. These are Augustine's thoughts. The insight that the good will exists only insofar as it is willed by God was just as self-evident to him . . . as the psychological fact that the will exists only in the form of free self-determination.[41]

Seeberg seems to be suggesting that Augustine's description of *liberum arbitrium* bypasses the "mystery"[42] of a human freedom that can effectively both deviate from, and at the same time remain subject to, God's predestining will. In response, McSorley quotes again from Seeberg: "If we look at man's life as a whole, then we can say that from the point of view of Augustine, man is always free in regard to his individual will acts, but these are conditioned by the total direction of his will. Thus the sinner is free, but the area in which his freedom operates is one dominated by evil. The justified man is free, but the area in which his freedom operates is one which is directed toward God."[43] It appears that this explanation is not inconsistent with Luther's explanation when he succinctly (if reductionistically) sums up the matter, declaring that "with God there simply is no contingency, but it is only in our eyes."

THE ESCHATOLOGICAL ELEMENT

Seeberg's description of "man [as] . . . always free in regard to his individual will acts" (see above) is an important point. That these acts "are conditioned by

---

41. *LW* 25:93.

42. The reference to "mystery" here refers back to a quotation from McSorley: "*Neither does the distinction explain the mystery* of the relation between divine and human activity. Rather, it enables us to state the mystery correctly and to retain it, affirming both God's transcendent, unfailing working and man's free will" (*Luther: Right or Wrong?*, 210 [emphasis added]).

43. Ibid.

the total direction of his will" (which is determined by God) eliminates the real possibility for an individual to choose in which "total direction" her will moves. And since it is this "total direction" that determines one's ultimate destiny (for saving faith is precisely the whole self, turned toward God rather than away), then it must be the case that God is determining that "total" or fundamental direction of the whole will. Thus it remains—God alone predetermines the condition that establishes the possibility of righteous willing. If this is a fair description of Augustine's approach to the matter of free will, then he seems to have provided precisely the description Luther was attempting to articulate when he spoke of a good tree bearing good fruit (and a bad tree bearing bad). "Freedom" here refers only to those choices derived from an overarching character that is determined solely by God; and this is because for Augustine, as for Luther, salvation (which implies choosing for and with God) can only be the work of God alone.

Luther's refusal to acknowledge responsibly effective human choice with regard to salvation entails a whole host of unfortunate theological consequences, not the least of which is the problem of making God apparently responsible for sin. If providence wholly overrides human responsibility in the matter of salvation, then we can no longer argue that human beings ultimately receive the end they deserve. Thus, McSorley concludes, Luther's emphatic rejection of free will is best explained as an unfortunate exaggeration—though, given Luther's historical context, an understandable one.

But is it? Given the aim of this project, which is to demonstrate, among other things, that Luther's theology both allows for, and even insists on, responsible human agency, it would make sense to stand with McSorley on this point. But that would entail ignoring Luther's own ongoing insistence that the question of free will, as it is related to salvation, cannot be sidestepped. And this is so (as has been noted) because "if I am ignorant of what, how far, and how much I can and may do in relation to God, it will be equally uncertain and unknown to me what, how far, and how much God can and may do in me."[44] Though one cannot ignore the importance of Luther's robust denial of human choice or responsibility with regard to salvation, it is also clear that to have abandoned his rejection would have meant losing everything else. Neither does Luther's insistence that salvation is the work of God alone mean that responsible agency must be undermined, as we shall argue. Luther identifies a tension in the Godhead itself that pulls human beings into engagement—rousing responsible agency awake. In that space, somewhere between the *Deus revelatus* on the one

44. *LW* 33:35.

hand (with the promise that salvation is for all) and the *Deus absconditus* on the other (before whom hope is crushed by doubt), persons are driven toward that relationship whereby they turn both to God and to themselves.

EXHORTATION TO ACTION: DEFLECTING THE DEVIL'S *ANFECHTUNGEN*

From the very beginning, well before Luther theologically embraced the temporal work of sanctification, he spoke of a personal, volitional struggle against the devil's assaults. Thus, even in his most prophetic period, Luther's discussion of his *Anfechtungen* suggested his unacknowledged presuppositions regarding a human capacity for willing *that makes a difference*. There is in Luther's work a burden on persons—a responsibility—to struggle against any passive resignation before the devil's assaults—to grasp the word that is offered. Even while he retained the *coram Deo* confession that these onslaughts are the result of a cosmic battle between God and Satan, Luther nevertheless also very clearly articulated his own experience (from below) with these demonic temptations as one that allows and, in the presence of possibility, encourages effective agency; and he offered this experience of struggle to others in his pastoral counsel.[45] This material on *Anfechtungen*, which spans Luther's entire career, stands in direct tension with the picture of Luther that McSorley derives from the *Bondage of the Will*, where, McSorley concludes, "we find that no divine call to conversion, no admonition to steadfastness in justice or to avoidance of sin, no struggle of man with Satan, no personal dialogue which presupposes a free response such as we find in Scripture, but only a domination

---

45. See *Luther: Letters of Spiritual Counsel*, ed. Theodore Tappert, Library of Christian Classics (Philadelphia: Westminster Press, 1955), 115–16: "Dear and virtuous Lady: Your brother Jerome Weller has informed me that you are sorely troubled about eternal election. . . . I know all about this affliction. I was myself brought to the brink of eternal death by it. . . . I shall show you how God helped me out of the trouble and by what means I now protect myself against it every day. First, you must firmly fix in your mind the conviction that such thoughts as yours are assuredly the suggestions and fiery darts of the wretched devil. . . . It is certain that these notions of yours come, not from God, but from the devil, who torments us with them to make us hate God and despair. God has strictly forbidden this in the First Commandment. He desires that we love, trust, and praise him by whom we live . . . in this way . . . does one learn how to deal properly with the question of predestination. It will be manifest that you believe in Christ. If you believe, then you are called. And if you are called, then you are most certainly predestined. Do not let this mirror and throne of grace be torn away from before your eyes. If such thoughts still come and bite like fiery serpents, pay no attention to the thoughts or serpents. Turn away from these notions and contemplate the brazen serpent."

of man's will by God or Satan without any free, personal action of man."[46] In fact, it is precisely Luther's insistence on a divine predestining will that one can trust absolutely—a will that cannot be manipulated—that provides the freedom out of which one discovers a new possibility. The *Deus revelatus* opens up the real possibility to engage Satan in an efficacious struggle. While the denial of free will makes the life-giving certainty of salvation possible, in Luther's vividly articulated descriptions of his *Anfechtungen* we discover the call that McSorley is looking for.

In his letter to Jonas von Stockhausen, for example, Luther wrote that the thoughts of the devil, "[which have been] forcibly inserted into your mind" must be sternly resisted. "Imagine that you are held fast and bound by chains and that you must work and sweat yourself out of their strangle hold by powerful exertions. . . . The darts of the devil cannot be removed pleasantly and without effort when they are so deeply imbedded in your flesh."[47] These "powerful exertions" in defense of faith (and the eternal well-being of the self) include a series of choices and actions that persons of faith are presumably capable of taking, in a cooperative efficacious agency made possible by the indwelling Spirit.[48] "Whenever the devil pesters you with these thoughts, at once seek out the company of men, drink more, joke and jest or engage in some other form of merriment. . . . If the devil should say, 'Do not drink,' you should reply to him, 'On this very account, because you forbid it, I shall drink, and what is more, I shall drink a generous amount.'"[49] Luther advises people to "despise" the devil's thoughts. Contempt, he says, is "the best and easiest method of winning over the devil."[50] In addition, those under assault are to "flee solitude . . . joke, and play games,"[51] make music, listen to Scripture, and pray. One may also enter into disputation with the devil. "When you are assailed by a temptation," Luther is reported to have said, "ask the devil, 'Devil, in what commandment is this written?' And if he cannot show you, say, 'Be gone, you wretch, and spare me your filthy talk.'"[52]

46. McSorley, *Luther: Right or Wrong?*, 338–39.
47. *Luther: Letters of Spiritual Counsel*, 89.
48. The indwelling power of the Spirit is presumably the factor that changes the required response of the faithful. Now the Spirit is aroused and at work, creating precisely this situation of the divided will. The call in this context is to choose with the Spirit—to cooperate, thus turning one's back on the devil. If, indeed, Luther really believed that the cooperation offered by persons was ultimately ineffective in itself, it would have made more sense for him to pray than to exhort.
49. *Luther: Letters of Spiritual Counsel*, 86.
50. Ibid., 85.
51. Ibid.
52. Ibid., 88.

The believer is also to be active in judging communications received through the conscience. Since the devil may appear under the guise of Christ, it is especially important to measure the content of any argument against the promise of the gospel.[53]

> If Christ appears in the guise of a wrathful judge or lawgiver who demands an accounting of how we have spent our lives, we should know for certain that this is not really Christ but the devil. For Scripture portrays Christ as our Propitiator, Mediator, and Comforter. . . . Therefore we should be on our guard, lest the amazing skill and infinite wiles of Satan deceive us into mistaking the accuser and mask of the false Christ, that is, of the devil.[54]

And, most importantly, he advises persons to actively seek out opportunities where God's Word of promise is delivered by way of the living voice. "Quickly recite comforting verses from the Scriptures," Luther advised the wife of a friend who was suffering from severe melancholy.[55]

In deflecting the devil's assaults, it is Christ's identification with sinners that provides the one and only effective weapon in the battle against demonic despair. It is a Word that Luther thought should be directed both toward the afflicted and toward the devil. To a suffering friend, Luther wrote, "Listen to the words of some good man as to the voice of God from heaven. And then preach the gospel back to the devil!"

> Begone, wretched devil! You are trying to make me worry about myself. But God declares everywhere that I should let him care for me. He says, "I am your God." This means, "I care for you; depend upon me, await my bidding, and let me take care of you." This is what Saint Peter taught, "Cast all our care upon him, for he cares for you." And David taught, "Cast your burden upon the Lord, and he shall sustain you."[56]

---

53. This can be compared to Staupitz's counsel to Luther, when the young monk was terrified by Christ's near presence in the monstrance. "It is not Christ," then, that you are thinking of, Staupitz told Luther. That is, if what you see is a terrible judge, then you are looking into the face of the devil rather than into the face of Christ.
54. *LW* 27:11–12.
55. *Luther: Letters of Spiritual Counsel*, 91.
56. Ibid., 116.

Luther emphasized the power of effective personal action in prayer, advising Valentine Hausmann to "call upon God and pray. . . . Fall upon your knees and cry out to heaven . . . even if . . . you think your prayers are unavailing and cold. Make a brave effort. Pray all the harder when you think it is to no purpose. You must learn to struggle until the terror lets up of its own accord. Do not simply remain passive . . . and suffer . . . for then your condition will get worse as time passes. . . . *God wants you to resist*" (emphasis added).[57]

In these *Anfechtungen* texts, we see Luther again and again urging against a submissive suffering, which is bound only to make matters worse. "God," he writes, "wants you to resist." God does not resist alone, replacing the human agent, but rather wants—and from where one stands, does not determine absolutely—that one actively wills, oneself, this resistance to evil. Note the emphasis in his statement above. It is not just that God *wants* something. It is that God wants *you* to resist. In these cases of inner temptation, related as they are to "things above," the resistance that God wants is effectively manifested, in Luther's view, through actions of the outer self—actions, that is, in relation to "things below," such as singing, seeking out friends, or generally engaging in social activities. And most importantly, Luther took these temporal volitional choices to be potentially efficacious in relation to the ultimate "things above." We shall see this integration of "things below" and "things above" in other cases as well, where Luther presupposes the capacity that he wishes to call a "self-will" (or *liberum arbitrium*) to be effectively agential in relation even to "things above." This freedom appears to be always open from the situation in which one stands.

Exhortation to Struggle against Temporal Temptations

"God, who protects and preserves us without our help . . . does not work in us without us," Luther writes, "because it is for this he has created and preserved us, that he might work in us and we might cooperate with him, whether outside his Kingdom through his general omnipotence, or inside his Kingdom by the special virtue of his Spirit."[58] Luther wrote these words in 1525, in the *Bondage of the Will*, in response to Erasmus's fear that a denial of *liberum arbitrium* would have disastrous moral and ethical consequences. In *Two Kinds of Righteousness*, written six years earlier, Luther had already spoken of that "second kind of righteousness [that] is our proper righteousness, *not because we alone work it,*

---

57. Ibid., 121.
58. *LW* 33:243.

but because we work with that first and alien righteousness. This is that manner of life spent profitably in good works, in the first place, in slaying the flesh and crucifying the desires with respect to the self" (emphasis added).[59]

Here, then, is the third kind of righteousness—one that points to the sort of personal transformation that Hampson is eager to recover. If the *civil* righteousness is applied to *apparently good* acts accomplished for temporal reward, and if *alien* or *passive* righteousness refers to that saving righteousness that Christ shares with the faithful, then *proper* righteousness refers to those authentically good acts, accomplished by the faithful in a cooperative alliance with the indwelling Spirit. Therefore, Luther admonishes, while it is true that "God gives everything freely . . . you have to [also] take hold and grab the ox by the horns . . . and provide the mask."[60] A mask, according to Luther's use of the word in this context, refers to a person who is faithfully clinging to and cooperating with the Spirit and thereby properly living out her Christian vocation in the temporal realm such that God's active and cooperating presence is at work in, with, and under her own agency. To be a mask does not mean that the created substance (be that a person or a tree) is eliminated or bypassed.[61] Like Adam and Eve in the garden, persons may choose from among all the many plants, with the exception of one. Likewise, human beings re-created in the "new Adam" can choose with the Spirit from among all the created possibilities. What they cannot choose, however, is the fundamental condition that characterizes every other choice. That is to say, they cannot choose to love God out of themselves. For this is the free gift of faith, whereby God chooses them, to become what they were not—members of the one body of Christ. Such a person is not *autonomous*, or apart from God, but *theonomous*, united in a cooperative agency, which is sustained and empowered by the indwelling Spirit.[62] We recall Luther's remarks in regard to Mary's participation in the birth of her son, Jesus. "Grace," Luther suggests, "does not destroy or impede nature

---

59. *LW* 31:297.

60. Martin J. Heineckin, "Luther and the 'Orders of Creation' in Relation to a Doctrine of Work and Vocation," *Lutheran Quarterly* (1952): 405–6.

61. This appears to be derived from Luther's understanding of Christ's presence in the eucharistic bread and wine, where the bread and wine remain real bread and wine even as Christ's true body and blood are also truly present. Notably, this description of a divine and created presence that are made manifest simultaneously suggests the possibility of a distinction, which allows a contingent will to operate fully according to its created ontology in concert with God's providence.

62. This is best reflected in Luther's eucharistic theology, where the real bread and wine remain earthly substances, made manifest together with the real body and blood of Christ. Neither are these created substances compromised by being transubstantiated into something higher. God's creative work is not diminished by God's redemptive work.

and nature's works. Indeed grace improves and promotes them."[63] Luther offers an illustration of that cooperating agency in his description of Mary's struggle to give birth to the baby Jesus.

Persistence, born of this cooperation between the Spirit and a will that *allows* itself to be led, are thus an expected dimension of the faithful response to all forms of temporal suffering (including that suffering related to passivity).[64] This is especially the case in Luther's later work, as he watched the freedom of the gospel become an opportunity for unbridled "fleshly" liberties. Again, we encounter Luther's pastoral exhortations to the faithful, who are expected to struggle actively in an explicitly synergistic relationship with the Spirit.

We have already encountered Luther's concern for those still "weak in faith," and in those situations where persons are only too aware of their failure to measure up. Observing that his parishioners were struggling, Luther shifted his focus. Where he had been working hard to undermine pride, he now turned his attention to a building-up in the Spirit. In these instances, we see Luther guiding his people into the faithful struggle as he encourages them to incrementally crucify their residual "flesh" in cooperation with the empowering Spirit.[65]

> Whoever belongs to Christ . . . crucifies the flesh with all its diseases and faults. . . . This takes place when they not only repress the wantonness of the flesh by fasting or other kinds of discipline, but when, as Paul said earlier, they walk by the Spirit; that is, when the threat that God will punish sin severely warns them and frightens

---

63. *LW* 52:11. Luther goes on, "We must stay with the gospel text which says [Mary] gave birth to [Jesus] . . . and with the article of the creed which says 'born of the Virgin Mary.' There is no deception here, but, as the words indicate, it was a real birth. Now we know, do we not, what the meaning of 'to bear' is and how it happens? The birth happened to her exactly as to other women, consciously with her mind functioning normally and with the parts of her body *helping along*, as is proper at the time of birth, in order that she should be his normal natural mother and he her natural normal son. For this reason her body did not abandon its natural functions which belong to childbirth, except that she gave birth without sin. . . . *For grace does not destroy or impede nature and nature's works. Indeed grace improves and promotes them*" (emphasis added).

64. This corresponds to Augustine's "cooperating grace."

65. It is precisely at this juncture that the present work of the Finnish school has argued that Luther spoke not only of the indwelling Spirit but more importantly of the indwelling Christ. That Luther did this is undeniable. For the purpose of this work, however, I refer to both, indwelling Spirit and indwelling Christ, interchangeably, even as Luther himself did. For more on this most interesting development in Luther studies, see Carl E. Braaten and Robert Jenson, eds., *Union with Christ: The New Finnish Interpretation of Luther* (Grand Rapids: Eerdmans, 1998).

them away from sinning and when instructed by the Word, by faith, and by prayer, they refuse to yield to the desires of the flesh. When they resist the flesh this way, they nail it to the cross with its passions and desires. Thus although the flesh is still alive and in motion, it cannot accomplish what it wishes, because it is fastened to the cross by its hands and feet.... Dressed in the armor of God, with faith, hope and the sword of the Spirit, they fight back at the flesh; and with these nails they fasten it to the cross, so that against its will it is forced to be subject to the Spirit.[66]

Here the cross is not delivered from without—but rather embraced internally—not to awaken suffering, but to overcome it! Here the cross is a tool of the believer who works with the Spirit to "nail" her unruly passions and desires to Christ's cross. Dressed for battle, she wields the sword of the Spirit, forcing that part of herself against which she has managed to effectively turn her will with the help of the Spirit within her. This is hardly the picture of a nonparticipant. She is decidedly more than a conduit for a volition not her own. The agent is the very one who, by her willing identification with the indwelling Spirit, assumes a transformed identity empowered and sustained by God.

Faith Active in Love

In faith, Luther said, such an overcoming is possible, not in passivity, but by way of an ongoing tenacious struggle. "Faith is never inactive."[67] By an "inward godliness we become Christ's heritage, and by sober and righteous living... good works are wrought."[68] By these good works, says Luther, we serve our neighbors and ourselves. Trying to learn exactly what God wants of us should not be a problem, Luther insists. "Look to your neighbor. There you will find enough to do, a thousand kind offices to render.... Do not suffer yourselves to be misled into believing you will reach heaven by praying and attending Church..., while you pass by your neighbor."[69] Lay hold of the Gospel, and "out of this grow love and praise to God.... This gives courage to do or leave undone."[70]

66. *LW* 27:96.
67. Martin Luther, "Sermon for Christmas Eve; Titus 2:11-15," in *The Sermons of Martin Luther*, trans. John Nicholas Lenker (Grand Rapids: Baker Book House, 1983), 6:135.
68. Ibid., 138.
69. Ibid., 125–26.

Leaving something undone raises important questions, especially for women. The Christian is called to discover her work by allowing God to lead; but she is not expected to allow herself to be manipulated by unhealthy or imprudent demands. Quoting from Paul, Luther declares, "If I were still pleasing men, I should not be a servant of Christ (Gal 1:10)." "Where saving grace of God comes," he continues, "the pernicious favor must be ignored. He who would taste the former must reject and forget the latter."[71] On the other hand, sloth is obviously not a good reason to leave a task undone. Discernment is key, and decisions must be made contextually, without succumbing to a new legalism in an effort to overcome old habits. "Faith must not be chained and imprisoned, nor bound by an ordinance to any work," Luther insists.[72] Christian freedom must not be allowed to become a new law. But taking our cue from Luther's own experience when he was busily tending to the spiritual needs of the sick and dying during the plague at Wittenberg, we can grasp the criterion by which he divided up his time and resources in ever-changing situations. Given the very great need for pastoral encouragement (and the relatively few pastors available to do it), Luther was not prepared to use valuable time and energy tending to someone so near death that they could not take in his counsel. We recall his rather fierce denunciation of those who waited until the last minute to call the pastor. Neither was he going to offer Communion to those who either had not bothered to learn what it meant or were, in their present state, incapable of learning. Luther specifically noted that the emotional needs of those close to the dying would not be a sufficient reason for him to make a pastoral call. The standard by which Luther appears to have made these pastoral decisions was whether salvation still remained an open possibility. He decided which neighbor to go to and which to leave alone, not on the basis of their pleas, but by determining himself how he could most effectively use his pastoral skills to bring people to a saving faith before they died.

Disappointing Results and a Refocusing of the Process

While Luther referred clearly and often to the necessary discipline and restraint of the "old Adam" in many of his earlier writings, and to the spontaneous nature of that love that springs from faith, his apparent surprise and disappointment at

---

70. Martin Luther, "Sermon for Christmas Eve; Titus 2:11-15 (paragraph 3),"
www.martinluthersermons.com/sermon14.html.
71. *LW* 52:29.
72. *LW* 51:76.

the meager social consequences of the newly liberated gospel message elicited from him an ever-more careful rendering of the process by which the "fruits of faith" are to be realized.

In 1522, Luther delivered a series of sermons in Wittenberg, hoping to quell the rising revolutionary spirit. Luther's description of a faith devoted to the building up of the faith community, rather than a focus on individual transformation, is notable in these sermons.

> It is true, you have the true gospel and the pure Word of God, but no one as yet has given his goods to the poor, no one has yet been burned. . . . Nobody extends a helping hand to another, nobody seriously considers the other person, but everyone looks out for himself and his own gain, insists on his own way, and lets everything else go hang. . . . Nobody looks after the poor to see how you might be able to help them. This is a pity. You have heard many sermons about it and all my books are full of it and have this one purpose, to urge you to faith and love.[73]

Luther's first set of lectures on Galatians provided him with the opportunity to revisit this matter in greater detail. In an early remark from these lectures, Luther complains that "the more we exhort and arouse our people to do good works, to practice love toward one another, and to get rid of their concern for the stomach, the more lazy and listless they become for any practice of godliness."[74] In this reversal of his earlier optimism Luther recognized that the situation called for pastoral attention. "The few," he concedes, "who acknowledge the glory of [Christian] freedom, who at the same time are ready to be the servants of others through love, and who know that according to the flesh they are debtors to the brethren—give us a happiness that is greater than the sadness that can be caused by the infinite number of those who abuse this freedom."[75] Unfortunately, Luther laments, most [people] smugly "shrug off this yoke and obligation of the flesh."[76]

> They transform the freedom of the Spirit into the license and lust of the flesh. Although they will not believe us but will make fun of us, we make this sure announcement to these smug despisers: If they

---

73. *LW* 51:96.
74. *LW* 27:53.
75. *LW* 27:51.
76. *LW* 27:50.

use their bodies and their powers for their own lusts—as they are certainly doing when they refuse to help the poor and to share, but defraud their brethren in business and acquire things by fair means or foul—then they are not free, as they loudly claim to be, but have lost both Christ and freedom, and are slaves of the devil, so that now, under the title of Christian freedom, their state is seven times as bad as it used to be.[77]

To his students, most of whom would become pastors, Luther suggested the following: "To those who are afraid and have already been terrified by the burden of their sins Christ the Savior and the gift should be announced, not Christ the example and the lawgiver. But to those who are smug and stubborn the example of Christ should be set forth, lest they use the Gospel as a pretext for the freedom of the flesh."[78]

Luther was, in those days, particularly concerned for the spiritual welfare of those who had lost their way in the translation of faith into love—to those in bondage to sloth, as well as to those who still struggled with anxiety and despair. Thus Luther proceeded to take up in his later Galatians lectures the problem of the *reluctant*, but nevertheless *faithful*, will—a will he had earlier described as apparently automatic or spontaneous under the power of faith.[79] But by this time, Luther was willing to concede on the basis of irrefutable

---

77. *LW* 27:50.

78. *LW* 27:35.

79. In his 1520 *The Freedom of a Christian*, Luther speaks of the "joyful zeal" of faith, and of "works [done] out of a *spontaneous love*." "That which is impossible for you to accomplish by trying to fulfill all the works of the law . . . you will accomplish quickly and easily through faith" (*LW* 31:349, 359). It is this early emphasis on the spontaneity of good works that has been appropriated as Luther's final word on the subject by those post-WWII theologians particularly devoted to retaining the absolute monergism of justification. In the process, however, they obscure the synergism of those works that follow from faith. Indeed, Helmut Thielicke even rejects the concept of causality, but prefers to think of faith as a single "Word-event" that entails spontaneous good works. Thielicke writes, for example, "We lay particular emphasis on the term *sponte* because it describes most felicitously the directness of the relation between justification and works. . . . The new obedience is 'automatic' in the sense that it cannot be otherwise" Thielicke, *Theological Ethics*, vol. 1, *Foundations*, trans. William H. Lazareth (Grand Rapids: Eerdmans, 1979), 63.[79] The freedom that is unleashed in faith is the "acquired freedom" to choose effectively (volitionally) for and with God. In Luther's famous opening lines of *The Freedom of A Christian*, he writes, "Many people have considered Christian faith an easy thing, and not a few have given it a place among the virtues. They do this because they have not experienced it and have never tasted the great strength there is in faith. It is impossible to write well about it or to understand what has been written about it unless one has at one time or another experienced the courage which faith gives a man when trials oppress him" (*LW* 31:343).

evidence that there was often a gap between understanding the gospel, on one hand, and living it out, on the other. And this, he now realized, he had failed to address in his earlier work. Then, in the wake of this less than perfect congruity between hearing and response, Luther applied himself to the pastoral task of facilitating not only the reception but also the *endurance* and *growth* of faith—the transformation of the faithful. Luther now framed personal transformation in the cosmic context of a battle waged against demons, with the devil at their head, determined to destroy the freedom and work of Christ.

ENDURANCE AND TRANSFORMATION IN CHRIST

"Every saint"[80] wrote Luther, "feels and confesses that his flesh resists the Spirit and that these two are opposed to each other, so that he cannot do what he would want to, even though he sweats and strains to do so."[81] "The good will is present, as it should be—it is, of course, the Spirit Himself resisting the flesh—and it would rather do good, fulfill the Law, love God and the neighbor, etc. But the flesh does not obey this will but resists it. . . . [While God] does not impute this sin . . . it does not follow . . . that you should minimize sin or think of it as something trivial."[82] "God hates sin," Luther cautioned. "Sin is really sin, regardless of whether you commit it before or after you have come to know Christ. . . . I say this to keep anyone from supposing that once faith has been accepted, sin should not be emphasized."[83] Luther did not expect perfection—what he expected was endurance. "It is one thing to be aroused by the flesh and not to tolerate its desires any further but to walk and to withstand by the Spirit; it is quite another thing to give in to the flesh and to do its works with a smug air, to persist in them, and yet at the same time to put on a pretense of piety. . . . Persistence in sin is the worst of all."[84] Indeed, Luther says in reference to Paul (Rom. 8:13), "If you forsake the guidance of the Spirit and follow the flesh, you will gratify the desires of the flesh, and you will die."[85] "What I am saying is that there are two contrary guides in you, the Spirit and the flesh. God has stirred up a conflict and fight in your body. . . . All I am requiring of you now—and, for that matter, all that you are able to produce—is

---

80. Luther here uses the title "saint" to refer to all baptized believers—those, that is, who have the Spirit.
81. *LW* 27:75.
82. *LW* 27:75.
83. *LW* 27:75.
84. *LW* 27:80.
85. *LW* 27:70.

that you follow the guidance of the Spirit."[86] We must struggle, and we have no rest. Nevertheless, Christ remains the victor and the Lord.[87]

Werner Elert seconds the point: "Struggling is not submission. Faith is never a resting."[88] It is precisely when one falls back from the struggle and passively acquiesces—when one relinquishes the faith—that the Spirit is lost. "It is," wrote Luther, "as though Paul were saying . . . 'Now *it is up to you* to be diligently on your guard.'"[89]

THE MYSTERY OF HUMAN FREEDOM IN THE CONTEXT OF GOD'S PROVIDENCE

What then shall we say about the interrelationship between "things above" and "things below"? Luther's exhortation to action suggests that, from where sinners stand, the will is always free to grasp God's outstretched hand. If the will could not do this, then Luther would do better to engage in intercessory prayer than to address his exhortations to an agency incapable of effective choosing and acting. Thus it appears that Luther does view the particular battle in which he (or someone else) is existentially engaged to be "open to both sides." The outcome from below is *not yet determined*.

McSorley suggests that Luther's unwillingness to use the language of freedom, even while confessing human responsibility for sin, expresses a voluntaristic view of God's justice—that is to say, whatever God commands must be good, no matter how unjust it seems to us. This attribution, as noted earlier, does not seem to be warranted. Luther is well aware of the "injustice" that seems inescapable in regard to God's predestining will, but "we have no right to inquire" why God acts in ways that seem, indeed *are*, unfair *from the human perspective*.[90] Nor is he prepared to downplay God's ultimate predestining will in what he takes to be a description of human freedom that is so easily and so often misconstrued by Christians in ways that put their faith (and ultimate destiny) in danger.

Is it possible to make sense out of Luther's absolute rejection of free will on the one hand and his exhortations to struggle in the Spirit on the other? Abundantly clear is the fact that Luther rejects the scholastic doctrine of free

---

86. *LW* 27:65.

87. Werner Elert, *The Structure of Lutheranism*, trans. Walter Hansen (Saint Louis: Concordia, 1962), 445.

88. Ibid.

89. *LW* 27:48, emphasis added.

will; but perhaps he does not reject the critical content that the doctrine is designed to protect—human responsibility. If people do have real responsibility, it is exercised in the context of *Anfechtungen*, as individuals are drawn into the cosmic conflict. We have seen Luther make the claim that the agency by which Christians faithfully take up their vocations comes not from the acting individual but from the call—from given relationships, need, and the person's ability—all of which help to determine what specific task is theirs. Nevertheless, a person must still chose to do it. While it is clear that Luther does understand people to be making effective choices within these contexts, his own prophetic and pastoral vocation encourages him to undermine human pride whenever possible, in the interests of driving sinners into the arms of Christ. The Wittenberg theology is for the sake of sinners, and so Luther is sometimes willing to speak in unusual and exaggerated ways, as we have seen. To support the doctrine of a free will is, in Luther's view, both impious and dangerous. At the same time, Luther recognizes and responds to the fact that individuals do in fact make agential choices with regard to their vocation; likewise, individuals do in fact make effective choices about whether to identify themselves with Christ or with the devil. In both cases, Luther lavishly dishes out pastoral exhortation in the hopes of effectively encouraging individual agents to make the right choice.

Anfechtungen are located in the conscience. One steps up to one's human responsibility when one enters the courtroom of the conscience to dispute. It cannot be avoided forever. The devil is the knave who comes knocking with an invitation that is irresistible—not because it is a delight but because one's very life is on trial. If the calling card is the law, the human response is the

---

90. It appears that Luther was wholly aware of what counts as "injustice," and we see his own cognitive struggle as he attempted to hold together God's predestining will on the one hand and his discomfort with Christian submission to that which is an "outrageous injustice" on the other. It is in the context of a hypothetical forced marriage that we see Luther struggling to both discover and come to terms with "God's will." It is important, in this context, to bear in mind the relationship Luther saw between the commandment to honor father and mother and the commandment to love God. Parental authority, like the authority of the state, is derived from divine authority, which works through these offices or orders of creation. Luther writes, "I would . . . advise those weak Christians who may be unable to comply with Christ's command, to seek and gain the good offices of princes, burghermasters, or other authorities, that they may put a stop to such *outrageous injustice, deprive the father of his devilish power, rescue the child from him, and restrict him to the proper use of his parental authority*. Although a Christian is in duty bound to tolerate injustice, the temporal authority is also under obligation to punish and prevent such injustice and to guard and uphold the right. *Should the government too prove to be negligent or tyrannical, as a last resort the child might flee to another land and abandon both parent and government, just as in former times certain weak Christians fled from tyrants into the wilderness*" (emphasis added) (*LW* 45:390–393).

recognition that one must justify oneself. In Luther's theology, this is where the fundamental choice is made, again and again.

The key dualism in Luther's thinking is life and death, where there is no middle ground. Neither is there middle ground between Christ and the devil, nor between the *Deus absconditus* and the *Deus revelatus*, nor between life as a glorious adventure and life as drudgery. It is the *Deus absconditus* who rules the courtroom insofar as Christ is absent. There is no joy here and no freedom. There is no debate. It is simply a matter of whether things are bad or worse, perhaps slightly better today than yesterday, but always short of the mark. Justification cannot be earned.

Christ—the Word—lives in both heaven and hell at the same time, in the world that is glorious and in the world that is despair and death. Christ comes to the dark side so as to provide a glimpse of what things look like where the *Deus revelatus* rules. Once one catches sight of it, there is no way to step back. Now the tension has been established between God and the devil, life and death, heaven and hell. Scripture is the swaddling clothes in which the Christ child is laid; Scripture is also the place where the word is stored if one can find it; or if it finds you—always alive, always ready to break out, but only able to do so by way of human beings who can speak and understand it. The promise of God must be delivered by a human being.

The encounter with the conscience is one of words and ideas, as in any debate; but it is the human being who provides the location, the language, and the purpose. This call into responsible being has been perfectly designed for humans. It is a courtroom that reason cannot avoid. Once one has glimpsed the *Deus revelatus* and heard the Word, one cannot avoid choosing; because with the coming of Christ, the *Anfechtung*-event is transformed. The devil continues to announce each appointment in the courtroom as he opens the law books. But with Christ, the space is rearranged. The judge behind the bench recedes, and Luther becomes the judge as Christ and the devil arrange their briefs on the desk. Luther is listening to, debating with, and at the same time judging the power of their arguments. The devil argues directly with Luther, but more importantly, through Luther, with Christ, who is standing nearby, coming and going, depending on whether Luther remembers to send for him in his confusion. As the devil hurls his threats at Luther, Christ is the sword in Luther's hand; but the sword does not win the battle without Luther wielding it well. The only way that Christ can overcome the devil is if Luther is convinced—if the argument holds. Luther is captive to the word of God—yes—but only if the word of God can stand against the devil's disputation.

Like the halter that controls the horse, some arguments hold better than others. A horse is not passive, but will escape the harness if it's not well made. Who has the stronger harness, God or the devil? Reason, like the horse, is by its very nature bound to test the strength of the harness. When Luther begs Cardinal Cajetan to engage in argument, it is because Luther wants to know what is true; he is eager to test his reading of the facts. If Cajetan will not engage Luther in argument, then Luther must decide what is true in isolation; it would be better for Luther if Cajetan would wage a good argument. Is Luther compelled to believe? If he doubts the truth of Christ's promise, he is done for; and human beings cannot avoid doubt, especially in regard to their own destiny. Luther must be convinced, and he must also hang on. Thus Luther is an agent in this believing. He is never passive, and the responsibility ultimately lies with him. God has sent forth the Word to fight for Luther, but Luther has to be convinced. It is his battle to lose, or to win.

While it is true, as McSorley points out, that as late as 1537, Luther "still held it to be 'nothing but error and stupidity' when 'scholastic theologians' taught that after the fall of Adam 'man has a free will, either to do good and refrain from evil or to refrain from good and do evil,'"[91] it is also the case that Luther was devoted to shifting the theological gaze away from human beings and back toward God. When Luther, in his 1537 Smalcald Articles, refuted the scholastics by making precisely the opposite claim, it might have been first and foremost a linguistic reversal intended to likewise reverse the direction of their gaze. It was also a reaffirmation of Augustine's "operating grace," not to mention a claim derivative of the biblical illustration Luther so loved to remind people of—only a good tree bears good fruit. None of these references seeks to make the actual experience of the Christian life, viewed from the temporal perspective, comprehensible; but rather, they have, as McSorley suggests, the structure of a confession.

It appeared good to Luther, in the presence of the living God, not to search too deeply into the divine majesty, but rather to hold firmly to that relationship with God in Christ, which he knew, from both Scripture and personal experience, to be the ground upon which everything else rested. It was Luther's gift (often experienced as a curse) to recognize the ubiquity of God—and, more importantly, to recognize, in faith, the power and promise of God's right hand extended in Christ. Indeed, as McSorley suggests, it was Luther's entirely Catholic contribution (which was often distorted by a polemical lack of charity on both sides) to prophetically recall us to that ground,

---

91. Theodore Tappert, ed., *The Lutheran Book of Concord: The Confessions of the Evangelical Lutheran Church* (Philadelphia: Fortress Press, 1959), 302.

out of which we are empowered to become the responsible, relational selves whom we are called by God to be.

The Inner Action of Choice: Coming Forth in Freedom

The faithful, as they come to recognize those new tasks to which they are called, realize ever more clearly the gap between the people they are and the people that their given vocations call them to be. Faith, says Luther, makes that which once seemed impossible possible; and in the power of that possibility, shortcomings are both recognized and transformed. Those who struggle in the faith are moved to do better; and they look for transformation through the power of the Spirit. They may wish to be more daring, more disciplined, more decisive, and more courageous in undertaking new challenges. What they seek is a new will to do those things to which they are drawn and from which they are simultaneously repelled by old fears and the hesitation this entails. There is a new desire—a new will—within them. It is not a will that is suddenly, miraculously whole, so that "works flow forth spontaneously."[92] But according to Luther, it is a good will that was not initially theirs. This is the will of the indwelling Spirit eliciting participation—drawing forth a reluctant will to join in willing what is difficult.

To make this more concrete, let us consider the case of a woman who wants to want x, where x is that vocational goal she takes to be God's will for her. This might be a Martha Quest, who has come to faith and begun to establish priorities. Or, in a more advanced situation, it is the case of the woman who is frightened to risk her relationship with her husband by taking up a career alongside her work as mother and homemaker. Still, she is convinced that God is calling her to new vocational tasks, by way of her talents and social location. Perhaps she sees a great need for trained nurses and doctors, and knows that this is something she can do. Perhaps this is Kari Malcolm's friend twenty-five years later.

In each of these cases, we begin with a person of faith—a person already alive to a sense of vocational obligation. There is gratitude at work as well, and a longing for wholeness and self-integration derived from her identity with God as her own unique gifts begin to be realized in effective and visible ways. She who had been in hiding begins to take on responsibility, or at least begins to see that this is a possibility, and that it would be good—both for her neighbor

---

92. "It is impossible for faith in Him to be idle; for it is alive, and it itself works and triumphs, and in this way works flow forth spontaneously" (*LW* 29:123).

and for herself. She is tentative but committed to God. She is a Christian who wants to want to do that which she believes she is called to. She is a theonomous self—in her sense of standing on and in God—but a theonomous self with lots of residual flesh still to overcome.

"Every saint," wrote Luther, "feels and confesses that his flesh resists the Spirit and that these two are opposed to each other, so that he cannot do what he would want to, even though he sweats and strains to do so."[93] Like the divided self, our example wants to do x, or at least she wants to want to do x; but other inclinations get in the way (such as wanting to avoid embarrassment, wanting to stay safe, or wanting to protect intimate relationships). Yet she at least wants to want x. This is the situation that Luther identifies with the indwelling Spirit battling against the residual flesh.

Where did this desire for x come from? asks Luther. Where "good will is present…it is, of course, the Spirit Himself resisting the flesh…."[94] Yet even where he identifies the "good will" with the Spirit, Luther does not deny the capacity for responsible choice and action. Addressing the individual who is in this situation, with a will that wants to x, or wants to want x, Luther writes, "All I am requiring of you now—and for that matter, all that you are able to produce—is that you follow the guidance of the Spirit."[95] But how does one actively participate in this process of synergistic willing? What is it that Luther is "requiring" the faithful to do? How does one decisively identify with one desire rather than with another?

One of the ways such a commitment might be made is by knowing that the decisive identification has already been made. That is to say, if the necessary action is identification with desire x and withdrawal of identification from desire y, and if the closest one can get to this is wanting to want to identify with x such that one is moved actually to will x, then to be convinced that one is *already* identified with x might be an empowering piece of information. It might make it possible to act on a will that seems to precede and support one's own. Now this recognition of the presence of such a prevenient will seems to be what Luther points to when he says that where "the good will is present . . . it is, of course, the Spirit Himself resisting the flesh."[96] In other words, if what you want is to will with God, then you should know that you are *already willing* with the will of God.

---

93. *LW* 27:75.
94. *LW* 27:75.
95. *LW* 27:65–66.
96. *LW* 27:75. See n106.

In the context of the battle between Spirit and flesh, as Luther drew it, what one wants is to be identified with the Spirit decisively enough to will x effectively in conformity with the Spirit. To recognize that the good will one has points to the Spirit already willing, allows one to rest in, rather than work toward, that identification with the new desire. The Spirit has already identified with the self, so the breech has been closed. What is necessary from the human side is consent and cooperation.[97] "When I have this faith," wrote Luther, "then I am certain God is fighting for me."[98] "I can defy the devil, death, hell and sin, and all the harm with which they threaten me. . . . You [must] believe that God steps in for you . . . as if He were saying, 'Fall in behind me without fear or delay, and then let us see what can harm you.'"[99]

Luther was working from Paul's description of the divided self as a battle of flesh against Spirit. "It is very useful to the faithful," he wrote, "to know this doctrine of Paul well and to meditate on it, because it gives wonderful comfort to [Christians] in their trial."[100] "If I had properly understood Paul's statements, 'The desires of the flesh are against the Spirit' . . . I would not have tortured myself to such a point."[101]

Having accepted what he takes to be Paul's understanding of the persisting problems of the "flesh," Luther focused not so much on the eradication of old, now-rejected desires that drive one to do what they "would not." What matters is faith (rather than works per se)—that is, one's relationship with the indwelling God the Spirit. "What I am saying," he wrote, "is that there are two contrary guides[102] in you, the Spirit and the flesh. God has stirred up a conflict and fight in your body."[103] Christians are expected to persist in the power of the Spirit. The faithful are called to struggle against their old (and now partially rejected) desires of the flesh. These characterized the old self from which one withdraws. Consent to the presence of the new will—to the recognition, that is, of the bridegroom, and God's empowering presence in, with, and under one's own—requires an active response from the one whom God invites. It

---

97. Whether this "consent" is itself an act that is free (insofar as one might or might not consent) is a critical question in the debate over free will. Yet, as I have argued here, Luther's passionate attempt to awaken such consent in his address to those who suffer their own *anfechtungen* suggests that he assumes the potential exists for his speaking to effect some response from them.

98. *LW* 51:93.

99. *LW* 51:93.

100. *LW* 27:73.

101. *LW* 27:73.

102. Notably, a "guide" leads by invitation rather than by necessity.

103. Gustaf Wingren, *Luther on Vocation*, trans. Carl C. Rasmussen (Philadelphia: Muhlenberg, 1957), 81.

requires a *decision to commit* oneself to that which seems to be "outside." Thus the responsible self is always agentially involved; and, as it was in the case of the *coram Deo anfechtungen*, this agency is particularly necessary in those situations where the illusion of alienation is most powerful. It is just when one seems to be looking at a hopelessly difficult goal that one is exhorted to cling actively to the Spirit that is already willing in concert with one's own.

To engage in this struggle is itself an act of prayer. It is to depend on the new will that has been given, to follow it in hope, and to pray to God for the faith and courage that are required to assume new responsibilities and new habits that point toward a renewed character—a transformed self. It is to have permission to stop identifying with old habits and to allow new ones to emerge.

Luther's growing interest and theological engagement in the struggles of the faithful against temporal temptations were not, as some seem to believe, an abandonment of his earlier emphasis on God's all-embracing grace given in Jesus Christ. While Luther's early theology, which focused on God's justifying work in Christ, downplayed any pious activity that encouraged a misplaced pride of accomplishment, it is a mistake to assume that his later interest in the incremental sanctification of the faithful was a departure from his early theocentric commitments. To overcome residual desires of the flesh, out of a new and good will—one that is elicited and sustained by the Spirit—is to enact faith over and over again in prayerful identity with the indwelling Spirit. Such a description of action rests on a most orthodox assertion that God's work precedes and supports one's own without at the same time denying one the freedom to resist the invitation of the Spirit. God's empowering presence is already enacted in a most personal and intimate way, already expressed in a new will. The human response—the reception of what already is, and the consent to it with one's own volition—is not superfluous or redundant. It is the limiting condition, and the locus of faith. It is the opening of the self to its theonomous ground—that ground out of which the self discovers courage and exercises independence. The struggle associated with the suffering that vocational challenges bring "urges faith to call upon God's name," wrote Luther. For "faith grows precisely by such prayer and praise to God and thereby recovers and strengthens itself."[104]

---

104. Wingren, *Luther on Vocation*, 119.

Conclusion

Luther's contentious theological claims—claims that ultimately resulted in his excommunication from the Church of Rome—are first and foremost the result of a different perspective. Like the problem of drawing a round world on a flat sheet of paper, everything depends on where you start. When historian and cartographer Dr. Arno Peters first introduced his "area accurate" map in 1974, it was met with indignation, especially by Europeans accustomed to the map they had always known. Peters argued that his new map represented a more accurate view of the land masses. The traditional map of the world—the 1569 Mercator map—had been drawn from the perspective of Western Europeans.[1] Politically, it seemed good to Peters to point out that Europe is not, in fact, the center of the world. Luther likewise drew his theological map knowing full well that it would be offensive; but like Peters, he was hoping to arouse a new consciousness. The church, he thought, was playing a dangerous game, and an impious one. If some were oblivious to God's terrifying gaze, Luther was not. He saw himself and the whole world teetering on the brink of eternal chaos and terror. But Luther drew his theological maps with God always in the center, and so tended to push everyone else out of the picture. As with Peters, the provocation was a serious one. Some worried that Luther's theological remapping would spur a dangerous moral collapse; others felt that his assertions were offensive to truth itself. God had set human beings into a position of responsibility from the very beginning. From the perspective of those Luther was trying to displace, his refusal to acknowledge the dignity, purpose, and value of human beings was an affront not only to them but also to God. But Luther was a man on a mission; and the mission was to put God back into the center. Like Peters, Luther was convinced that his approach to the theological remapping represented a more accurate rendering of what is real. For Luther, this was a matter of infinite importance; he believed he was dealing

---

1. The Mercator map was particularly helpful for navigation because the lines on Mercator's map matched the compass readings that ships in those days used to find their way. The size and shape of the land masses reflected a choice made by Mercator to draw the land according its real shape as these land masses actually appear in nature. If Mercator had opted instead to draw them according to size he would have had to distort their shape in order to do it. Thus it was not an error but a conscious choice to make the land masses smaller so as to maintain their natural shape. (See http://www.petersmap.com/page2.html, accessed January 2013.)

with nothing less than the future of humanity, judged and condemned, under the wrath and the mercy of Almighty God.

Luther was certainly not the first to see things this way. He was the bearer of a tradition within the church that boasted a very prominent lineage, but a lineage that had, in those days, fallen out of favor. And so, in his own day, he sounded like a prophet. He not only (inadvertently) started a reformation, but he also ignited a new religious enthusiasm. Luther's prophetic voice effectively renewed and enlivened the faith of many; but it is also the case that from the very start there were those who thought his pronouncements were excessive and dangerous. The most recent have been offended by his teaching with regard to gender issues in particular. For those already on the margins, Luther's theological therapy has sometimes been experienced as destructive rather than restorative. He was aiming at the people who put themselves in God's place; but his scattershot hit many who didn't, and don't. Thus the focus of this project has been to consider these concerns and look for resources within the Lutheran tradition that might be helpful.

I began in the introduction by highlighting some of the key issues in Luther's theology that have concerned feminist theologians. Daphne Hampson, reflecting the teaching of prominent post–World War II Luther scholars, has cogently identified key anthropological factors that complicate Luther's theology, particularly for women. Luther, in Hampson's assessment, fails to provide the ontic structures required for a self that can persist through time. And, she explains, this presents a grave difficulty for women, given the feminist goal of self-empowerment. I have suggested that her reading of Luther is the result of a tradition that defines itself systematically on the basis of article 4 in the Augsburg Confession—the article, many believe, by which "the church stands or falls"[2]—namely, justification by faith alone. I have suggested here in these chapters that it is the overwhelming dominance of Luther's inner, relational anthropology among those who identify Luther with his early theology of justification that has resulted in Hampson's analysis.

The apparent failure of Luther to provide the necessary anthropological capacities for human agency is one of the primary challenges that I've attempted to address in these pages, arguing that Luther's early description of temporal capacities as "nothing"[3] reflects his biblical (rather than philosophical) starting point. We have seen that Luther had no doubt that the "natural man" does exist, with all the usual capacities one expects to find; but Luther was reluctant

---

2. "The Augsburg Confession," art. 4, in *The Book of Concord: The Confessions of the Evangelical Lutheran Church*, ed. and trans. Theodore Tappert (Philadelphia: Fortress Press, 1959), 30.

3. *LW* 27:93.

to identify these capacities philosophically. Luther thought philosophy, when applied to theological questions, was not only incorrect but also impious *coram Deo*, and, therefore, dangerous *coram hominibus*; thus he would have no part in it. But Luther's early dismissal of creation did not persist. Once Luther was engaged in life outside the monastery, he began to appreciate it more and more.

The deafening silence on Luther's developing appreciation of both world and self appears to be the result of a tradition that, following Luther, took the work of theology to be first and foremost for the sake of salvation rather than systematic clarity. And since (until the recent feminist insights) salvation has been understood by Lutheran theologians to begin universally with an attack on self-assertion, the tradition has frequently attempted to apply this traditional theological therapy to those whom, as Hampson says, "it should never have been directed."[4] As I hope to have demonstrated here, Luther paid close attention to the results of his preaching; when he observed that the Word was not producing the effect he had expected, Luther adjusted his presuppositions, teaching that pastors needed to pay attention to their audience.[5] For some, Luther concluded, it would be better to teach the traditional imitation of Christ, with its emphasis on the law. The preaching of free justification should be reserved for those already humbled.[6] And while neither of these approaches addresses the form of sin that has been most recently linked to the experience of women, Luther's discovery—that sin takes more than one form—is an important one, often overlooked.

Luther had identified two responses to the one underlying sin of human alienation from God—pride, in the case of those not yet aware of their situation, and terror among those who were. What neither he nor the tradition in general noticed (given the fact that women were by and large denied a seat at the theological round table) is a third manifestation of the sin with which we are concerned today. In some sense it is a situation that seems to precede the other two. What some have called the sin of self-abnegation consists essentially in a reluctance to acknowledge that human dignity, which entails responsibility–a refusal to step into that light, whereby pride or terror is generated before God.

---

4. Daphne Hampson, "On Power and Gender," *Modern Theology* 4, no. 3 (April 1988): 234–50 (239).

5. "In our churches where the true doctrine of good works is at forth with great diligence, it is amazing how much sluggishness and lack of concern prevails. The more we exhort and arouse our people to do good works . . . the more lazy and listless they become" (*LW* 27:53).

6. "To those who are afraid and have already been terrified by the burden of their sins Christ the Savior and the gift should be announced, not Christ the example and the lawgiver. But to those who are smug and stubborn the example of Christ should be set forth, lest they use the Gospel as a pretext for the freedom of the flesh and thus become smug" (*LW* 27:35).

But one must know what God expects before attempting to avoid it. This holds back, refusing to stand before the face of God, not authentic immaturity so much as a kind of reactive, immature stance. Recognizing that responsibility attends maturity, the sin of self-abnegation appears to mimic the child who, though old enough to be capable of assuming an appropriate degree of self-care, is nevertheless unwilling to step aside for the sake of a younger sibling, reverting rather to more childish behavior. This sort of behavior, unbecoming to a person who should know better, is affectionately condoned in the young. The sin of self-abnegation, then, might be understood as the reluctance of an individual to metaphorically leave the nursery.[7] What is but a brief setback for the child can become the adopted (false) identity of an adult, where the cost is considerably higher. For to fail in this is to relinquish many of the natural goods of mature personhood. Thus "to come to oneself," as both Hampson and Plaskow put it, requires the acknowledgment of what one already knows to be the case with the addition of something new that allows one to get on with life. The recognition that something is being avoided must precede the act of courage by which one steps into the light. Notably, this two-part approach to redemption parallels Luther's assumed process by which redemption takes place; the law "kills" what is old so as to clear the way for the reception of the gospel promise. Our question here has been whether Luther's brand of theology is more or less appropriate to the theologically therapeutic intervention that women are looking for—and I am suggesting that it is. Hampson is clearly convinced it is not, whereas Plaskow asks "whether the Protestant doctrine of justification *per se* is . . . more relevant to men's than to women's experience." One thing seems to be clear, however—any theology that further encourages the avoidance of God by insisting on a notion of self that is autonomous from its divine ground will succeed only in moving a person from immaturity into pride or terror rather than into that restoration of relationship with God that salvation implies. When Hampson says, for example, that it is "not natural" for one to look outside the self for oneself, she appears to be adopting a view of "inner" and "outer" that reflects an outdated understanding of persons as cut apart from one another, each separate in his or her self.

In opposition to Hampson's position on this matter (if I understand her rightly), Luther's understanding of God's "right hand" suggests that the power of God is ubiquitous; God is in, with, and under everything that is. "The

---

7. Why this appears to be the favored form of sin among women may be the result of collusion with the socially received message that women and children have much in common, as Judith Plaskow suggests. This form of manipulation, however, could not arise without the maturity to recognize the call to responsibility one is so assiduously avoiding.

power of God cannot be so determined and measured," writes Luther, "for it is uncircumscribed and immeasurable, beyond and above all that is or may be."[8] In the face of such a God, concepts like "inside" and "outside" are meaningless. Luther's understanding of God's presence contrasts markedly with Calvin's view (which to a large degree attempts to retain the spatial and material laws of this world).[9] From a feminist perspective, Luther's understanding of a truly ubiquitous God may provide some interesting possibilities even as it raises concerns about agency. Not only does it arguably sacramentalize the world, but it also suggests that God is present to the self in the most intimate way possible. For, Luther writes, the power of God "must be essentially present at all places, even in the tiniest tree leaf. The reason is this: It is God who creates, effects, and preserves all things through his almighty power and right hand . . . [Thus] he himself must be present in every single creature in its innermost and outermost being, on all sides, through and through, below and above, before and behind, so that nothing can be more truly present and within all creatures than God himself with his power."[10]

The presence of a theonomous self in Luther's thinking is central. "As little as God's being ever ceases," writes Luther, "so little does His speaking ever cease, through which all creatures came into being. But God speaks still, and without pause, since no creature exists on its own."[11] Not only is this an important part of Luther's personal experience of God, but it also reflects his Christology, which takes seriously the "totally human, totally divine" Christ of the historic creeds. In a time when we are struggling to find ways to address the growing ecological crisis, a retrieval of this link between the Eucharist and the world is a valuable component of Luther's thinking.

---

8. *LW* 37:57–58.

9. Elert, *Structure of Lutheranism*, 416. As an example of the tension between these two positions, see the following from a Reformed preacher named Georg Spindler: "The Father, they say, is everywhere. Now ascending into heaven and going to the Father are one and the same thing. Therefore ascending into heaven is tantamount to being everywhere, since, of course, going to the Father does not mean to come to the essence of the Father, because he always was with the Father, and the Father always was with Him, but to come where God's throne is. . . . In addition, they maintain that heaven, into which Christ ascended and wants to take us to Himself, is everywhere too and extends through heaven, earth, and hell, and that for this reason the Lord did not need to ascend a hairbreadth from earth in order to come to the Father with His body. For in their heaven, which is everywhere, angels and devils run around higgledy-piggledy, and the angels carry their heaven around with them, just as the devils carry their hell around with them. This is horrible to hear."

10. *LW* 37:58. For a fuller account of God's ubiquity, see *LW* 37:57–64.

11. George Forell, *Faith Active in Love: An Investigation of the Principles Underlying Luther's Social Ethics* (Minneapolis: Augsburg, 1954), 66.

But while Luther's ubiquitous Christ may be a helpful theological move from the perspective of ecology, the question here is whether or not his emphasis on God's efficacious presence is really good news for those still hesitant to become responsibly accountable adults. We have seen that Luther sometimes explicitly denies human agency in the presence of God's effective power. At the same time, however, Luther always holds human beings responsible. Like Augustine, Luther takes a view that volition is authentically free to choose one thing or another in the temporal realm, though always in accordance with the fundamental direction of the will (which is already at work).[12] As for the cooperating will with regard to temporal matters, we recall Luther's remarks about the birth of Jesus in the Christmas Eve sermon (chapter 2). There he talks about Mary's full participation in this event, even as women ordinarily participate in every birth. God's grace (or presence), he explains, does not obliterate nature, but rather perfects it. Likewise, in his descriptions of vocation, Luther will speak of God as effectively accomplishing whatever task is done. Yet he also talks about God's cooperating agency: "You are to plow and plant," Luther writes, "and then ask his blessing and pray, 'Now let God take over.' . . . He could give children without man and woman. But he does not want to do this."[13]

While one may hear Luther's language as intended to overthrow pride (and thus undermine human empowerment), this is but one way to hear him. The other is to understand the presence of God not as a threat but rather as gift. The way one receives the information about God's cooperating presence reflects whether one lives under the law and the *Deus absconditus*, or in Christian freedom, under the promise of the *Deus revelatus*. If you look around your house and "every corner seems empty," Luther tells us, you are not seeing things as they really are, but rather you see them under the aspect of the law (which, in

---

12. While Luther (and often Augustine) argues strenuously that it is God's work alone to determine the overall direction of the will, one cannot miss the fact that once Luther begins to speak of resisting the flesh in the power of the Spirit, he is quick to raise the danger of losing faith, not by failing to accomplish the discipline, but by failing to try. As with his pastoral letters written to people suffering from the temptation to despair, Luther calls upon them to fight actively against the devil, presumably with the presupposition that one can effectively resist through one's own willing. In a letter to Jerome Weller, for example, Luther writes, "Try as hard as you can to despise those thoughts which are induced by the devil. In this sort of temptation and struggle, contempt is the best and easiest method of winning over the devil. Laugh you adversary to scorn and ask who it is with whom you are talking. This devil is conquered by mocking and despising him. . . . Therefore, Jerome, joke and play games with my wife and others. In this way you will drive out your diabolical thoughts and take courage" (*Luther: Letters of Spiritual Counsel*, Library of Christian Classics, ed. and trans. Theodore Tappert [Philadelphia: Westminster, 1955], 85).

13. *LW* 14:114 (CD-ROM).

our fallen state, makes us anxious). But "if you look upon Him, you will never notice whether a corner is bare; everything will appear to you to be full, and will indeed be full. And if it is not full it is your vision which is at fault."[14] The common laborer, once she understands herself and her work as part of God's larger story, becomes nothing less than the mask of God; it is a calling, once grasped, that dignifies both self and work. Similarly, in the letter to Jerome Weller, in which Luther exhorts the young man to stand fast against the devil's temptations, not only does he suggest a number of activities, but he also assures Weller that for him to be so tempted suggests that Weller, too, must have an important role to play in God's cosmic drama. Explaining that it was Staupitz who had reassured Luther (saying that "God does not exercise you thus without reason. You will see that he intends to use you as his servant to accomplish great things"), Luther now passes on the same counsel to Weller: "I have no doubt that this will happen to you too. You will become a great man. Just see to it that you are of good courage in the meantime, and be persuaded that such utterances, especially those which fall from the lips of learned and great men, are not without prophetic quality."[15] "The hand which you reach out in order to relieve the brother's need is the hand of God," Luther writes. In a priesthood of all believers, every priest become God's effective Word, in her action and in her speaking. "The mouth of the pious teacher is the mouth of God."[16]

For the people of Luther's world who struggled to get by—those for whom life was little more than daily drudgery—the good news was the promise that their lives had meaning. Mary Stewart van Leeuwen tells the story of Queen Esther's courageous defense of her people. When her uncle first asks her to intercede for the Jews, she is more than reluctant. Life will be considerably easier if she just quietly steps aside. There is certainly no point in arousing the king's fierce anger against her if she can escape it; but Mordecai's threat suggests that Esther cannot deny who she is. "Think not that in the king's palace you will escape any more than all the other Jews. God will bring deliverance to the Jews in some other way, but you will perish" (Esther 4:13-14 RSV). Denying who you are is a dangerous business. This news might be heard as a threat; but it could also be heard as a gift. "Who knows," Mordecai asks, "whether you have not come to the kingdom for such a time as this?" (v. 15). Like the children in C. S. Lewis's *The Lion, the Witch and the Wardrobe*,[17] who find their

---

14. *LW* 45:324.
15. Tappert, *Letters of Spiritual Counsel*, 86.
16. *LW* 31:41.
17. C. S. Lewis, *The Lion, the Witch and the Wardrobe*, The Chronicles of Narnia (London: Geoffrey Bles, 1950).

way through an opening in the back of a closet only to discover they are very important people in a very big story, chosen by God to serve a great good, Mordecai reminds Esther that her life has infinite importance in the context of another, much larger story. Thus Esther stops hiding from herself. Out of her recovered identity she also recovers her agency, acting on behalf of God with great courage; and so Esther "comes to herself," as she steps into responsible adulthood.

Without the compass that comes with the recognition of who we really are, we are left with only the natural biological influences to guide our choice. Thus we are reduced to seeking survival and pleasure as the only goals we can understand. When she hears Mordacai's address and comes to recognize who she is in relation to God, Esther is drawn to God. Grateful to find that her life has meaning and purpose beyond measure, she wishes to respond, to please this God who has chosen her. Thus, Esther finds her voice; she steps into her real identity. Less freely, she might make a choice not because she really wants to but out of obedience or even fear. The first way described above, where Esther finds herself in the larger story, she responds as to a gift—life under the *Deus revelatus*; a second way of responding is, conversely, the result of an obedient and disciplined will; this is life lived out under the law. While Calvin might see this as a graced response to the "third use of the law," in Luther's view, the law "always accuses." Both responses require courage to carry through, but in the first instance, it is a courage that is standing on God; in the second, it is a courage that is drawn from self-discipline.[18] The manner in which Esther hears and embraces Mordecai's words demonstrates the specific sort of situation in which faith and courage are two sides of the same coin.

Luther's theology calls us into a life that looks with the eyes of faith for the promise, even when it is hidden under rebuke and warning. Mordacai's message to Esther was both an invitation to find herself in the larger story and a threat; she must do something now that will put her life at risk. Esther appears to move out of a new power that comes from knowing God is with her. These eyes of faith, which can find the fullness of God in every corner that is otherwise bare, reflect Luther's understanding of Christian vocation understood as an expression of the promise rather than of the law.

Could this work for Martha Quest, our real test case? Martha Quest,[19] "drifts in and out of relationships and cannot commit herself to be. . . . There is no Martha Quest as a responsible, willing being." Martha marries because

---

18. I have spoken of some apparent anomalies in Luther's overarching understanding of law and gospel; but these do not, in themselves, overturn his primary approach—in this case, the notion that the law always accuses.

the possibility is in front of her; and, after all, on what basis could she say no? Without a functional self to guide her choices, Martha has no basis for judging what she wants, and so passively receives whatever is in the offing. As Martha is alienated from herself and from God, her problems seem considerably more serious than those of Malcolm's friend, who chose marriage over the mission field. Presumably, Martha's name (i.e. Martha Quest) tells us something about her situation: Martha is looking for herself. Since she cannot find any determinative identity within to use as a standard, she is incapable of choosing. Thus Martha must attach herself, first to one person, and then another—whoever strikes her as most reliably identified with something true. She must, as Ralph Waldo Emerson suggested long ago, "hitch her wagon to [some] star" because she can find no star within herself to guide her. Chameleon-like, she assumes the identity of that to which she clings. What could function for Martha as Mordecai's words did for Esther? It would have to be something that would convince her that she—and no one else—really was being called by God into the great story for some enormously important purpose. "Who knows whether you have not come to the kingdom for such a time as this," Mordecai suggests.

Luther's theology of vocation leaves no one out of the cast. Everyone has a role to play, and Luther is quick to tell them so. These roles may shift and intertwine; they may layer up on each other, or a calling may suddenly emerge as something entirely new. Every situation is distinctive, because, for Luther, God is in the world, busily working through every created thing toward that great day when the devil will be banished forever and all of creation will come into its own. Luther appears to have had a sense of his own place in God's vast and infinitely important drama fairly early; and it was confirmed in this again and again, as he interpreted the various controversies as signs of the devil's death pangs. That those around Luther found this convincing is clear enough, for they quickly fell in, taking up their assigned roles with the same keen sense of purpose that Luther exhibited. Perhaps one of the great fascinations with Luther is this sense of prophetic certainty that he exuded—the high drama that he read into every event—and the absolute necessity to stand strong against the devil, which, in Luther's view, is the first and most important task of every true Christian. Luther, like Moredcai, calls individuals into the dangerous and important life that God has designed for each one of them.

19. Mary Stewart van Leeuwen, "The Christian Mind and the Challenge of Gender Relations," in *Sexuality and the Sacred: Sources for Theological Reflection*, ed. Sandra Longfellow and James B. Nelson (Louisville: Westminster John Knox Press, 1994), 128.

When Katie and the other nuns slipped out of the convent unobserved, they were doing a very courageous thing. Luther had been busily writing tracts that challenged the monastics to take up the real work of this world—work that was not something made-up, but the real, everyday things that God wants to accomplish so that this world can survive another day. When the young nuns landed on Luther's doorstep, he took this as a sign that God expected him to care for them and to find them husbands. When all the vocational pointers indicated to Luther that he was to "spite the devil" by marrying Katie, he did. And so they both undertook a new marriage that was not just difficult because learning to be married to someone else always is, and it was not just tricky because by then Luther was a very well-known man—a man people watched and talked about. It was challenging because theirs was a relationship understood by them both as something that was part of God's overarching plan. God was in the very midst of that marriage, down to the tiniest detail, because as Luther saw it, this all mattered infinitely to God. Luther's own sense of having been called into God's drama seems to have pervaded his life to such an extent that anyone caught in the vortex could have hardly failed to re-envision his or her own existence against the same backdrop.

This is the body of Christ "for you" on which Luther insists in the Eucharist. But the "for you" of redemption was matched in Luther's thinking by a similar "for you" that he applied to vocation. This is the marriage "for you," Katie; the child "for you." This is the schoolmaster's job "for you," or the plowing of this particular field—"for you." Might Martha Quest have been able to find herself had she heard the "for you" of the gospel and, perhaps even more, the "for you" of vocation? Perhaps—because to discover that one is already assigned an important role in a very important drama is much like discovering that one is already "saved." Justification and vocation both have a "by God alone" element to them that is pure gift for those with ears to hear. And would the discovery of such a theonomous self—brought to being by God's call, sustained and empowered by Spirit—fail to be a full self?

When Luther stepped out of the courtroom in Worms, a condemned man, with every reason to suppose he would soon die a horrible death, he threw his arms into the air and shouted with delight, "I've come through, I've come through!"[20] He did not say, "God has come through," or even "we have come through," though all these were true enough. But in saying, "I've come through," Luther spoke of himself—a self that includes God's presence. Neither "God" nor "we"—but "I"—Luther's words point toward himself as that

20. Martin Brecht, *Martin Luther: His Road to Reformation: 1483–1521*, trans. James L. Schaaf (Philadelphia, Fortress Press, 1985), 461.

in which he delights; a theonomous self that recognizes its ground and is empowered by it. Thus Luther stood his ground and shouted out with joy, having courageously enacted the task that it was his, alone with God, to do.

Index

Luther's Writings by Date and Name of Work

1513–1514
Mid-August 1513–Fall 1515: *First Lectures on the Psalms 1–75*......37, 39, 84f
    Psalm 2......37
    Psalm 9......37
    Psalm 64......39
    Psalm 69......37

1513–1515
First Lectures on the Psalms......9–10, 37, 38, 39, 45, 52, 84, 86, 87
    Psalm 115......162
For later works on the Psalms, see years 1519, 1521, 1525, 1530, 1531, 1538.

1515–1516
Lectures on Romans
    From Summer 1515......9–10, 37–39, 48, 86–87, 91–92
    Winter 1515–1516......166
        Romans 4 and 8......31–32
        Romans 8......18–19
    Summer 1516
        Romans 9......40–41, 119
        Romans 15......120–21

1516–1518
The anthropology associated with justification......86, 87–89, 90–94

1516
Bernhardi Theses......47, 48, 51

Letter to George Spalatin......37, 48

1517

Disputation Against Scholastic Theology......46, 49, 50, 52, 54, 89, 196
    Thesis 2......159
April 1517–March 1518: *Lectures on Hebrews*......51, 186
Letter to Cardinal Abrecht, Archbishop of Mainz......44, 46, 56–57
Ninety-Five Theses Against Indulgences......46, 54, 55–59, 63–64, 68, 89
    Theses 42–51, Thesis 49, Thesis 62......58
Saint Matthew's Day Sermon......55

1518

Explanations of the Ninety-Five Theses......43–44, 58, 98
    Thesis 5......57
    Theses 42–51......58, 59
    Thesis 62......58
Heidelberg Disputation......46, 47, 49, 51, 66, 67, 90, 155–56, 158, 160–62, 197
    Thesis 2......159
    Thesis 5......57, 161, 162
    Thesis 13 (on free will) 155, 156, 158–59
    Thesis 20......15
    Thesis 21......15
    Thesis 34......161
Lenten Sermon......120
Letter to George Spalatin (Feb. 15) 44
Letter to George Spalatin (Nov. 25)......64
Preface to the Complete The German Theology (anonymously written fragment, introduction by Luther)......38–39
Proceedings at Augsburg......61–64, 66, 77
Sermon on Indulgences and Grace......60
Sermon on the Man Born Blind, Jn 9:1-38......148
Sermon on March 28, 1518......44–45
Sermon on Threefold Righteousness Philippians 2......162

1519

Collected works translated from Latin to German (published in Basel)......67

The Leipzig Debate......67, 68, 69, 70–71, 72
Letter to George Spalatin......49, 65, 70
Lectures on Galatians......134–35, 173, 79–180, 181–82, 186–88, 192–93. See also 1535 for *Lectures on Galatians*
Psalm 1......32
Series of writings on penance, baptism, Eucharist, and good works......72
A Sermon on the Estate of Marriage......143
Two Kinds of Righteousness......45, 175

1520

The Freedom of A Christian......10f, 18, 20, 39, 76, 87, 88, 89, 92, 97, 121–23, 125, 180f
To the German Nobility......73, 74–75, 143
Treatise on Good Works......75, 76, 102
Why the Books of the Pope Were Burned......76, 77

1521

Against Latomus......91–92, 164
Church Postil......123
Defense and Explanation of All the Articles......18f, 35, 58, 91, 92
The Gospel for Christmas Eve, Luke 2:1-14......104, 196, 177
Judgment of Luther on Monastic Vows......123
Psalm 68......112
Psalm 101......133f.
Psalm 110......51
Psalm 111......109
Sermon on the Mount and the Magnificat......30f, 108
Sermon for Christmas Eve, Titus 2:11-14......177

1522

The Estate of Marriage......148
Sermons at Wittenberg
    The First Sermon, March 9, 1522, Invocavit Sunday......46
    The Second Sermon, March 10, 1522, Monday after Invocavit......178
    The Sixth Sermon, March 14, 1522, Friday after Invocavit......188

The Seventh Sermon, March 15, 1522, Saturday before Reminiscere......179

1523

Letter to George Spalatin......138–39
Ordinance of a Common Chest......113–14, 124, 126
On Temporal Authority......135, 136, 182
That Maidens May Honorably Leave Their Cloisters, a public letter......139–40

1524

Exposition of Psalm 127......113–14, 197
Letter to George Spalatin......140, 142
Parents and the Marriage of Their Children......133, 134, 136, 182

1525

Against the Robbing and Murdering Hordes of Peasant......141
The Bondage of the Will......58, 71, 103–4, 107, 116, 153f, 155–57, 158f, 159f, 163f, 164, 170, 171, 174
Exposition of Psalm 127......113–14, 197
Letter to John Rühel......141, 144f
Lectures on the Minor Prophets: Jonah......107
Letter to Nicholas von Amsdorf (May 30)......17, 141–42
Letter to Nicholas von Amsdorf (June 21)......142, 144–45

1527

Letter to George Spalatin......147
Whether One May Flee the Deadly Plague......125, 127–32, 137

1528

Letter to Nicholas Hausmann......149

1529

Letter to Nicholas von Amsdorf......149

1530

The Beautiful Confitemini......32
Letter to Mrs. Luther......147, 150
Letter to (Hans) John Luther......147
Sermons on the Gospel of Saint John (Chapters 6–8)......32
Sermon on Keeping Children in School......110
Sermons on Matthew 5–7......122f, 135, 148f

1531

Psalm 147......114

1532

Letter to Jonas von Stockhausen......172

1535

Lectures on Galatians......13, 113, 119, 134, 179, 180

1536

The Disputation Concerning Man......105

1537

Sermons on the Gospel of Saint John (Chapters 1–4) 32, 33
Sermons on the Gospel of Saint John (Chapter 14) 108
Sermons on the Gospel of Saint John (Chapters 16) 51

1538

The Psalm Miserere......52, 84

1542

Letter to Marcus Crodel......147

1545

Preface to the *Complete Edition of Luther's Latin Writings*......41f, 42

Themes in Luther's Writings

doctrine on free will......13, 18, 19, 66f, 70, 89, 90, 104f, 114, 132f, 155–59, 160, 163–66, 167–70, 171–72, 183, 185
gift of grace......35, 44, 58, 62f, 63, 91–92, 98, 121, 153, 167
theology of the cross......14, 46, 48, 52, 54–55, 93, 117, 176–77
theology of justification (by faith) 11, 21, 44, 82, 86, 88, 92, 96, 97, 107, 121, 123, 133, 167
theology of work and vocation......11, 14, 16–18 , 21, 46, 83, 99f, 104f, 105, 111, 113–16, 129, 147–48, 153, 154f, 156–57, 165, 168, 175, 183, 185–86, 189, 196, 198–200